Lecture Notes in Artificial Intelligence 7169

Subseries of Lecture Notes in Computer Science

Chiaki Sakama Sebastian Sardina
Wamberto Vasconcelos Michael Winikoff (Eds.)

Declarative Agent Languages and Technologies IX

9th International Workshop, DALT 2011
Taipei, Taiwan, May 3, 2011
Revised Selected and Invited Papers

Volume Editors

Chiaki Sakama
Wakayama University, Dept. of Computer and Communication Sciences
930 Sakaedani, Wakayama 640-8510, Japan
E-mail: sakama@sys.wakayama-u.ac.jp

Sebastian Sardina
RMIT University, School of Computer Science and Information Technology
PO Box GPO Box 2476V, Melbourne, VIC, 3001, Australia
E-mail: sebastian.sardina@rmit.edu.au

Wamberto Vasconcelos
University of Aberdeen, Dept. of Computing Science
Meston Building, Aberdeen, AB24 3UE, UK
E-mail: w.w.vasconcelos@abdn.ac.uk

Michael Winikoff
University of Otago, Dept. of Information Science
PO Box 56, Dunedin, 9054, New Zealand
E-mail: michael.winikoff@otago.ac.nz

ISSN 0302-9743 e-ISSN 1611-3349
ISBN 978-3-642-29112-8 ISBN 978-3-642-29113-5 (eBook)
DOI 10.1007/978-3-642-29113-5
Springer Heidelberg Dordrecht London New York

Library of Congress Control Number: 2012933973

CR Subject Classification (1998): I.2.11, C.2.4, D.2.4, D.2, D.3, F.3.1

LNCS Sublibrary: SL 7 – Artificial Intelligence

Typesetting: Camera-ready by author, data conversion by Scientific Publishing Services, Chennai, India

Printed on acid-free paper

Springer is part of Springer Science+Business Media (www.springer.com)

Preface

This volume contains revised papers presented at the International Workshop on Declarative Agent Languages and Technologies (DALT 2011). In addition to these technical contributions, this volume also revisits the most influential papers of past DALT editions, through a "retrospective" in which the authors themselves appraise the impact of the research in the field and how it led to future developments.

DALT 2011 was the ninth and most recent edition of the ongoing series of events aimed at promoting declarative approaches and technologies for software agents and multiagent systems. DALT 2011 took place in Taipei, Taiwan, on May 3, and was held as a satellite workshop of the 10th International Joint Conference on Autonomous Agents and Multiagent Systems (AAMAS 2011). Past editions were held in 2003 in Melbourne, Australia; in 2004 in New York, USA; in 2005 in Utrecht, The Netherlands; in 2006 in Hakodate, Japan; in 2007 in Honolulu, USA; in 2008 in Estoril, Portugal; in 2009 in Budapest, Hungary; and in 2010 in Toronto, Canada. The post-workshop proceedings for all these were published in the *Lecture Notes in Artificial Intelligence* series as volumes 2990, 3476, 3904, 4327, 4897, 5397, 5948, and 6619, respectively.

Business and pleasure activities increasingly benefit from computer networks to share information and processes. Software to support such activities thus need to be distributed (i.e., many independent pieces of hardware, communicating via message-passing), open (i.e., components may come and go) and heterogeneous (i.e., components have been developed independently by different parties using different technologies). Moreover, as solutions become more sophisticated, they need to become more *autonomous*, being able to function with little or no human interference. Software agents and multiagent systems help make this class of applications a reality.

Engineering such systems brings about exciting challenges for which declarative approaches offer much. Declarative formalisms (e.g., functions and logics), and their associated mechanisms, can be used to specify, verify, analyze and, in many cases, actually program software agents and multiagent systems. Declarative approaches, with their well-understood and robust mathematical foundations, provide abstractions with which to explore computational phenomena.

The series of international workshops on Declarative Agent Languages and Technologies (DALT) has been organized as a forum in which theoreticians and practitioners come together for scientific exchange on declarative approaches to specifying, verifying, programming, and running software agents and multiagent systems. A main theme of the DALT series is to advance the state of the art in declarative specification and verification techniques, to address large, expressive and realistic classes of software agents and multiagent systems.

We have included in this volume five papers presented at DALT 2011; the authors have revised their papers in light of the comments and suggestions they received from the reviewers and during the workshop. The papers are:

1. *A Formal Framework for Reasoning about Goal Interactions*, by Michael Winikoff
2. *Plan Indexing for State-Based Plans*, by Louise Dennis
3. *Probing Attacks on Multiagent Systems using Electronic Institutions*, by Shahriar Bijani, David Robertson, and David Aspinall
4. *Formalizing Commitments Using Action Languages*, by Tran Cao Son, Enrico Pontelli, and Chiaki Sakama
5. *Detecting Conflicts in Commitments*, by Akin Gunay and Pinar Yolum

In addition to these original contributions, we also have a retrospective of the best papers of the DALT series, by the respective authors themselves, explaining how the research developed and how it influenced and impacted the community, the state of the art and subsequent work. The best papers of the DALT series were selected based on their number of citations given by Google Scholar.[1] The papers are:

1. *Coo-BDI: Extending the BDI Model with Cooperativity*, by Davide Ancona and Viviana Mascardi (DALT 2003)
2. *Extending the Operational Semantics of a BDI Agent-Oriented Programming Language for Introducing Speech-Act Based Communication*, by Álvaro F. Moreira, Renata Vieira, and Rafael H. Bordini (DALT 2003)
3. *A Lightweight Coordination Calculus for Agent Systems*, by David S. Robertson (DALT 2004)
4. *A Distributed Architecture for Norm-Aware Agent Societies*, by Andrés García-Camino, Juan-Antonio Rodríguez-Aguilar, Carles Sierra, and Wamberto W. Vasconcelos (DALT 2005)
5. *Producing Compliant Interactions: Conformance, Coverage, and Interoperability*, by Amit K. Chopra and Munindar P. Singh (DALT 2006)
6. *Specifying and Enforcing Norms in Artificial Institutions*, by Nicoletta Fornara and Marco Colombetti (DALT 2008)
7. *Social Commitments in Time: Satisfied or Compensated*, by Paolo Torroni, Federico Chesani, Paola Mello, and Marco Montali (DALT 2009)

In 2011, there was also a DALT Spring School, held during April 10-15 in Bertinoro (Forlì-Cesena), Italy. The school, organized by Paolo Torroni and Andrea Omicini, aimed at giving a comprehensive introduction to the DALT research topics and disseminating the results of research achieved in an 8-year-long workshop activity, with a perspective on the future. The 5-day school program included five courses:

– *Agent Reasoning: Knowledge, Plans and Flexible Control Cycles* by Francesca Toni

[1] `http://scholar.google.com/`

- *Agent Reasoning: Goals and Preferences*, by Birna van Riemsdijk
- *Agent Interaction: Languages, Dialogues and Protocols*, by Peter McBurney
- *Agent and Multi-Agent Software Engineering: Modelling, Programming, and Verification*, by Rafael Bordini
- *Organization, Coordination and Norms for Multi-Agent Systems*, by Wamberto Vasconcelos

There was also a student session, organized by Federico Chesani in two tracks: for junior and senior students. The initiative was a success, with more than 30 students attending, and it received very positive feedback. The DALT school was very conveniently co-located with the Third ALP/GULP International School on Computational Logic. Additional information and course materials are available for download at the website: `http://lia.deis.unibo.it/confs/dalt_school/`. The DALT school is represented in this volume by two invited contributions from DALT lecturers: a short course report by Rafael Bordini, and a technical article by Wamberto Vasconcelos and colleagues.[2]

We would like to take this opportunity to thank the authors for their contributions, the members of the Steering Committee for support and guidance, and the members of the Program Committee for timely and high-quality reviews. We would also like to thank Wiebe Van der Hoek (Department of Computer Science, University of Liverpool, UK), for his invited talk "Control and Delegation;" we are very happy to include in this volume an extended abstract for this talk.

August 2011

Chiaki Sakama
Sebastian Sardina
Wamberto Vasconcelos
Michael Winikoff

[2] We thank Paolo Torroni for providing us with this summary text on the DALT 2011 Spring School for inclusion in this preface.

Organization

Organizing Committee

Chiaki Sakama	Wakayama University, Japan
Sebastian Sardina	RMIT University, Australia
Wamberto Vasconcelos	University of Aberdeen, UK
Michael Winikoff	University of Otago, New Zealand

Steering Committee

Matteo Baldoni	Università di Torino, Italy
Andrea Omicini	Alma Mater Studiorum – Università di Bologna, Italy
M. Birna van Riemsdijk	Delft University of Technology, The Netherlands
Tran Cao Son	New Mexico State University, USA
Paolo Torroni	Alma Mater Studiorum – Università di Bologna, Italy
Pinar Yolum	Bogazici University, Turkey
Michael Winikoff	University of Otago, New Zealand

Program Committee

Thomas Ågotnes	University of Bergen, Norway
Marco Alberti	Universidade Nova de Lisboa, Portugal
Natasha Alechina	University of Nottingham, UK
Cristina Baroglio	Università di Torino, Italy
Rafael Bordini	Federal University of Rio Grande do Sul, Brazil
Jan Broersen	University of Utrecht, The Netherlands
Federico Chesani	Alma Mater Studiorum – Università di Bologna, Italy
Amit Chopra	Università di Trento, Italy
Francesco M. Donini	Università della Tuscia, Italy
James Harland	RMIT University, Australia
Andreas Herzig	Paul Sabatier University, France
Koen Hindriks	Delft University of Technology, The Netherlands
João Leite	New University of Lisbon, Portugal
Yves Lespérance	York University, Canada
Viviana Mascardi	Università di Genova, Italy

Nicolas Maudet	LAMSADE, Université Paris-Dauphine, France
John-Jules Meyer	University of Utrecht, The Netherlands
Peter Novák	Czech Technical University in Prague, Czech Republic
Fabio Patrizi	Università "La Sapienza" di Roma, Italy
Enrico Pontelli	New Mexico State University, USA
David Pym	University of Aberdeen, UK
Michael Rovatsos	The University of Edinburgh, UK
Flavio Correa da Silva	Universidade de Sao Paulo, Brazil
Guillermo Simari	Universidad Nacional del Sur, Argentina
Tran Cao Son	New Mexico State University, USA
Marina De Vos	University of Bath, UK

Additional Referees

Federico Chesani
Marco Montali
Michal Čáp

Table of Contents

DALT 2011 Papers

Best of DALT

DALT Spring School 2011

Control and Delegation*

Wiebe van der Hoek**

University of Liverpool, United Kingdom
wiebe@csc.liv.ac.uk

The context of the talk is an interest and a need to reason about issues related to *co-operation* in multi-agent systems, where, given the notion of a coalition (that is, a group of agents), questions arise regarding the coalitional power (*what can the coalition achieve?*), coalition formation (*which coalitions will form?*) and the result of cooperation (*how will the coalition act?*). Coalition Logics provide a tool to analyse some of those questions. They took off with two important developments, namely with Pauly's formulation of Coalition Logic CL [2], and the work on Alternating-time Temporal Logic (ATL) by Alur, Henzinger and Kupferman [1].

Basic concept in both systems is the *cooperation modality*: $\langle\langle C\rangle\rangle\varphi$ meaning 'coalition C can cooperate to ensure that φ'. Formally, this is defined to hold as 'the members of C can each chose a strategy, such that, no matter what the agents outside C decide to do, φ will be true in all remaining computations' (more precisely: $\exists\sigma_C : \forall\sigma_{\bar{C}} : out(\sigma_C, \sigma_{\bar{C}}) \models \varphi$ — what matters for now is the $\exists\forall$ pattern). This is the so-called α*-ability*.

In CL and ATL however, no answer is given to the question as to *where the agents' powers arise from*. In our work on *Coalition Logic for Proposition Control* (CL-PC), we give one possible answer to this: we assume that every agent i is uniquely assigned a set of propositional atoms $\mathbb{A}_i$: the agent has complete control over the truth values. So the choices or powers available to agents correspond to the valuations over their variables that are possible. Here is the basic semantics: a model M is a tuple

$$M = \langle \mathcal{AG}, \mathbb{A}, \mathbb{A}_1, \ldots, \mathbb{A}_n, \theta\rangle, \text{ where}$$

- $\mathcal{AG} = \{1, \ldots, n\}$ is a finite, non-empty set of *agents*;
- $\mathbb{A} = \{p, q, \ldots\}$ is a finite, non-empty set of *propositional variables*;
- $\mathbb{A}_1 \ldots, \mathbb{A}_n$ is a partition of $\mathbb{A}$ among the members of Ag, with the intended interpretation that $\mathbb{A}_i$ is the subset of $\mathbb{A}$ representing those variables under the control of agent $i \in \mathcal{AG}$; for $C \subseteq Ag$, let $\mathbb{A}_C = \cup_{c\in C}\mathbb{A}_c$, and finally,
- $\theta : \mathbb{A} \to \{\top, \bot\}$ is a propositional valuation. For $C \subseteq Ag$, define $\theta' = \theta \bmod C$ iff for all $p \notin \mathbb{A}_C$, $\theta'(p) = \theta(p)$.

We then define $M \models \Diamond_C\varphi$ iff $\exists\theta_C(\theta_C = \theta \bmod C$ and $M \dagger \theta_C \models \varphi)$, where $M \dagger \theta_C$ is like M, but with θ replaced by θ_C. With $\Box_C$ defined as $\neg\Diamond_C\neg\varphi$, we can then define α-ability as $\langle\langle C\rangle\rangle_\alpha\varphi \leftrightarrow \Diamond_C\Box_{\bar{C}}\varphi$ ('C can chose values for their variables, so that, no matter what the complement $\bar{C}$ of C choses for theirs, φ holds' and β-ability as $\langle\langle C\rangle\rangle_\beta\varphi \leftrightarrow \Box_{\bar{C}}\Diamond_C\varphi$ ('for any choice of the others, C can respond with a valuation for their atoms, such that φ'). Define $controls(C, \varphi)$ as $\Diamond_C\varphi \wedge \Diamond_C\neg\varphi$ (obviously, for atoms p this coincides with $p \in \mathbb{A}_C$).

---

* Abstract of a talk given at DALT2011, Taipei, Taiwan.

** Based on work with Thomas Ågotnes, Nicolas Troquard, and Michael Wooldridge.

C. Sakama et al. (Eds.): DALT 2011, LNAI 7169, pp. 1–2, 2012.

In [5], we

1. Provide a Kripke semantics for CL-PC
2. Give a sound and complete axiomatisation of CL-PC
3. Give a syntactic characterisation of $controls(C, \varphi)$
4. settle the computational complexity of model checking and satisfiability of CL-PC.

In CL-PC, the 'ownership' of atoms is *fixed*: in DCL-PC [4] we add a notion of *delegation*, which is formalised through programs of the form $i \leadsto_p j$, which have the effect that in the resulting model, $p \in \mathbb{A}_j$, if originally $p \in \mathbb{A}_i$. An example of a statement in DCL-PC is thus $\langle \textbf{while } \neg\Diamond_j\varphi \textbf{ do } \bigcup_{p\in\mathbb{A}_i} i \leadsto_p j\rangle\top$ ('it is possible that i passes on control of his atoms to j, until j can eventually achieve φ'). [4] offers a sound and complete axiomatisation of DCL-PC, and establishes its model checking and satisfiability complexity. Model checking appears to be hard, due to the very succinct representation of our models.

Then, in [3] we relax CL-PC's assumption regarding complete information of the agents.

- agents may be uncertain about the *values* of the variables.
  E.g., if agent i's goal is $p \leftrightarrow \neg q$ he can achieve this if (1) he *controls* at least one of the variables, and (2) if he controls one of them, he *knows* the value of the other
- there may also be uncertainty about *who controls what*
  (1) agents may be uncertain about which atoms are controlled by other agents or even by themselves; and (2) agents may be uncertain who to join coalitions with.

These two assumptions about partial information give rise to ECL-PC(PO) (Epistemic CL-PC with Partial Observability) and ECL-PC(UO) (ECL-PC with Uncertainty about Ownership). In the former, one can for instance express $K_a\Diamond_a(p \leftrightarrow q) \wedge \neg\Diamond_a(p \wedge q)$ (think of a having control over p, but not knowing the truth value of q), and in the latter logic, an example would be $K_a\Box_{\{a,b\}}\Diamond_{\{a,b\}}(p \leftrightarrow q) \wedge K_b\Box_a\Diamond_b(p \leftrightarrow q)$ (suppose a and b are the only two agents, a being fully ignorant of who controls what, but b having the information that both p and a are under his control). In [3], we extend CL-PC to cope with these two types of uncertainty, and provide a sound and complete axiomatisation for this.

References

1. Alur, R., Henzinger, T.A., Kupferman, O.: Alternating-time temporal logic. In: IEEE Symposium on Foundations of Computer Science, pp. 100–109 (1997)
2. Pauly, M.: A modal logic for coalitional power in games. Journal of Logic and Computation 12(1), 149–166 (2002)
3. van der Hoek, W., Troquard, N., Wooldridge, M.: Knowledge and control. In: Tumer, K., Yolum, P., Sonenberg, L., Stone, P. (eds.) Proc. of 10th Int. Conf. on Autonomous Agents and Multiagent Systems (AAMAS 2011), pp. 719–726 (2011)
4. van der Hoek, W., Walther, D., Wooldridge, M.: Reasoning about the transfer of control. JAIR 37, 437–477 (2010)
5. van der Hoek, W., Wooldridge, M.: On the logic of cooperation and propositional control. Artificial Intelligence 64, 81–119 (2005)

Plan Indexing for State-Based Plans

Louise A. Dennis

Department of Computer Science, University of Liverpool, UK
L.A.Dennis@liverpool.ac.uk

Abstract. We consider the issue of indexing plans (or rules) in the implementation of BDI languages. In particular we look at the issue of plans which are not triggered by the occurence of specific events. The selection of a plan from such a set represents one of the major bottle-necks in the execution of BDI programs. This bottle-neck is particularly obvious when attempting to use program model checkers to reason about such languages.

This paper describes the problem and examines one possible indexing scheme. It evaluates the scheme experimentally and concludes that it is only of benefit in fairly specific circumstances. It then discusses ways the indexing mechanism could be improved to provide wider benefits.

1 Introduction

The implementation of the theory of Beliefs, Desires and Intentions [10] as programming languages has led to a family of languages with many similarities to resolution based logic programming languages and resolution based first-order theorem provers.

A key component of programs written in these languages is the plan or rule base, consisting of programmer designed procedures for achieving intentions. For simplicity we will here refer to these procedures as *plans* and the set of such procedures as the *plan library*.

At given points in the execution of a BDI agent's reasoning cycle the plan library will be accessed in order to determine which plans are applicable given the agent's current set of beliefs and intentions. There are two types of plans used in these languages: *triggered plans* are activated by the occurence of some event (normally the acquisition of a belief or a goal) while *state-based plans* may become active at any time a particular set of beliefs and goals are held. Both types of plans typically have a *guard* – a set of beliefs and goals – that the agent must either believe or intend before the plan is deemed applicable. Both triggers and guards may (and indeed commonly do) contain free variables which are instantiated by unification against the current events, beliefs and goals. A naive implementation of plan selection involves accessing all the plans in the library and then checking each one in turn to see if its trigger event has occurred (in the case of triggered plans) and its guard is satisfied by the agent's state. The time involved in doing this, especially in the presence of large plan libraries, represents a significant bottle-neck in agent execution.

C. Sakama et al. (Eds.): DALT 2011, LNAI 7169, pp. 3–15, 2012.

This paper investigates an indexing mechanism for plans in the hope this will reduce the time spent checking guards for applicability. A preliminary implementation is presented and the results of testing this implementation are discussed. The results reveal that there are complex tradeoffs and attention needs to be paid to the efficiency of retrieval from the index if the process is to be of use outside a small number of situations.

1.1 Plans in BDI Languages

The design of plans in BDI languages owes much to logic programming and the semantics of plan applicability is generally similar to that of guarded horn clauses. The guards on plans are checked against the agent's *belief base*, Σ, and, in some cases, also against the *goal base*, Γ. In the tradition of logic programming these guards are expressed as first-order predicates with free variables which are instantiated by unification with the goal and belief bases.

In some languages the guards may also be more complex and contain logical formulae constructed using negation, conjuction and disjunction. There may even be deductive rules that operate on the belief and goal bases allowing the agent to conclude that it has some derived belief or goal from the explicit ones stored in its database.

Notation: In what follows we will write triggered plans as $trigger : \{guard\} \leftarrow$ *body* and state-based plans as $\{guard\} \leftarrow$ *body*. We will refer to the individual forumulae contained in guards as *guard statements*. Where a guard statement states that something is *not* believed by the agent or is *not* a goal of the agent we will refer to this as a *negative guard statement*. Where a guard statement can be deduced using rules we will refer to it as a *deductive guard statement*. All other guard statements, i.e. those that can be inferred directly by inspection of Σ or Γ we will refer to as *explicit guard statements*. Our interest here is primarily in the use of explicit guard statements as a filter on plan selection.

A naive implemention of plan selection retrieves all plans from the agent's plan library and then iterates over this set checking each trigger and guard in turn for applicability. This involves the construction of unifiers and, in some cases, logical deduction, typically in a PROLOG-style. This represents a significant bottle-neck in execution of the agent program. Figure 1 shows profile information generated using the JProfiler tool [1] from running a program written in the GOAL language [5,8] as implemented in the AIL toolkit [2]. The procedure matchPlans selects all plans and then checks their guards in turn. In the example shown, this procedure is taking up 40% of the execution time. Of the constituent calls within matchPlans most are involved in the checking of guards (ail.syntax.Guards$1.hasNext). We performed similar profiling on all the examples in the AIL GOAL distribution (fewer than half a dozen, sadly). The percentage of time spent on plan selection shown in figure 1 is typical of the programs we examined.

In many agent programs the time taken for plan selection is not of major concern. It typically only becomes a problem in the presence of an extremely large

Call Tree

Session: SimpleJunkMAS
Time of export: Tuesday, October 19, 2010 4:05:09 PM BST
JVM time: 00:48

View mode: Tree
Thread selection: All thread groups
Thread status: Runnable
Aggregation level: Methods

```
61.3% - 751 ms - 3 inv. mcapl.MCAPLAgent.run
  61.3% - 751 ms - 44 inv. mcapl.MCAPLAgent.reason
    60.6% - 742 ms - 44 inv. ail.semantics.AILAgent.MCAPLreason
      60.6% - 742 ms - 44 inv. ail.semantics.AILAgent.reason
        43.3% - 530 ms - 36 inv. goalc.PlanWithActionRule.checkPreconditions
          40.8% - 500 ms - 36 inv. ail.semantics.AILAgent.appPlans
            40.8% - 499 ms - 36 inv. ail.semantics.AILAgent.matchPlans
              25.2% - 309 ms - 560 inv. ail.syntax.Guard$1.hasNext
              12.9% - 158 ms - 456 inv. ail.syntax.Plan.clone
              1.2% - 14,461 µs - 456 inv. ail.syntax.ConstraintLibrary.check_constraints
              0.3% - 3,314 µs - 456 inv. ail.semantics.AILAgent.believes
              0.2% - 1,911 µs - 492 inv. ail.semantics.Intention.empty
              0.1% - 1,480 µs - 36 inv. goalc.GOALAgent.getAllReactivePlans
                0.1% - 1,314 µs - 36 inv. ail.syntax.PlanLibrary.getAllReactivePlans
                  0.1% - 1,282 µs - 36 inv. java.util.Collections.sort
                    0.1% - 745 µs - 420 inv. ail.syntax.Plan.compareTo
                      0.0% - 295 µs - 840 inv. ail.syntax.Plan.getID
                0.0% - 18 µs - 36 inv. goalc.GOALRC.getStage
                0.0% - 17 µs - 36 inv. ail.semantics.AILAgent.getReasoningCycle
                0.0% - 15 µs - 36 inv. java.lang.String.equals
```

Fig. 1. Profiling the Execution of a GOAL Program

plan library and there are relatively few examples of the use of BDI-programs in such cases. However there is considerable interest in the community in the use of program model checking for BDI programs [9,3]. A program model checker uses the actual program as the model which is checked against some property. This causes individual segments of code to be executed many times as the model checker investigates all execution paths and exacerbates the effects of any inefficiences in the program or the underlying language interpreter.

1.2 Indexing

An indexing system allows the fast retrieval of data from a large set by organising the data in some way. For instance, the data can be stored in tuples where some subset of the data is indexed by a key. Data is retrieved by deriving a *query key* (or key set) from the current problem and using that to traverse the index, returning only that data associated with the key in a tuple.

Clearly an index is only of value if the cost of storing data in the index, computing query keys and retrieving data using those keys is lower than the cost of examining the entire set of data and computing the relevance of each item on the fly.

2 Related Work

2.1 Plan Indexing in *Jason*

The *Jason* implementation of AgentSpeak [4] uses triggered plans. Each event is represented by a predicate and the *Jason* implementation generates a *predicate indicator* from these predicates. The predicate indicator is the name of the predicate plus the number of arguments it takes represented as a string.

Consider, for instance the plan: $see(X) : \{garbage(X)\} \leftarrow remove(X)$. This states that if an agent sees some garbage then it removes the garbage. This plan would be indexed by the predicate indicator `see/1` (predicate `see` with 1 argument). *Jason* stores all its plans in tuples of the trigger predicate indicator and a list of all the plans with that trigger. When plans are retrieved the list of predicate indicators alone is searched (using string matching) and then only the plans in the associated tuple are returned.

By indexing plans by their triggers *Jason* is able to considerably speed up the plan selection process. The guards are checked only for those plans whose trigger matches the current event. In our example unifiers for X are only determined and the plan's guard checked, when the agent has just acquired a belief that it can see something, not when any other event occurs.

Jason gains considerable speed up in the plan selection process by this means, and this indexing style is used in many implementations of languages that have triggered plans (e.g. GWENDOLEN [6]).

Unfortunately not all languages use triggered plans. GOAL, for instance, has *state-based plans*, called *conditional actions* which have no trigger and consist of a guard and a plan body alone. The absense of a trigger means that these can not be indexed in the same way.

Aside: It is of note that *Jason* also indexes its belief base with predicate indicators allowing the rapid filtering out of irrelevant beliefs during the checking of plan guards. This technique is trivially applicable in the case of state-based plans and, indeed, the implementation of GOAL discussed in section 4 uses indexing of the belief base in this style.

2.2 Term Indexing

First order theorem provers have long investigated a similar problem, indexing horn clauses for retrieval against a given literal in a variety of situations [11]. This is a similar problem to that addressed by *Jason*. Theorem provers typically work with horn clauses with a single head literal which must be matched to a single literal in the problem at hand.

In our case we are considering a set of literals (the guard) all of which need to match a set of literals in the belief base, but the belief base may also contain literals irrelevant to the current problem.

Theorem provers also deal with a far larger number of clauses which need to be retrieved and much of the research in theorem proving has focused on efficient term representations in order to minimize time searching the index. In situations where we consider agents which may have plans numbering in the tens of thousands the advanced techniques for term indexing developed in the theorem proving field may have a contribution to make to the problem of plan indexing, particularly in languages which have triggered plans.

3 Data Structures

We have chosen to index our plans using a tree-based indexing scheme. Plans are stored as sets at the leaves of a tree data structure and the tree is traversed with reference to the current agent state in order to retrieve plans.

We do not generate an explicit query key before traversing the tree but instead refer to indexing information stored in the agent's belief base. However there is no reason why a query key should not be generated and, indeed, the pseudo-code in the appendices assumes this.

3.1 Plan Keys

We slightly extend the notion of a predicate indicator from *Jason*'s plan indexing algorithm to that of a *plan key.* A plan key is a tuple, (pi, τ) of a predicate indicator, pi, and a type, τ, which refers to the type of entity the associated guard refers to – in the examples we have considered these are either beliefs or goals.

Plan guards are thus associated with a list of plan keys. This list contains a plan key for each explicit guard statement. Negative and deductive guard statements are ignored. We call this list the guard's *index list.*

3.2 Plan Index Trees

We store all our plans in a tree data structure. Each node in the tree is labelled with a plan key and has two subtrees. One subtree contains all plans which have the plan key in their index list, the *must have branch*, and the other subtree contains all the plans which do not, the *don't care branch.* More complex logical formulae and predicates which can be deduced are ignored[1] partly for simplicity and partly because plan keys alone do not provide sufficient information to tell that some guard statement is *not* true in the current agent state. For ease of indexing the plan keys are ordered as the levels in the tree descend [2]. The leaves of the tree are populated with the set of plans which exist on that tree branch.

Say for instance we have three plans:

$$\begin{aligned}
\textbf{plan1} &: \{\mathcal{B}a, \mathcal{B}b\} \leftarrow body \\
\textbf{plan2} &: \{\mathcal{B}b, \mathcal{B}c\} \leftarrow body \\
\textbf{plan3} &: \{\mathcal{B}c\} \leftarrow body
\end{aligned}$$

Where a statement $\mathcal{B}b$ means that the agent must believe b for the plan to apply. These would be stored as shown in figure 2.

[1] In the languages we consider deduction is performed by resolution using horn clauses stored in a *rule base* so we simply exclude all predicates that appear in the head of any of the listed horn clauses. It may be that in some languages it is harder to identify and exclude these predicates.

[2] Details of this are discussed in appendix A.

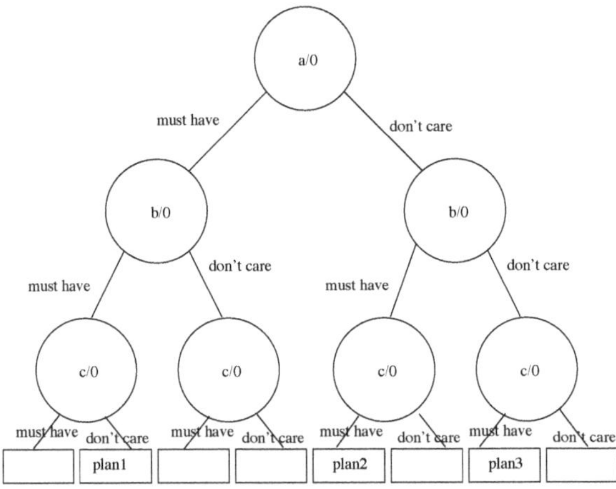

Fig. 2. Example of a Plan Tree

In order to select plans, the program traverses the tree. At each node it checks Σ or Γ (as relevant) for the presence of the appropriate plan key. If it exists then both plans that require that element and plans that do not require that element may be applicable to the current state. As a result, the program searches both sub-trees for relevant plans. If the plan key doesn't exist in the relevant set then only plans that do not require that guard statement will be applicable and the program *only* searches the don't care branch of that node.

So if the belief base contained both a and c then plan 3 would be returned and the branches of the tree highlighted in figure 3 would be explored.

We include pseudo-code for the algorithms to insert plans into the tree and look plans up from the tree in the appendices.

4 Results

We implemented two versions of our plan indexing algorithm in the AIL-based implementation of the GOAL language[3]. The code used in the implementation is available from the author and via the MCAPL sourceforge distribution [4].

The first version indexed by predicate indicators alone and considered only guard statements that referred to beliefs. The second version used plan keys and considered also guard statements referring to goals. We then conducted some simple experiments with the system to see whether the overhead associated with storing and accessing plans from the tree data structure was off-set by the gains

[3] AIL is, among other things, a prototyping tool for BDI-languages [2]. The version of GOAL used was based on the semantics described in [8].

[4] `http://mcapl.sourceforge.net`

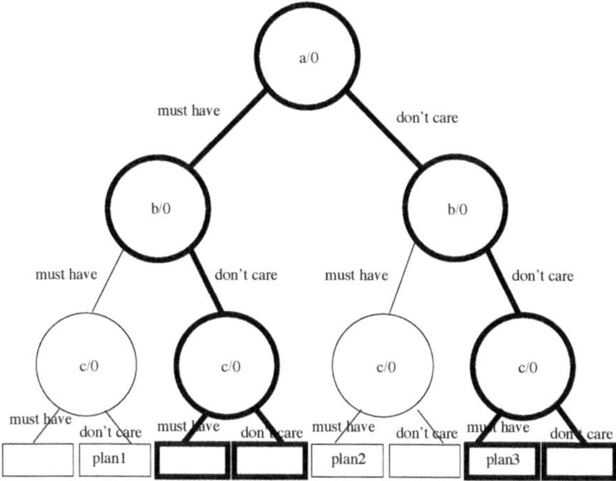

Fig. 3. Example of a Plan Tree Lookup

in time reduced spent checking the plan guards. In all the experiments the only differences between the code run was the way in which the plans in the library were stored and retrieved, all other parts of the system were identical.

4.1 Experiment 1: Junk Code

In the first example we studied a simple program in which a lead agent communicated with two others simply to ascertain their existence. When they received a query they responded with a simple "ping" message and the program was done. To this were added plans for a Dining Philosopher program which were irrelevant to achieving the goal at hand and these "junk" plans were duplicated n times. The average run time of the system was then plotted against the number of duplications of the redundant code in the system.

We ran each version of the code 100 times and averaged the time taken in order to allow for differences in running time caused by different scheduling behaviour between the agents.

Results. The graph in figure 4 shows the result of running the program with up to 24 duplications of the redundant code.

The graph shows that the fastest performance is achieved by the system that organises its plan library as a tree indexed by plan keys that refer to both beliefs and goals and that the performance gain increases as the number of plans increase.

4.2 Experiment 2: Generic Contract Net with Many Goals

The second example we considered was a contract net style program with three agents. One agent wished to achieve a number of goals, none of which it could do

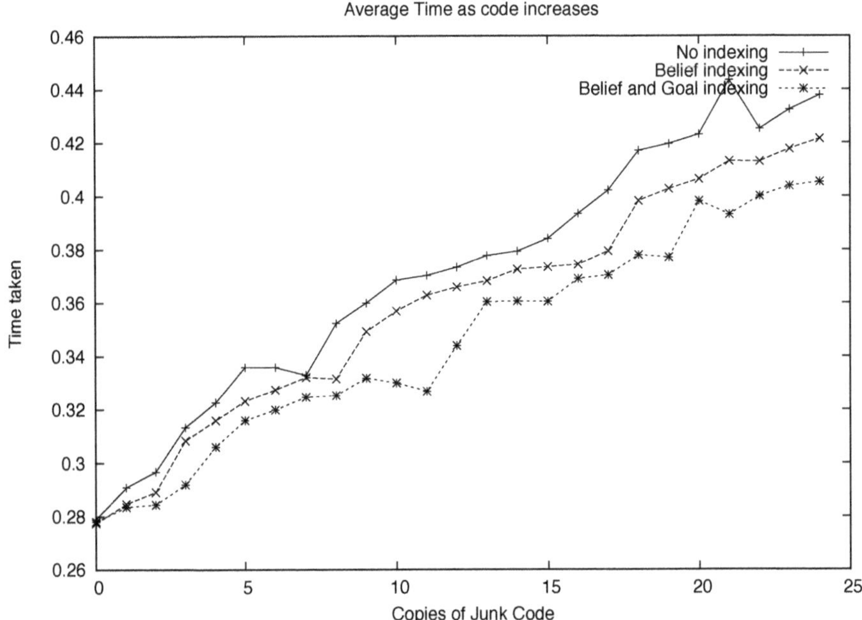

Fig. 4. Plan Indexing Performance in the presence of Redundant Plans

on its own. The other two agents could both achieve these goals and would "bid" for them. Whichever bid was received first was awarded the "contract" for the goal.

Results. Figure 5 shows the results, averaged over 100 runs of the program, as the number of goals to be achieved increases.

In this case it can be seen that the traditional approach of testing all plans is working considerably better than the plan indexing variety and indeed, that as the number of goals increases the efficiency gap between the two methods is going to get significantly worse. This result is obviously disappointing.

4.3 Discussion of the Results

The results are obviously disappointing but it is of interest to consider the differences between the two experimental set ups. Clearly as the guards on plans contain more statements, especially if those statements require further deduction to check, then the system slows down. At the same time as the number of plan keys in the plan tree increases[5] the computation required to traverse the tree also increases and, again, the system slows down.

[5] by this we mean the size of the plan tree increases from experiment to experiment, not within any particular run of the program. That said, if plans were to be added dynamically to the agent then dynamic changes to the indexing tree would also be necessary.

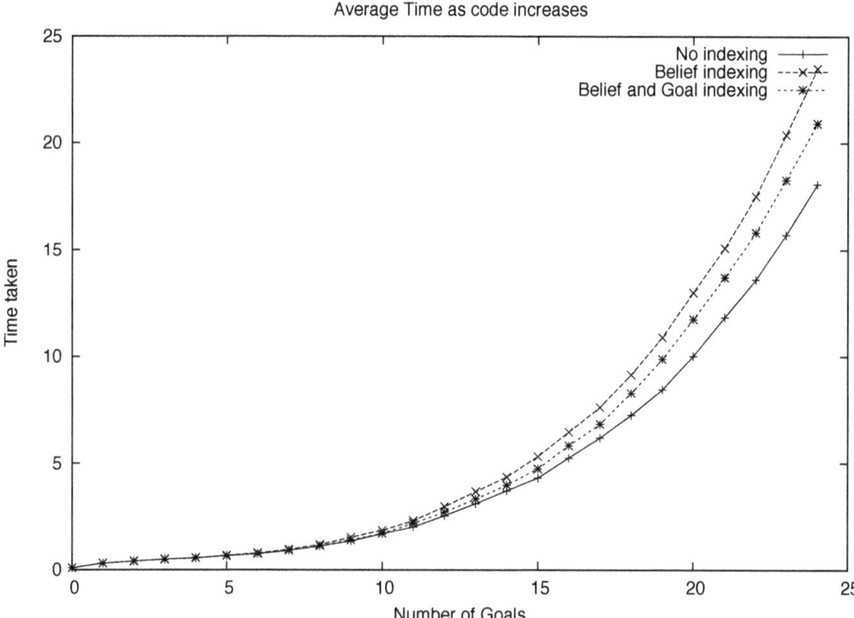

Fig. 5. Plan Indexing Performance in the presence of Multiple Goals

In the first experiment the system contained an increasing number of plans that were never applicable in the agent's current state. Since the plans were duplicated a relatively small number of plan keys were involved in the plan tree. In the second example each new goal introduced into the problem introduced a new plan key into the plan tree, and the increased traversal overhead clearly more than offset any gains being made by filtering out the plans before the guards were considered.

Tentatively, therefore, it seems that plan indexing in this style may be of benefit in programs were there are a large number of plans which refer to a comparatively small number of predicates.

5 Further Work

This paper represents a preliminary investigation into the indexing of state-based plans.

The programs we investigated contained a number of the plan guards involving negative and deductive guard statements. The plan index ignored such guards when indexing the plans. It would be desirable to have a quick way to eliminate plans based on these types of guards, particularly because they are more complex to check than explicit guard statements. Deductive rules require the (sometimes recursive) checking of the truth of their bodies, while negative guard statements require exhaustive checking of either Σ or Γ.

An obvious extension to the indexing proposed would be to investigate ways to incorporate consideration of these guards into the indexing scheme. A problem with both is that plan keys, alone, are in general not sufficient to provide a quick check of the applicability of the guard. For instance in the case of negative guard statements, simply knowing that there *is* a predicate in the belief base does not necessarily imply *for certain* that the guard statement is true since there may be no unifier that satisfies both it and any other guard statements with which it shares free variables. However it might be possible to perform some limited indexing of negative guards using predicate indicators so long as the guard, itself, had no parameters. Similarly, in the case of ground guards, it might be possible to match directly against the belief base.

Similarly it might be possible to represent belief rules in such a way (assuming the rule bodies do not contain any negative literals) that a judgement could be quickly drawn that the rule *was not* applicable (e.g. as a list of the plan keys that referred to explicit predicates appearing within the rule and which would need to hold for the rule to apply).

A further extension would be to look at techniques from term indexing for sharing subterms and, in particular, free variables. Some of these techniques allow unifiers to be constructed as part of the term lookup process. This would allow plan trees to return *only* plans that matched, together with relevant unifiers and so remove the need for checking the guards at all once the list were found.

Obviously all these approaches run the risk that the plan lookup process becomes even more inefficient when compared to simply iterating over the list of all plans in order to check the guards. Another important aspect of further work is improving the data structure and lookup process currently used for storing the plans. An adaptation of the RETE algorithm [7] would appear to be a promising approach in this direction.

6 Conclusions

This work represents an initial approach to the indexing of plans for retrieval in the plan selection phase of a BDI interpreter. The proposed scheme represents efficiency gains for GOAL-like languages in situations where an agent's plan library contains a large number of plans referring to a small number of predicates. However the scheme is less efficient in situations where many predicates are used. Therefore some care should be taken before deciding to implement such an indexing method.

It seems plausible that the indexing of state-based plans can be improved, even if the approach presented here has not yielded good results. Such improvements would supply gains both in terms of the efficiency of BDI-programs in large scale settings, and in terms of the model checking of such programs.

References

1. JProfiler, `http://www.ej-technologies.com/products/jprofiler/overview.html`
2. Bordini, R.H., Dennis, L.A., Farwer, B., Fisher, M.: Automated Verification of Multi-Agent Programs. In: Proceedings of the 23rd IEEE/ACM International Conference on Automated Software Engineering (ASE), L'Aquila, Italy, pp. 69–78 (September 2008)
3. Bordini, R.H., Dennis, L.A., Farwer, B., Fisher, M.: Automated Verification of Multi-Agent Programs. In: Proc. 23rd Int. Conf. Automated Software Engineering (ASE), pp. 69–78. IEEE CS Press (2008)
4. Bordini, R.H., Hübner, J.F., Vieira, R.: Jason and the Golden Fleece of Agent-Oriented Programming. In: Bordini, R.H., Dastani, M., Dix, J., El Fallah Seghrouchni, A. (eds.) Multi-Agent Programming: Languages, Platforms and Applications, ch. 1, pp. 3–37. Springer, Heidelberg (2005)
5. de Boer, F.S., Hindriks, K.V., van der Hoek, W., Meyer, J.-J.C.: A Verification Framework for Agent Programming with Declarative Goals. J. Applied Logic 5(2), 277–302 (2007)
6. Dennis, L.A., Farwer, B.: Gwendolen: A BDI Language for Verifiable Agents. In: Löwe, B. (ed.) AISB 2008 Workshop, Logic and the Simulation of Interaction and Reasoning, Aberdeen, AISB (2008)
7. Forgy, C.L.: Rete: A fast algorithm for the many pattern/many object pattern match problem. Artificial Intelligence 19, 17–37 (1982)
8. Hindriks, K.V., van Riemsdijk, M.B.: A Computational Semantics for Communicating Rational Agents Based on Mental Models. In: Braubach, L., Briot, J.-P., Thangarajah, J. (eds.) ProMAS 2009. LNCS, vol. 5919, pp. 31–48. Springer, Heidelberg (2010)
9. Jongmans, S.-S.T.Q., Hindriks, K.V., van Riemsdijk, M.B.: Model Checking Agent Programs by Using the Program Interpreter. In: Dix, J., Leite, J., Governatori, G., Jamroga, W. (eds.) CLIMA XI 2010. LNCS, vol. 6245, pp. 219–237. Springer, Heidelberg (2010)
10. Rao, A.S., Georgeff, M.P.: BDI agents: From theory to practice. In: Proceedings of the First International Conference on Multi-Agent Systems (ICMAS), San Francisco, USA, pp. 312–319 (June 1995)
11. Sekar, R., Ramakrishnan, I.V., Voronkov, A.: Term Indexing. In: Handbook of Automated Reasoning, vol. 2, pp. 1853–1964. North Holland (2001)

A Insertion Code

Notation: Both the algorithms presented in these appendices recurse through a tree structure. Each node in this tree contains a plan key and two subtrees, the must have branch and the don't care branch. The leaves of the plan tree contain a list of plans. We will treat both nodes and leaves as plan trees. We abuse object oriented notation and refer to the plan key of a plan tree, pt, as pt.pk, the must have branch as pt.musthave, the don't have branch as pt.donthave and the list of plans as pt.plans.

The insertion code recurses through a list of plan keys generated from the guard of a plan, p, and inserts the plan into a pre-existing plan tree (which could be empty). However where the plan contains a plan key that does not already exist in the tree the tree must be modified with new nodes for that plan key.

The algorithm takes as inputs the list of plan keys associated with the guard of plan, p, and the pre-existing plan tree into which the plan is to be inserted.

Code fragment 1.1 Insert a Plan into an Index Tree

```
addPlan(PlanKey List pks, Plan p, PlanTree pt)
  if (pks is empty)
    if (pt is a leaf)
       add p to pt.plans
       return pt
    else
       replace pt.dontcare with addPlan(pks, p, pt.dontcare)
       return pt
  else
    if (pt is a leaf)
       create a new plan tree node, n,  where
         n.pk equals the head of pks
         n.dontcare is a plantree leaf where
                n.plans = pt.plans
         n.musthave is the result of
                addPlan(tail of pks, p, new plantree leaf)
       return n
    else
       if pt.pk equals the head of pks
          replace pt.musthave with
             addPlan(tail of pks, p, pt.musthave)
          return pt
       else if the head of pks is ordered after pt.pk
          replace pt.dontcare with
             addPlan(pks, p, pt.dontcare)
          return pt
       else
         create a new plan tree node, n,  where
            n.pk equals the head of pks
            n.dontcare is pt
            n.musthave is the result of
                addPlan(tail of pks, p, pt.musthave)
         return n
```

B Lookup Code

Notation: The notation used in this code is explained in appendix A.

The algorithm takes a list of plan keys (generated from the agent's belief and goal bases) and which have been ordered according to some ordering on plan keys. The algorithm recurses through the tree comparing the plan key at each node against the supplied list of plan keys.

Code fragment 2.1 Look up plans in the Index

```
lookup(PlanKey List pks, Plan Tree pt)
  if (pt is a leaf)
     return pt.plans
  else
     if pt.pk is in pks
        return
          lookup(pks, pt.musthave)
          AND
          lookup(pks, pt.dontcare)
     else
        return lookup(pks, pt.dontcare)
```

An Integrated Formal Framework for Reasoning about Goal Interactions

Michael Winikoff*

Department of Information Science,
University of Otago,
Dunedin, New Zealand
michael.winikoff@otago.ac.nz

Abstract. One of the defining characteristics of intelligent software agents is their ability to pursue goals in a flexible and reliable manner, and many modern agent platforms provide some form of goal construct. However, these platforms are surprisingly naive in their handling of *interactions* between goals. Most provide no support for detecting that two goals interact, which allows an agent to interfere with itself, for example by simultaneously pursuing conflicting goals. Previous work has provided representations and reasoning mechanisms to identify and react appropriately to various sorts of interactions. However, previous work has not provided a framework for reasoning about goal interactions that is generic, extensible, formally described, and that covers a range of interaction types. This paper provides such a framework.

1 Introduction

One of the defining characteristics of intelligent software agents is their ability to pursue goals in a flexible and reliable manner, and many modern agent platforms provide some form of goal construct [1]. However, these platforms are surprisingly naive in their handling of *interactions* between goals in that few implemented agent platforms provide support for reasoning about interactions between goals. Platforms such as Jason [2], JACK [3], 2APL [4] and many others don't make any attempt to detect interactions between goals, which means that agents may behave irrationally. Empirical evaluation [5] has shown that this can be a serious issue, and that the cost of introducing limited reasoning to prevent certain forms of irrational behaviour is low, and consistent with bounded reasoning.

There has been work on providing means for an agent to detect various forms of interaction between its goals, such as resource contention [6], and interactions involving logical conditions, both positive [7] and negative (e.g. [8]). However, this strand of work has not integrated the various forms of reasoning into a single framework: each form of interaction is treated separately. Although more recent work by Shaw and Bordini [9] does integrate a range of interaction reasoning mechanisms, it does so indirectly, by translation to Petri nets, which makes it difficult to extend, to determine whether the reasoning being done is correct, or to relate the reasoning back to the agent's goals and plans (traceability).

* This work was partly done while the author was employed by RMIT University.

C. Sakama et al. (Eds.): DALT 2011, LNAI 7169, pp. 16–32, 2012.

This paper provides a framework for extending BDI platforms with the ability to reason about interactions between goals. The framework developed improves on previous work by being generic and by being formally presented. Thus, the key criteria for evaluating our proposed framework is its ability to deal with the different types of interaction between goals. The sorts of goal interactions that we want to be able to model and reason about include the following.

Resources: goals may have resource requirements, including both reusable resources such as communication channels, and consumable resources such as fuel or money. Given a number of goals it is possible that their combined resource requirements exceed the available resources. In this case the agent should realise this, and only commit to pursuing some of its goals or, for reusable resources, schedule the goals so as to use the resources appropriately (if possible). Furthermore, should there be a change in either the available resources or the estimated resource requirements of its goals, the agent should be able to respond by reconsidering its commitments. For example, if a Mars rover updates its estimate of the fuel required to visit a site of interest (it may have found a shorter route), then the rover should consider whether any of its suspended goals may be reactivated.

Conditions: goals affect the state of the agent and of its environment, and may also at various points require certain properties of the agent and/or its environment. An agent should be aware of interactions between goals such as:

- After moving to a location in order to perform some experiment, avoid moving elsewhere until the experiment has been completed.
- If two goals involve being at the same location, schedule them so as to avoid travelling to the location twice.
- If there are changes to conditions then appropriate re-planning should take place. For example, if a rover has placed equipment to perform a long-running experiment but the equipment has malfunctioned, then the rover should respond to this.

In summary, the challenge is to provide mechanisms that allow for:

- Specification of the dependencies between goals/plans and resources/conditions. To be practical, dependencies must be specified in a local and modular fashion where each goal or plan only needs to specify the resources/conditions that it is directly affected by.
- Reasoning about conditions and resources so as to detect situations where there is interaction between goals.
- Having a means of specifying suitable responses to detected interactions. Possible responses include suspending or aborting a goal, changing the means by which a goal is achieved (e.g. travelling by train rather than plane to save money), and scheduling goals (e.g. to avoid double-booking a reusable resource).

Section 2 reviews the goal framework and agent notation that we will build on. Section 3 presents our framework for reasoning about goal interactions, and Section 4 completes the framework by extending the agent notation. In Section 5 we evaluate the framework by showing how it is able to deal with the various types of goal interaction under consideration. We conclude in Section 6.

2 Conceptual Agent Notation with Generic Goals

We now briefly present the Conceptual Agent Notation (CAN) [10, 11]. CAN is used as a representative for a whole class of BDI agent languages which define agent execution in terms of event-triggered plans, where multiple plans may be relevant to handle a given event, and where failure is handled by reposting events. It is similar to AgentSpeak(L) [12] in that it uses a library of event-triggered plans which have a specified trigger, context condition, and plan body. CAN differs from AgentSpeak(L) in that it provides additional constructs, and in that it uses a particular failure handling mechanism (event reposting) which is common to BDI languages.

In order to extend goals into "interaction-aware goals" that are able to detect and respond to interactions with other goals we will use a variant of CAN which uses the generic goal construct of van Riemsdijk *et al.* [1]. Their framework defines a goal type with certain default life-cycle transitions, and provides a mechanism for adding additional life-cycle transitions. A goal type is defined in terms of a set C of condition-response pairs $\langle c, S\rangle$ where c is a condition to be checked that, if true, changes the goal's state to S. For example, a goal to achieve p includes $\langle p, \text{DROPPED}\rangle$ which specifies that when p becomes true the goal should be dropped. Condition-response pairs come in two flavours: "continuous", checked at all times, and "end", checked only at the start/end of plan execution. A goal instance $\mathsf{g}(C, \pi_0, S, \pi)$ specifies a set of condition-response pairs C, an initial plan π_0, a current state S (e.g. ACTIVE, DROPPED, SUSPENDED), and a current plan π.

The default goal life-cycle of van Riemsdijk *et al.* [1] is that goals are adopted into a suspended state, and they are then repeatedly activated and suspended until they are dropped. Active goals are subjected to means-end reasoning to find an abstract plan for pursuing the goal, and this plan is then executed (as long as the goal remains active).

We integrate this generic goal construct into CAN, replacing its more limited goal construct. The resulting language defines an agent in terms of a set Π of plans of the form $e : c \leftarrow \pi$ where e is the triggering event, c is a context condition (a logical formula over the agent's beliefs), and π is a plan body (we will sometimes refer to plan bodies as "plans"):

$$\pi ::= \epsilon \mid a \mid e \mid \pi_1; \pi_2 \mid \pi_1 \| \pi_2$$

We denote the empty plan body by ϵ, and an event is written as e. For simplicity we define a generic action construct, a, which has a pre-condition pre_a and post-condition defined in terms of non-overlapping addition and deletion sets add_a and del_a. A number of previously defined CAN constructs can be viewed as special cases of this, for example $+b$ can be defined as an action with $pre_{+b} = true$, $add_{+b} = \{b\}$ and $del_{+b} = \emptyset$. Similarly, $-b$ has $pre_{-b} = \{b\}$, $add_{-b} = \emptyset$, $del_{-b} = \{b\}$ and $?c$ has $pre_{?c} = \{c\}$ and $add_{?c} = del_{?c} = \emptyset$. We assume that events e and actions a can be distinguished. An agent configuration is a pair $\langle B, G\rangle$ where B is the agent's current beliefs, and G is a set of goals.

Figures 1 and 2 provide formal semantics for this language (based on previously presented semantics for CAN [1, 10, 13]) in structured operational semantics style [14] where the premise (above the line) gives the conditions under which the transition below the line may take place. We define a number of different transition types. Firstly, $\rightarrow$ as

$$\frac{S = \text{ACTIVE}}{\mathsf{g}(C, \pi_0, S, \epsilon) \overset{e}{\Rightarrow} \mathsf{g}(C, \pi_0, S, \pi_0)}\ 1 \qquad \frac{\pi \overset{e}{\Rightarrow} \pi' \quad S = \text{ACTIVE}}{\mathsf{g}(C, \pi_0, S, \pi) \overset{e}{\Rightarrow} \mathsf{g}(C, \pi_0, S, \pi')}\ 2$$

$$\frac{\langle c, S', f\rangle \in C \quad B \models c \quad S \neq S' \quad ok(f, \pi)}{\mathsf{g}(C, \pi_0, S, \pi) \overset{u}{\Rightarrow} \mathsf{g}(C, \pi_0, S', \pi)}\ 3$$

$$\frac{g \in G \quad \langle B, g\rangle \overset{e}{\Rightarrow} \langle B', g'\rangle}{\langle B, G\rangle \overset{e}{\rightarrow} \langle B', (G \setminus \{g\}) \cup \{g'\}\rangle}\ 4 \qquad \frac{g \in G \quad g \overset{u}{\Rightarrow} g'}{\langle B, G\rangle \overset{u}{\rightarrow} \langle B, (G \setminus \{g\}) \cup \{g'\}\rangle}\ 5$$

$$\frac{\langle B, G\rangle \overset{u}{\rightarrow}^{*} \langle B, G'\rangle \quad \langle B, G'\rangle \overset{u}{\not\rightarrow} \langle B, G''\rangle}{\langle B, G\rangle \overset{u}{\twoheadrightarrow} \langle B, \{g | g \in G' \wedge g \neq \mathsf{g}(C, \pi_0, \text{DROPPED}, \pi)\}\rangle}\ 6$$

$$\frac{\langle B, G\rangle \overset{u}{\twoheadrightarrow} \langle B, G''\rangle \quad \langle B, G''\rangle \overset{e}{\rightarrow} \langle B', G'\rangle}{\langle B, G\rangle \rightarrow \langle B', G'\rangle}\ 7$$

Fig. 1. Formal semantics for CAN with generic goals

being a transition over a *set* of goals (i.e. $\langle B, G\rangle$), and $\Rightarrow$ is defined as being a transition over a *single* goal/plan (i.e. $\langle B, g\rangle$ where $g \in G$). Furthermore, we use letters to denote particular transition types (e for execute, u for update) and a superscript asterisk ($*$) denotes "zero or more" as is usual. For conciseness we abbreviate $\langle B, g\rangle$ by just g, for example the bottom of rule 9 abbreviates $\langle B, e\rangle \overset{e}{\Rightarrow} \langle B', (\!|\Gamma|\!)\rangle$, and similarly for rules 1-3.

Figure 1 defines the semantics of goals. The first two rules specify that an active goal can be executed by replacing an empty plan with the initial plan π_0 (rule 1) or by executing the goal's plan (rule 2) which makes use of the rules for plan execution (Figure 2). The next rule (3) defines a single goal update: if an update condition holds, update the goal's state, subject to two conditions: firstly, the new state should be different ($S \neq S'$), secondly, the condition c should be active given the f tag[1] and the plan π; formally $ok(f, \pi) \equiv ((f = end \wedge \pi = \epsilon) \vee (f = mid \wedge \pi \neq \epsilon) \vee f = all)$. Rules 4 and 5 define respectively execution (rule 4) and update (rule 5) of a set of goals by selecting a single goal and respectively executing it or updating it. Rule 6 defines a complete update cycle $\overset{u}{\twoheadrightarrow}$ which performs all possible updates, and deletes goals with a state of "DROPPED". Rule 7 defines a single top-level transition step of a set of goals: first perform all possible updates ($\overset{u}{\twoheadrightarrow}$) and then perform a single execution step ($\overset{e}{\rightarrow}$). We require that all possible updates are done in order to avoid ever executing a goal that has a pending update to a non-active state.

Figure 2 defines a single execution step ($\overset{e}{\Rightarrow}$) for various CAN plan constructs. Rule 8 defines how an action a is executed in terms of its precondition and add/delete sets. Rule 9 defines how an event is replaced by the set of guarded relevant plan instances $(\!|\Gamma|\!)$. Rule 10 selects an applicable plan instance from a set of plans, using the auxiliary

[1] We have compressed the two sets C and E of van Riemsdijk *et al.* [1] into a single set of triples $\langle c, S, f\rangle$ where f is a flag specifying when the condition should be checked: when the plan is empty (end), when the plan is non-empty, i.e. during execution (mid) or at all times (all). E.g. $\langle c, S\rangle \in C$ in their framework translates to $\langle c, S, all\rangle$.

$$\frac{B \models pre_a}{\langle B,a\rangle \overset{e}{\Rightarrow} \langle (B\cup add_a)\setminus del_a, \epsilon\rangle}\ 8 \qquad \frac{\Gamma = \{c\theta{:}\pi\theta \mid (e'{:}c{\leftarrow}\pi) \in \Pi \wedge \theta = \mathsf{mgu}(e,e')\}}{e \overset{e}{\Rightarrow} (\!|\Gamma|\!)}\ 9$$

$$\frac{(c_i{:}\pi_i) \in \Gamma \quad B \models c_i\theta \quad \pi_i\theta \overset{e}{\Rightarrow} \pi'}{(\!|\Gamma|\!) \overset{e}{\Rightarrow} \pi_i\theta \rhd (\!|\Gamma \setminus \{c_i{:}\pi_i\}|\!)}\ 10 \qquad \frac{P_1 \overset{e}{\Rightarrow} P'}{P_1; P_2 \overset{e}{\Rightarrow} \overline{P'; P_2}}\ 11 \qquad \frac{P_1 \overset{e}{\Rightarrow} P'}{P_1 \| P_2 \overset{e}{\Rightarrow} \overline{P' \| P_2}}\ 12$$

$$\frac{P_2 \overset{e}{\Rightarrow} P'}{P_1 \| P_2 \overset{e}{\Rightarrow} \overline{P_1 \| P'}}\ 13 \qquad \frac{P_1 \overset{e}{\Rightarrow} P'}{P_1 \rhd P_2 \overset{e}{\Rightarrow} \overline{P' \rhd P_2}}\ 14 \qquad \frac{P_1 \not\overset{e}{\Rightarrow} P' \quad P_2 \overset{e}{\Rightarrow} P_2'}{P_1 \rhd P_2 \overset{e}{\Rightarrow} P_2}\ 15$$

Fig. 2. Formal semantics for CAN plan constructs

construct $\rhd$ to indicate "try π, but if it fails, use the set of (remaining) relevant plans". Rule 11 simply defines the semantics of sequential execution ";", rules 12 and 13 define parallel execution "$\|$", and rules 14 and 15 define "try-else" ($\rhd$). The function denoted by an overline (e.g. $\overline{\pi_1; \pi_2}$) cleans up by removing empty plan bodies: $\overline{\epsilon; \pi} = \overline{\epsilon \| \pi} = \overline{\pi \| \epsilon} = \pi$, and $\overline{\epsilon \rhd \pi} = \epsilon$, otherwise $\overline{\pi} = \pi$.

Note that the semantics model failure as an inability to progress, i.e. a failed plan body π is one where $\pi \not\Rightarrow \pi'$. This simplifies the semantics at the cost of losing the distinction between failure and suspension, and creating a slight anomaly with parallelism where given $\pi_1 \| \pi_2$ we can continue to execute π_2 even if π_1 has "failed". Both these issues are easily repaired by modelling failure separately (as is done by Winikoff *et al.* [10]), but this makes the semantics considerably more verbose.

We can now define a (very!) simple Mars rover that performs a range of experiments at different locations on the Martian surface. The first plan below for performing an experiment of type X at location L firstly moves to the appropriate location L, then collects a sample using the appropriate measuring apparatus.

$$\begin{array}{lll} exp(L,X) : \neg locn(L) & \leftarrow & goto(L)\ ;\ sample(X) \\ exp(L,X) : locn(L) & \leftarrow & sample(X) \end{array}$$

We assume for simplicity of exposition that $goto(L)$, and $sample(X)$ are primitive actions, but they could also be defined as events that trigger further plans. The action $goto(L)$ has precondition $\neg locn(L)$ and add set $\{locn(L)\}$ and delete set $\{locn(x)\}$ where x is the current location.

3 Reasoning about Interactions

We provide reasoning about interactions between goals by:

1. Extending the language to allow goal requirements (resources, conditions to be maintained etc.) to be specified (Section 3.1).
2. Providing a mechanism to reason about these requirements, specifically by aggregating requirements and propagating them (Section 3.2).

3. Defining new conditions that can be used to specify goal state transitions, and adding additional state transition types that allow responses to detected interactions to be specified. These are then used to extend CAN with interaction-aware goals (Section 4).

3.1 Specifying Requirements

There are a number of ways of specifying requirements. Perhaps the simplest is to require each primitive action to specify its requirements. Unfortunately this is less flexible since it does not allow the user to indicate that a plan, perhaps combining a number of actions, has certain requirements. We thus extend the language with a construct $\tau(\pi, R)$ which indicates that the plan π is tagged ("τ") with requirements R. It is still possible to annotate actions directly, $\tau(a, R)$, but it is no longer the only place where requirements may be noted.

However, in some cases, the requirements of a goal or plan can only be determined in context. For example, the fuel consumed in moving to a location depends on the location, but also on the current location, which is not known ahead of time. We thus provide a second mechanism for dynamic tagging where the requirements of a goal/plan are provided in terms of a procedure that computes the requirements, and a condition that indicates when the procedure should be re-run. This is denoted $\tau(\pi, f, c)$ where f is a function that uses the agent's beliefs to compute the requirements, and c is a re-computation condition. Once the requirements have been propagated (see next section) this becomes $T(\pi, R, f, c)$ (the difference between τ and T is discussed in Section 3.2) we need to retain f and c so the requirements can be re-computed (if c becomes true). Otherwise $T(\pi, R, f, c)$ behaves just like $T(\pi, R)$.

We define R as being a pair of two sets, $\langle L, U \rangle$, representing a lower and upper bound. For convenience, where a requirement R is written as a set $R = \{\ldots\}$ then it is taken to denote the pair $\langle R, R \rangle$. Each of the sets can be defined in many ways, depending on the needs of the domain and application. Here we define each set as containing a number of the following requirement statements:

- $re(r/c, t, n)$ where the first argument in the term is either r or c, denoting a reusable or consumable resource, t is a type (e.g. fuel), and n is the required amount of the resource.
- $pr(c)$ where c is a condition that must be true at the *start* of execution (i.e. a precondition)
- $in(c)$ where c is a condition that must be true *during* the *whole* of execution (including at the start). For the computation of summaries we also define a variant in_s which means that c must be true *somewhere* during the execution but not necessarily during the whole execution.

In the Mars rover example we have the following requirements:

1. $goto(L)$ computes its requirements based on the distance between the destination and current location. This needs to be re-computed after each goto. We thus specify the requirements of the $goto(L)$ action as $\tau(goto(L), f(L), c)$ where $f(L)$ looks up the current location $locn$ in the belief base, and then computes the distance between

it and L; and where $c = \Delta locn(x)$ (informally, Δc means that the belief base has changed in a way that affects the condition c; formally, if B is the old belief base and B' the updated belief base, then $\Delta c \equiv \neg(B \models c \Leftrightarrow B' \models c)$);

2. $sample(X)$ requires that the rover remains at the desired location, hence we specify an in-condition (in) that the location ($locn$) remains L: $\tau(sample(X), \{in(locn(L))\})$.

We thus provide requirements by specifying the following plan body (for the first plan), where f is a function that is given a location L and computes the fuel required to reach the location.
$\tau(goto(L), f(L), c); \tau(sample(X), \{in(locn(L))\})$

3.2 Propagating Requirements

We define a function Σ that takes a plan body and tags it with requirements by propagating and aggregating given requirements. We use ε to denote the empty requirement. The function returns a modified plan which contains tags of the form $T(\pi, R)$: this is different from $\tau(\pi, R)$ in that τ is used by the user to provide requirements for a plan, not including the requirements of the plan's sub-plans, but T *does* include the requirements of sub-plans. Observe that Σ is defined compositionally over the plan, and that computing it is not expensive in the absence of recursive plans [5].

$\Sigma(\epsilon) = T(\epsilon, \varepsilon)$
$\Sigma(a) = T(a, \{pr(pre_a)\})$
$\Sigma(e) = T(e, \langle L_1 \sqcap \ldots \sqcap L_n, U_1 \sqcup \ldots \sqcup U_n\rangle)$, where $T(\pi_i', \langle L_i, U_i\rangle) = \Sigma(\pi_i)$
and $\pi_1 \ldots \pi_n$ are the plans relevant for e.
$\Sigma(\pi_1; \pi_2) = T(\pi_1'; \pi_2', \langle L_1 \fatsemi L_2, U_1 \fatsemi U_2\rangle)$, where $T(\pi_i', \langle L_i, U_i\rangle) = \Sigma(\pi_i)$
$\Sigma(\pi_1 \| \pi_2) = T(\pi_1' \| \pi_2', \langle L_1 \talloblong L_2, U_1 \talloblong U_2\rangle)$, where $T(\pi_i', \langle L_i, U_i\rangle) = \Sigma(\pi_i)$
$\Sigma(\pi_1 \rhd \pi_2) = T(\pi_1' \rhd \pi_2', \langle L_1, U_1 \fatsemi U_2\rangle)$, where $T(\pi_i', \langle L_i, U_i\rangle) = \Sigma(\pi_i)$
$\Sigma((\!|\Gamma|\!)) = T((\!|\Gamma'|\!), \langle L_1 \sqcap \ldots \sqcap L_n, U_1 \sqcup \ldots \sqcup U_n\rangle)$, where $T(\pi_i', \langle L_i, U_i\rangle) = \Sigma(\pi_i)$
and $\Gamma = \{b_1{:}\pi_1, \ldots, b_n{:}\pi_n\}$ and $\Gamma' = \{b_1{:}\pi_1' \ldots, b_n{:}\pi_n'\}$.
$\Sigma(\tau(\pi, \langle L, U\rangle)) = T(\pi', \langle L' \oplus L, U' \oplus U\rangle)$, where $T(\pi', \langle L', U'\rangle) = \Sigma(\pi)$
$\Sigma(\tau(\pi, f, c)) = \Sigma(T(\pi, f(B), f, c))$, where B is the agent's beliefs.
$\Sigma(T(\pi, R)) =$ if $\pi' = T(\pi'', \varepsilon)$ then $T(\pi'', R)$ else π', where $\pi' = \Sigma(\pi)$

The requirements of an action are simply its pre-condition. The requirements of an event are computed by taking the requirements of the set of relevant plans and combining them: the best case is the minimum of the available plans ($\sqcap$), and in the worse case (represented by the upper bound) we may need to execute all of the plans and so we take the (unspecified sequential) maximum of the requirements of the available plans using $\sqcup$. The requirements for $\pi_1; \pi_2$ and $\pi_1 \| \pi_2$ are determined by computing the requirements of π_1 and of π_2 and then combining them appropriately with auxiliary functions $\fatsemi$ and $\talloblong$ which are both variants on $\sqcup$: $\fatsemi$ treats pre-conditions of the first requirement set as pre-conditions, since we *do* know that they occur at the start of execution; and $\talloblong$ is like $\sqcup$ except that, because execution is in parallel, we cannot reuse resources. The lower bound requirements for $\pi_1 \rhd \pi_2$ are just the (lower bound) requirements for π_1, since, if all goes well, there will be no need to execute π_2. However, in the worse case (upper bound) both π_1 and π_2 will need to be executed (sequentially, hence $\fatsemi$). The requirements for a user-tagged plan, $\tau(\pi, R)$ are determined by computing the requirements of π and then adding ($\oplus$) this to the provided R. Finally, when re-computing the requirements of $T(\pi, R)$ we simply replace R with the newly computed requirements.

The case for events (e) is interesting: in the worst case, we may need to execute all of the available plans. In the best case, only one plan will be executed. However, when computing the initial estimate of requirements we don't know which plans are applicable, so we overestimate by using all relevant plans, and later update the estimate (see below).

The function Σ is defined in terms of a number of auxiliary functions: $\oplus$, $\sqcup$, $\sqcap$, $\fatsemi$ and $[\!]$. By defining what can appear in R as well as these functions the agent designer can create their own types of reasoning. We have defined an example R in the previous section, and briefly and informally given the intended meaning of the auxiliary functions above. The appendix contains precise formal definitions of these auxiliary functions.

We integrate requirements propagation into the operational semantics of CAN by defining operational semantics for the $T(\pi, R)$ construct which captures the process of updating requirements:

$$\frac{\pi \Rightarrow \pi' \quad \pi \neq \epsilon \quad R \neq \varepsilon}{T(\pi, R) \Rightarrow \Sigma(\pi')} \qquad \frac{\pi \neq \epsilon}{T(\pi, \varepsilon) \Rightarrow \pi} \qquad \frac{}{T(\epsilon, R) \Rightarrow \epsilon}$$

The first rule is the general case: if π executes one step to π' then $T(\pi, R)$ can also be stepped to $\Sigma(\pi')$. The next rule specifies that tagging with an empty requirement set can be deleted. The final rule allows an empty plan body with requirements to be resolved to the empty plan body. Finally, we modify the goal initialisation rule (first rule in figure 1) to compute requirements by replacing the right-most π_0 with $\Sigma(\pi_0)$:

$$\frac{S = \text{ACTIVE}}{\mathsf{g}(C, \pi_0, S, \epsilon) \overset{e}{\Rightarrow} \mathsf{g}(C, \pi_0, S, \Sigma(\pi_0))}$$

Alternatively, as is done by Thangarajah *et al.* [6], we could modify the agent's plan set by replacing π with $\Sigma(\pi)$ at compile time.

Returning to the Mars rover, let $\pi = \tau(goto(L), f, c); \tau(sample(X), \{in(locn(L))\})$ then the following requirements are computed (recall that $T(\pi, R)$ where R is a set is short for $T(\pi, \langle R, R\rangle)$, and we assume that f returns 20 for the fuel requirement of reaching L from the starting location):

$$\begin{aligned}
\Sigma(\pi) &= T(\pi_2; \pi_3, \{re(c, fuel, 20), in_s(locn(L)), pr(\neg locn(L))\}) \\
\pi_2 &= T(goto(L), \{re(c, fuel, 20), pr(\neg locn(L))\}, f, c) \\
\pi_3 &= T(sample(X), \{in(locn(L))\})
\end{aligned}$$

After the first action (π_2) has completed we have: $\Sigma(\pi') = \pi_3$.

4 Using Requirements to Deal with Interactions

The work of the previous sections allows us to specify requirements, and to compute and update them. In this section we consider how this information can be used to avoid undesirable interactions and (attempt to) ensure desirable interactions. For goals, we do this by defining a new goal type, an "interaction-aware goal", which has additional condition-response triples. But first, we define a number of new conditions, and new responses.

4.1 Conditions

The language of conditions is extended with new constructs: rok ("resources are ok"), $culprit$, and $interfere$.

The new condition $rok(G)$ means that there are enough resources for all of the goals in G. Informally we define $rok(G)$ by computing the resource requirements of the active goals in G and comparing it with the available resources. If the available resources exceed the resource requirements of the active goals, then clearly $rok(G)$ is true. If not, then we need to work out which goals should be suspended. We define the condition $culprit(g)$ to indicate that the goal g is responsible for a lack of sufficient resources. Informally, $culprit(g)$ is true if removing g from G makes things better[2] i.e., $culprit(g) \equiv rok(G \setminus \{g\}) \wedge \neg rok(G)$. See the appendix (definitions 4 and 5) for the (correct) formal definitions of rok and $culprit$.

The new condition $interfere(g)$ is true if g is about to do something that interferes with another goal. Informally, this is the case if one of the actions that g may do next (denoted $na(g)$, defined in the appendix) has an effect that is inconsistent with another goal's in-condition (where both goals are active). Formally[3] $interfere(g) \equiv \exists g' \in (G \setminus \{g\}), c \in getin(g'), a \in na(g) \;.\; g.S = g'.S = \text{ACTIVE} \wedge \mathit{eff}_a \supset \neg c$ where G is the agent's goals, we use $g.S$ to refer to the state of the goal g, we use $\supset$ to denote logical implication (to avoid confusion with transitions), and we define $getin$ to return the in-conditions of a goal, plan or requirements set:

$$
\begin{aligned}
getin(\mathsf{g}(C, \pi_0, S, \pi)) &= getin(\pi) \\
getin(T(\pi, \langle L, U \rangle)) &= \{c \mid in(c) \in L\} \\
getin(\pi) &= getin(\Sigma(\pi)), \text{ if } \pi \neq T(\pi', R)
\end{aligned}
$$

We also define eff_a to be a logical formula combining add_a and del_a as a conjunction of atoms in add_a and the negations of atoms in del_a. For example, for $goto(L)$ we have $\mathit{eff}_{goto(L)} = locn(L) \wedge \neg locn(x)$.

We can also define a similar condition that detects interference with pre-conditions. In order to avoid suspending goals unnecessarily, we only consider interference to be real if the pre-condition being affected currently holds. In other words, if the precondition c of goal g' does *not* currently hold, then there is not a strong reason to suspend goal g which makes c false because c is *already* false. This gives $interfere_{pre}(g) \equiv \exists g' \in (G \setminus \{g\}), c \in getpre(g'), a \in na(g) \;.\; B \models c \wedge g.S = g'.S = \text{ACTIVE} \wedge \mathit{eff}_a \supset \neg c$ where $getpre$ retrieves the pre-conditions, similarly to $getin$ (see appendix definition 2).

[2] In fact, as discussed in the appendix, this isn't entirely correct.

[3] We use a period "." to denote "such that", i.e. $\exists a \in A, b \in B \;.\; p$ is read as "there exists a in A and b in B such that p".

4.2 Responses

Responses to interactions can be either "subtle": influencing existing choices, but not changing the semantics, i.e. "subtle" responses can be viewed as refining the semantics by reducing non-determinism. Alternatively, responses can be "blunt" responses which change the semantics.

So-called "subtle" responses apply where there is a choice to be made in the execution. This is the case in the following places: when selecting which (top-level) goal to execute, when selecting which plan to use from a set of alternatives ($(\!|\Gamma|\!)$), and when selecting which parallel plan to execute ($\pi_1 \| \pi_2$). Note that only the first case involves goals: the second and third involve plan bodies.

Influencing the choice of goal can be done by a range of means, including suspending goals and giving certain goals higher priority. Suspending goals can be done using the generic goal mechanism. In order to allow a goal to be given a higher priority we define a new *response* (not goal state) PICKME (below).

Influencing the selection of a plan from a set of possible plans ($(\!|\Gamma|\!)$) can be done by modifying the selection rule (it can't be done using the generic goal mechanism because plan selection occurs within a single goal). For example, we could require that an applicable plan is not selected if a cheaper plan exists. This can be formalised by adding to the rule for plan selection the following additional condition (the relation $\prec$ and function *getres* are defined in the appendix in definitions 1 and 3):

$$\frac{(c_i{:}\pi_i) \in \Gamma \quad B \models c_i\theta \quad \neg\exists(c_j{:}\pi_j) \in \Gamma . getres(\pi_j) \prec getres(\pi_i)}{(\!|\Gamma|\!) \overset{e}{\Rightarrow} \pi_i\theta \rhd (\!|\Gamma \setminus \{c_i{:}\pi_i\}|\!)}$$

However, we do not consider plan selection to be particularly useful in preventing resource issues, because the set of applicable plans will typically not contain a wide range of options.

The third case, influencing the scheduling of parallel plans ($\pi_1 \| \pi_2$) we consider to be less useful and leave it for future work.

Turning now to the so-called "blunt" responses we have a number of possible responses including: (a) dropping a goal, and (b) adding a new goal. The former may be used to permanently eliminate a goal that cannot be achieved (although suspension may be a more sensible response). The second may be used to create a new goal (or plan), for example, if a resource shortage is detected, a plan may be created to obtain more of the resource (e.g. re-fuelling).

We thus define the following additional responses:

- $!\pi$ which executes π (we can define synchronous and asynchronous variants of this)
- PICKME which specifies that this goal should be given priority when selecting which goal to execute (but, since more than one goal may be flagged as PICKME, cannot guarantee that the goal will be selected next). More generally, we could have a priority mechanism and have responses that raise/lower the priority of the goal.

These are defined formally as follows. Although they appear in condition-response triples, the semantics of these two constructs aren't just changing the state of the goal, and so we revise the existing rule so it does not apply to these two responses:

$$\frac{\langle c, S', f\rangle \in C \quad S' \in asd \quad B \models c \quad S \neq S' \quad ok(f, \pi)}{\mathsf{g}(C, \pi_0, S, \pi) \overset{u}{\Rightarrow} \mathsf{g}(C, \pi_0, S', \pi)} \; 3'$$

where $asd = \{\text{ACTIVE}, \text{SUSPENDED}, \text{DROPPED}\}$.

Because we want a PICKME to only last while the corresponding condition is true, we do not update the goal's state to PICKME, but instead modify the selection rule (rule 4) by adding the following additional condition (premise, where we use $\supset$ to denote logical implication) which requires that if any active goals are prioritised, then the selected goal must be a prioritised one: $((\exists \mathsf{g}(C', \pi_0', \text{ACTIVE}, \pi') \in G \,.\, \langle c', \text{PICKME}\rangle \in C' \wedge B \models c') \supset (\langle c, \text{PICKME}\rangle \in g.C \wedge B \models c))$. Where g is the goal being selected, and where we use $g.C$ to denote the C set of g (i.e. $g = \mathsf{g}(C, \pi_0, S, \pi)$).

We now turn to $!\pi$. A response of the form $!\pi$ transforms the goal from $\mathsf{g}(C, \pi_0, S, \pi')$ to the variant $\mathsf{g}_\pi(C, \pi_0, S, \pi')$:

$$\frac{\langle c, !\pi\rangle \in C \quad B \models c}{\mathsf{g}(C, \pi_0, S, \pi') \overset{u}{\Rightarrow} \mathsf{g}_\pi(C, \pi_0, S, \pi')} \; 16$$

We then define the semantics of this as follows:

$$\frac{\pi \overset{e}{\Rightarrow} \pi_1}{\mathsf{g}_\pi(C, \pi_0, S, \pi') \overset{e}{\Rightarrow} \overline{\mathsf{g}_{\pi_1}(C, \pi_0, S, \pi')}} \; 17$$

where $\overline{\mathsf{g}_\epsilon(C, \pi_0, S, \pi)} = \mathsf{g}(C, \pi_0, S, \pi)$, and for $g = \mathsf{g}_\pi(\ldots)$ with $\pi \neq \epsilon$ we have $\overline{g} = g$.

4.3 Interaction-Aware Goals

Finally, we are in a position to define a new goal type which uses the conditions and responses defined, along with the underlying infrastructure for specifying and propagating requirements, in order to deal with interactions as part of the agent's goal reasoning process.

We extend goals into interaction-aware goals by simply adding to their C set the following condition-response triples, where *culprit* is short for $culprit(g)$ with g being the current goal, and similarly for *interfere*. The condition *notculprit* differs from $\neg culprit$ in that it includes the current goal g in the computation of resources (whereas *culprit* treats it as not having any resource requirements, since it is suspended). Formally $notculprit(\mathsf{g}(C, \pi_0, \text{SUSPENDED}, \pi)) \equiv \neg culprit(\mathsf{g}(C, \pi_0, \text{ACTIVE}, \pi))$. Similarly, *notinterfere* differs from $\neg interfere$ by considering the current goal as being hypothetically active, i.e. $notinterfere(\mathsf{g}(C, \pi_0, \text{SUSPENDED}, \pi)) \equiv \neg interfere(\mathsf{g}(C, \pi_0, \text{ACTIVE}, \pi))$.

$$\mathcal{I} = \{\langle culprit, \text{SUSPENDED}, all\rangle, \langle notculprit, \text{ACTIVE}, all\rangle,$$
$$\langle interfere, \text{SUSPENDED}, all\rangle, \langle notinterfere, \text{ACTIVE}, all\rangle\}$$

An alternative, if there is a plan π_r which obtains more of a needed resource, is to use it instead of suspending: $\mathcal{I}' = \{\langle culprit, !\pi_r, all\rangle, \ldots\}$.

5 Motivating Scenarios Revisited

We now consider how the different forms of reasoning discussed at the outset can be supported. We define

$$gexp(l,x) \equiv g(\mathcal{I} \cup \{\langle locn(l), \text{PICKME}, all\rangle\}, exp(l,x))$$

that is, $gexp(l,x)$ is an interaction-aware goal which uses the initial plan body (which is actually just an event) $exp(l,x)$. Finally, we suppose that the Mars rover has been asked to perform three experiments: experiment 1 of type T_1 at location L_A (i.e. $g_1 = gexp(L_A, T_1)$) experiment 2 of type T_1 at location L_B (i.e. $g_2 = gexp(L_B, T_1)$), and experiment 3 of type T_2 at location L_A (i.e. $g_3 = gexp(L_A, T_2)$).

Let us now briefly consider how the Mars rover deals with the following cases of interaction:

1. **A lack of resources causes a goal to be suspended, and, when resources are sufficient, resumed:** since the goals are interaction-aware, suspension and resumption will occur as a result of the conditions-responses in $\mathcal{I}$. Specifically, should the resources available be insufficient to achieve all goals, then some of goals will be suspended by the $\langle culprit, \text{SUSPENDED}, all\rangle$ condition-response triple. Note that since updates are performed one at a time, this will only suspend as many goals as are needed to resolve the resource issue.

   If further resources are obtained, then the suspended goals will be re-activated ($\langle notculprit, \text{ACTIVE}, all\rangle$). In the case of reusable resources, the suspension/resumption mechanism will realise scheduling of the reusable resources amongst goals: once a goal has completed and releases the (reusable) resources it has been using, another goal that requires these resources can then resume.
2. **A lack of resources, instead of suspending, may trigger a plan to obtain more resources:** if the goals are defined using $\mathcal{I}'$ rather than $\mathcal{I}$, then a lack of resources will cause a plan body π_r to be used to obtain more resources. In this domain, where the main resource is fuel, a sensible choice for π_r would be to re-fuel.
3. **Once the Mars rover has moved to location L_A, it avoids moving again until the sampling at L_A has completed:** once goal g_1 has executed $goto(L_A)$ then, as discussed at the end of Section 3.2, its requirement is updated to include the in-condition $locn(L_A)$. Should goal g_2 get to the point of being about to execute its action $goto(L_B)$, then this next action interferes with the in-condition, and goal g_2 will then be suspended, using the condition-response triple $\langle interfere,$ $\text{SUSPENDED}, all\rangle$, preventing the execution of $goto(L_B)$. Once g_1 has concluded the experiment, then it no longer has $locn(L_A)$ as an in-condition, and at this point g_2 will be re-activated ($\langle \neg interfere, \text{ACTIVE}, all\rangle$).
4. **Once it has moved to location L_A, the rover also performs g_3 before moving elsewhere:** when it reaches L_A the PICKME response of g_3 (and g_1) is triggered which prioritises selecting these goals over g_2, and thus the rover will remain at L_A until g_1 and g_3 are both completed.

As can be seen, interaction-aware goals — which are defined in terms of the additional condition and response types, which themselves rest on the resource specification and propagation mechanism defined in Section 3 — are able to deal with a range of goal-interaction scenarios.

6 Discussion

We have provided a framework for reasoning about goal interactions that is: **generic**, i.e. can be customised to provide the reasoning that is needed for the application at hand; **presented formally**, and hence precisely, avoiding the ambiguity of natural language; and that **integrates** different reasoning types into one framework. We have also defined a wider range of conditions and responses than previous work.

Our work can be seen as a rational reconstruction of earlier work [6–8] which formalises and makes precise the English presentation in these papers. However, we do more than just formalise existing work: we provide a generic framework that allows for other forms of reasoning to be added, and for the existing forms to be integrated.

In addition to work on reasoning about interactions between an agent's goals, there has also been work on reasoning about interactions between the goals of different agents [15, 16]. This work has a somewhat different flavour in that it is concerned with the cost of communication between agents. However, in some other aspects, such as the use of requirements summaries, it is similar to the single agent case.

Also related is the work by Horty and Pollack [17] which looked at the cost of plans in context (i.e. taking into account the agent's other plans). Although the paper is ostensibly concerned with cost, they do also define various notions of compatibility between plans. However, their plans are composed only of primitive actions.

Thangarajah *et al.* [18] consider the goal adoption part of goal deliberation: should a candidate goal (roughly speaking, a desire) be added to the agent's set of adopted goals? They embed the goal adoption problem in a BDI setting into a soft constraint optimisation problem model and discuss a range of factors that can be taken into account in making decisions. However, while promising, this is early work: the presentation is informal and a precise definition of the mapping to soft constraint optimisation problems is not given.

There are three main directions for future work that we would like to pursue: implementation, evaluation, and extending to further interaction scenarios.

What this paper presents can be seen as an extended BDI programming language with interaction-aware goals. One area for future work is how to implement this extended language using a standard BDI platform (such as Jason, Jadex, JACK etc.) that doesn't have a generic goal construct, or resource/condition management. One possibility is to transform the agent program, Π, into a variant that uses existing constructs (such as maintenance goals) to realise the desired behaviour. Another possibility, if the platform provides an API for manipulating the state of goals, is to realise generic goals by two parallel goals: one that executes the plan π, and another (with higher priority) that monitors for conditions and updates the first goal's state. Finally, a third approach is to use a meta-interpreter [19]. An implementation would allow for an evaluation to be done in order to assess the benefits, and also the real practical computational cost.

An interesting scenario which we have not yet investigated is "achieve then maintain", where a particular condition is achieved (e.g. booking a hotel), but then for some period of time (e.g. until the travel dates) the condition is maintained and updated should certain changes take place (e.g. budget reductions or changes to travel dates).

References

1. van Riemsdijk, M.B., Dastani, M., Winikoff, M.: Goals in agent systems: A unifying framework. In: Proceedings of the Seventh International Joint Conference on Autonomous Agents and Multiagent Systems (AAMAS), pp. 713–720 (2008)
2. Bordini, R.H., Hübner, J.F., Wooldridge, M.: Programming multi-agent systems in AgentSpeak using Jason. Wiley (2007) ISBN 0470029005
3. Busetta, P., Rönnquist, R., Hodgson, A., Lucas, A.: JACK Intelligent Agents - Components for Intelligent Agents in Java. Technical report, Agent Oriented Software Pty. Ltd., Melbourne, Australia (1998), `http://www.agent-software.com`
4. Dastani, M.: 2APL: a practical agent programming language. Autonomous Agents and Multi-Agent Systems 16(3), 214–248 (2008)
5. Thangarajah, J., Padgham, L.: Computationally effective reasoning about goal interactions. Journal of Automated Reasoning, 1–40 (2010)
6. Thangarajah, J., Winikoff, M., Padgham, L., Fischer, K.: Avoiding resource conflicts in intelligent agents. In: van Harmelen, F. (ed.) Proceedings of the 15th European Conference on Artificial Intelligence, pp. 18–22. IOS Press (2002)
7. Thangarajah, J., Padgham, L., Winikoff, M.: Detecting and exploiting positive goal interaction in intelligent agents. In: Proceedings of the Second International Joint Conference on Autonomous Agents and Multiagent Systems (AAMAS), pp. 401–408. ACM Press (2003)
8. Thangarajah, J., Padgham, L., Winikoff, M.: Detecting and avoiding interference between goals in intelligent agents. In: Proceedings of the 18th International Joint Conference on Artificial Intelligence (IJCAI), pp. 721–726 (2003)
9. Shaw, P.H., Bordini, R.H.: Towards Alternative Approaches to Reasoning About Goals. In: Baldoni, M., Son, T.C., van Riemsdijk, M.B., Winikoff, M. (eds.) DALT 2007. LNCS (LNAI), vol. 4897, pp. 104–121. Springer, Heidelberg (2008)
10. Winikoff, M., Padgham, L., Harland, J., Thangarajah, J.: Declarative & procedural goals in intelligent agent systems. In: Proceedings of the Eighth International Conference on Principles of Knowledge Representation and Reasoning (KR 2002), Toulouse, France, pp. 470–481 (2002)
11. Sardiña, S., Padgham, L.: A BDI agent programming language with failure handling, declarative goals, and planning. Autonomous Agents and Multi-Agent Systems 23(1), 18–70 (2011)
12. Rao, A.S.: AgentSpeak(L): BDI Agents Speak Out in a Logical Computable Language. In: Perram, J., Van de Velde, W. (eds.) MAAMAW 1996. LNCS (LNAI), vol. 1038, pp. 42–55. Springer, Heidelberg (1996)
13. Sardina, S., Padgham, L.: Goals in the context of BDI plan failure and planning. In: Proceedings of the Sixth International Joint Conference on Autonomous Agents and Multiagent Systems (AAMAS), pp. 16–23 (2007)
14. Plotkin, G.: Structural operational semantics (lecture notes). Technical Report DAIMI FN-19, Aarhus University (1981(reprinted 1991))
15. Clement, B.J., Durfee, E.H.: Identifying and resolving conflicts among agents with hierarchical plans. In: AAAI Workshop on Negotiation: Settling Conflicts and Identifying Opportunities, Technical Report WS-99-12 (1999)
16. Clement, B.J., Durfee, E.H.: Theory for coordinating concurrent hierarchical planning agents using summary information. In: Proceedings of the Sixteenth National Conference on Artificial Intelligence, pp. 495–502 (1999)
17. Horty, J.F., Pollack, M.E.: Evaluating new options in the context of existing plans. Artificial Intelligence 127(2), 199–220 (2001)

18. Thangarajah, J., Harland, J., Yorke-Smith, N.: A soft COP model for goal deliberation in a BDI agent. In: Proceedings of the Sixth International Workshop on Constraint Modelling and Reformulation, ModRef (September 2007)
19. Winikoff, M.: An AgentSpeak Meta-interpreter and Its Applications. In: Bordini, R.H., Dastani, M.M., Dix, J., El Fallah Seghrouchni, A. (eds.) PROMAS 2005. LNCS (LNAI), vol. 3862, pp. 123–138. Springer, Heidelberg (2006)

A Definitions

Definition 1 ($\prec$). *We define an ordering on requirement sets as follows. We say that R_1 is less than R_2 ($R_1 \preceq R_2$) if, intuitively, R_2 requires more than R_1. Formally, we define this by recognising that for a given condition c we have that $in_s(c) \preceq pr(c) \preceq in(c)$, i.e. a requirement that a condition hold for some unspecified part of the execution is less demanding than insisting that it hold at the start, which in turn is less demanding than insisting that it hold during the whole of execution (including at the start). We thus define $R_1 \preceq R_2$ to hold iff:*

- $re(f,t,n_1) \in R_1 \supset (r(f,t,n_2) \in R_2 \wedge n_1 \leq n_2)$
- $in(c) \in R_1 \supset (in(c') \in R_2 \wedge c' \supset c)$
- $pr(c) \in R_1 \supset ((pr(c') \in R_2 \vee in(c') \in R_2) \wedge c' \supset c)$
- $in_s(c) \in R_1 \supset ((in_s(c') \in R_2 \vee pr(c') \in R_2 \vee in(c') \in R_2) \wedge c' \supset c)$

We next define na ("next action") which takes a plan body and returns a set of possible next actions. Note that na is an approximation: it doesn't attempt to predict which actions might result from a set of plans $(\!|\Gamma|\!)$. A more accurate approach is to wait until an action is about to be executed before checking for interference.

$$\begin{aligned} na(a) &= \{a\} \\ na(\pi_1;\pi_2) &= na(\pi_1) \\ na(\pi_1 \| \pi_2) &= na(\pi_1) \cup na(\pi_2) \\ na(\pi_1 \rhd \pi_2) &= na(\pi_1) \\ na(e) &= \emptyset \\ na((\!|\Gamma|\!)) &= \emptyset \end{aligned}$$

Definition 2 (*getpre*). *getpre returns the pre-condition of a goal/plan.*

$$\begin{aligned} getpre(\mathsf{g}(C,\pi_0,S,\pi)) &= getpre(\pi) \\ getpre(T(\pi,\langle L,U\rangle)) &= \{c \mid pr(c) \in L\} \\ getpre(\pi) &= getpre(\Sigma(\pi)),\ \textit{if}\ \pi \neq T(\pi',R) \end{aligned}$$

Definition 3 (*getres*). *Calculating resource requirements only uses active goals, we ignore goals that are suspended or are executing responses triggered by* $!\pi$.

$$\begin{aligned} getres(\mathsf{g}(C,\pi_0,S,\pi)) &= getres(\pi),\ \textit{if}\ S = \textsc{Active} \\ getres(\mathsf{g}(C,\pi_0,S,\pi)) &= \varepsilon,\ \textit{if}\ S \neq \textsc{Active} \\ getres(\mathsf{g}_{\pi}(C,\pi_0,S,\pi)) &= \varepsilon \\ getres(T(\pi,\langle L,U\rangle)) &= \{re(f,t,n) \mid re(f,t,n) \in U\} \\ getres(\pi) &= getres(\Sigma(\pi)),\ \textit{if}\ \pi \neq T(\pi',R) \end{aligned}$$

Definition 4 (rok). *In defining $rok(G)$ we need to sum the resource requirements of the set of goals, and then check whether the available resources are sufficient. As discussed by Thangarajah et al. [6], there are actually a number of different cases. Here, for illustrative purposes, we just consider the case where there are sufficient resources to execute the goals freely as being an rok situation. We thus define the collected resource requirements of a goal set $G = \{g_1, \ldots, g_n\}$ as being $getres(G) = U_1 \talloblong \ldots \talloblong U_n$ where $U_i = getres(g_i)$. Finally, we define $rok(G) \equiv getres(G) \preceq \mathcal{R}$ where $\mathcal{R}$ is the available resources.*

Definition 5 ($culprit$). *In defining $culprit(g)$ one situation to be aware of is where removing a single goal is not enough. In this situation the definition given in the body of the paper will fail to identify any goals to suspend. To cover this case we need a slightly more complex definition. Informally, the previous definition is correct except where there does not exist a single goal that can be removed to fix the resource issue ($\neg\exists g \in G.rok(G \setminus \{g\})$). In this case we consider $culprit(g)$ to be true if removing g and one other goal will fix the problem. This generalises to the situation where one must remove n goals to fix a resource issue:*

$$\begin{aligned}
&culprit(g) \equiv \exists n \,.\, (\;\; (\exists G' \subseteq G.|G'| = n \wedge rok(G \setminus G') \wedge \neg rok(G) \wedge g \in G') \\
&\quad \wedge \;\; (\neg\exists G'' \subseteq G.|G''| < n \wedge rok(G \setminus G'') \wedge \neg rok(G)))
\end{aligned}$$

We now turn to defining the various auxiliary functions that are needed. We assume that requirements definitions, R_i, are *normalised*, i.e. that they contain (a) exactly one $re(f, t, n)$ for each resource type t that is of interest (where n may be 0); and (b) exactly one in, one in_s and one pr. We also assume that resource reusability is consistent, i.e. that a resource type t is not indicated in one place as being consumable and in another as being reusable.

The intended meaning of the auxiliary functions (based on where they are used in the definition of Σ) is as follows: $\oplus$ adds resources without changing the intervals; $\sqcup$ is used to collect the upper bound for a set of plans which are executed sequentially in an unknown order; $\sqcap$ computes the minimal (lower bound) requirements of a set of alternative plans; $\fatsemi$ corresponds to a sequential join of two intervals, and $\talloblong$ corresponds to the parallel composition of two intervals. Formally, they are defined as follows:

$$\begin{aligned}
&R_1 \oplus R_2 = \\
&\quad \{re(f, t, n_1 + n_2) \mid re(f, t, n_1) \in R_1 \wedge \; re(f, t, n_2) \in R_2\} \cup \\
&\quad \{in(c_1 \wedge c_2) \mid in(c_1) \in R_1 \wedge in(c_2) \in R_2\} \cup \\
&\quad \{in_s(c_1 \wedge c_2) \mid in_s(c_1) \in R_1 \wedge in_s(c_2) \in R_2\} \cup \\
&\quad \{pr(c_1 \wedge c_2) \mid pr(c_1) \in R_1 \wedge pr(c_2) \in R_2\}
\end{aligned}$$

$$\begin{aligned}
&R_1 \sqcup R_2 = \\
&\quad \{re(r, t, \max(n_1, n_2)) \mid re(r, t, n_1) \in R_1 \wedge \; re(r, t, n_2) \in R_2\} \cup \\
&\quad \{re(c, t, n_1 + n_2) \mid re(c, t, n_1) \in R_1 \wedge \; re(c, t, n_2) \in R_2\} \cup \\
&\quad \{in_s(c_1 \wedge c_2 \wedge c_3 \wedge c_4 \wedge c_5 \wedge c_6) \mid in(c_1) \in R_1 \\
&\qquad\quad \wedge in(c_2) \in R_2 \wedge in_s(c_3) \in R_1 \wedge in_s(c_4) \in R_2 \\
&\qquad\quad \wedge pr(c_5) \in R_1 \wedge pr(c_6) \in R_2\}
\end{aligned}$$

$$
\begin{aligned}
&R_1 \sqcap R_2 = \\
&\quad \{re(f,t,\min(n_1,n_2)) \mid re(f,t,n_1) \in R_1 \wedge\ re(f,t,n_2) \in R_2\} \cup \\
&\quad \{in(c_1 \vee c_2) \mid in(c_1) \in R_1 \wedge in(c_2) \in R_2\} \cup \\
&\quad \{in_s(c_1 \vee c_2) \mid in_s(c_1) \in R_1 \wedge in_s(c_2) \in R_2\} \cup \\
&\quad \{pr(c_1 \vee c_2) \mid pr(c_1) \in R_1 \wedge pr(c_2) \in R_2\}
\end{aligned}
$$

$$
\begin{aligned}
&R_1 \mathbin{;} R_2 = \\
&\quad \{re(r,t,\max(n_1,n_2)) \mid re(r,t,n_1) \in R_1 \wedge\ re(r,t,n_2) \in R_2\} \cup \\
&\quad \{re(c,t,n_1+n_2) \mid re(c,t,n_1) \in R_1 \wedge\ re(c,t,n_2) \in R_2\} \cup \\
&\quad \{in_s(c_1 \wedge c_2 \wedge c_3 \wedge c_4 \wedge c_5) \mid in(c_1) \in R_1 \wedge\ in(c_2) \in R_2\ \wedge in_s(c_3) \in R_1 \\
&\qquad\qquad \wedge\ in_s(c_4) \in R_2 \wedge pr(c_5) \in R_2\}\ \cup \{pr(c) \mid pr(c) \in R_1\}
\end{aligned}
$$

$$
\begin{aligned}
&R_1 \mathbin{[\!]} R_2 = \\
&\quad \{re(f,t,n_1+n_2) \mid re(f,t,n_1) \in R_1 \wedge\ re(f,t,n_2) \in R_2\} \cup \\
&\quad \{in_s(c_1 \wedge c_2 \wedge c_3 \wedge c_4 \wedge c_5 \wedge c_6) \mid in(c_1) \in R_1 \\
&\qquad\qquad \wedge\ in(c_2) \in R_2 \wedge in_s(c_3) \in R_1 \wedge\ in_s(c_4) \in R_2 \wedge pr(c_5) \in R_1 \wedge pr(c_6) \in R_2\}
\end{aligned}
$$

Probing Attacks on Multi-Agent Systems Using Electronic Institutions

Shahriar Bijani[1,2], David Robertson[1], and David Aspinall[1]

[1] Informatics School, University of Edinburgh, 10 Crichton St. Edinburgh, UK
[2] Computer Science Dept., Shahed University, Persian Gulf Highway, Tehran, Iran
{s.bijani,david.aspinall}@ed.ac.uk,
dr@inf.ed.ac.uk

Abstract. In open multi-agent systems, electronic institutions are used to form the interaction environment by defining social norms for group behaviour. However, as this paper shows, electronic institutions can be turned against agents to breach their security in a variety of ways. We focus our attention on probing attacks using electronic institutions specified in the Lightweight Coordination Calculus (LCC) language. LCC is a choreography language used to define electronic institutions in agent systems. A probing attack is an attack against the confidentiality of information systems. In this paper, we redefine the probing attack in conventional network security to be applicable in a multi-agent system domain, governed by electronic institutions. We introduce different probing attacks against LCC interaction models and suggest a secrecy analysis framework for these interactions. The proposed framework could be used to detect the possibility of certain probing attacks and to identify some forms of malicious electronic institutions.

Keywords: Multi-Agent Systems, Electronic Institutions, Interaction Models, Security, Probing Attack, Information Leakage, Lightweight Coordination Calculus (LCC).

1 Introduction

One way to build large-scale multi-agent systems is to develop open architectures in which agents are not pre-engineered to work together and in which agents themselves determine the social norms that govern collective behaviour. Open multi-agent systems have growing popularity in the Multi-agent Systems community and are predicted to have many applications in the future [1]. A major practical limitation to such systems is security because the openness of such systems negates many traditional security solutions.

An electronic institution [2] is an organisation model for multi-agent systems that provides a framework to describe, specify and deploy agents' interaction environments [3]. It is a formalism which defines agents' interaction rules and their permitted and prohibited actions. Lightweight Coordination Calculus, LCC [4, 5], is a declarative language to execute electronic institutions in a peer to peer style. In LCC,

C. Sakama et al. (Eds.): DALT 2011, LNAI 7169, pp. 33–50, 2012.

electronic institutions are called *interaction models.* While electronic institutions can be used to implement security requirements of a multi-agent system, they also can be turned against agents to breach their security in a variety of ways, as this paper shows.

Although openness in open multi-agent systems makes them attractive for various new applications, new problems emerge, among which security is a key. This is because we can make only minimum guarantees about identity and behaviour of agents. The more these systems are used in the real world, the more the necessity of their security will be obvious to users and system designers. Unfortunately there remain many potential gaps in the security of open multi-agent systems and relying on security of low level network communications is not enough to prevent many attacks on multi-agent systems. Furthermore, traditional security mechanisms are difficult to use in multi-agent systems directly, because of their social nature. Confidentiality is one of the main features of a secure system and there are various attacks against this. In this paper, we focus our attention on probing attacks against confidentiality from agents on agents using electronic institutions specified in the LCC language.

Most work on security of multi-agent systems directly or indirectly focuses on mobile agents and many of the solutions have been proposed for threats from agents to hosts or from hosts to agents (e.g.[6-8]). But little research has been done on attacks from agents on agents in open multi-agent systems. A survey of possible attacks on multi-agent systems and existing solutions for attack prevention and detection can be found in [9]. None of these solutions address the probing attacks introduced in this paper.

Xiao et al. [10] have proposed multilevel secure LCC interaction models for health care multi-agent systems. A security architecture for the *HealthAgents* system and a security policy set using LCC have been suggested in [11]. Hu et al. [12] have developed a system to support data integration and decision making in the breast cancer domain using LCC and briefly addressed some security issues. They have all used constraints and message passing in LCC interaction models to implement security solutions for access control and secure data transfer, but they have not addressed inference of private data based on our defined probing attack.

In this paper, we introduce a new attack against the confidentiality of agents' local knowledge, inspired by the concept of probing attack in conventional computer networks. We introduce an attack detection method by proposing a conceptual representation of LCC interaction models and adapting an inference system from credential-based authorisation policies [13] to electronic institutions. We also suggest countermeasures to prevent probing attacks on the systems using the LCC language.

2 Lightweight Coordination Calculus (LCC)

LCC is a compact executable specification to describe the notion of social norms [5]. It is a choreography language based on π-calculus [14] and logic programming. We use LCC to implement interaction models for agent communication. An interaction model (an electronic institution) in LCC is defined as a set of clauses, each of which specifies a role and its process of execution and message passing. The LCC syntax is shown in Fig. 1.

```
Interaction Model := {Clause,...}
Clause := Role::Def
Role := a(Type, Id)
Def := Role | Message | Def then Def | Def or Def | null ← Constraint
Message:=  M => Role   | M => Role <- Constraint  |  M <= Role |
         M <= Role <- Constraint
Constraint:= Constant | P(Term,...) | Constraint ∧ Constraint |
             Constraint ∨ Constraint | ¬Constraint
Type := Term
Id := Constant | Variable
M := Term
Term := Constant | Variable | P(Term,...)
Constant := lower case character sequence or number
Variable := upper case character sequence or number
```

Fig. 1. LCC language syntax; principal operators are: outgoing and incoming messages (=>*and* <=), conditional (<–), sequence (then) and committed choice (or). Functor *P* is a non-numeric constant and variable names in a clause are local.

An interaction model in LCC is a set of clauses each of the form *Role :: Def*, where *Role* denotes the role in the interaction and *Def* is the definition of the role. Roles are of the form a(Type, Id), where Type gives the type of role and Id is an identifier for the individual peer undertaking that role. The definition of performance of a role is constructed using combinations of the sequence operator (then) or choice operator (or) to connect messages and changes of role. Messages are either outgoing to another peer in a given role (=>) or incoming from another peer in a given role (<=). Message input/output or change of role can be governed by constraints (connected by the "<–" operator) which may be conjunctive or disjunctive. Constraints can be satisfied via shared components registered with a website (e.g. www.openk.org), so that complex (possibly interactive) solving methods can be shared along with interaction models; or they can be calls to services with private data and reasoning methods. Variables begin with upper case characters.

Role definitions in LCC can be recursive and the language supports structured terms in addition to variables and constants so that, although its syntax is simple, it can represent sophisticated interactions. Notice also that role definitions are "stand alone" in the sense that each role definition specifies all the information needed to complete that role. This means that definitions for roles can be distributed across a network of computers and (assuming the LCC definition is well engineered) will synchronise through message passing while otherwise operating independently. Matching of output messages from one peer to input messages of another is achieved by simple structure matching (as in Prolog), since (although operating independently) the roles were originally defined to work together. More sophisticated forms of input/output matching have been defined for LCC (to allow for more sophisticated ontology matching) but these are not the subject of this paper. For a more detailed introduction to LCC, see [4].

For different applications, agents may use their own interaction model or download an existing one. When an agent selects an interaction model and a role in it, its behaviour in that interaction is then determined by the constraints attached to message sending/receiving events specified in the definition of that role. Agents may be involved in any number of interactions (specified by interaction models) simultaneously.

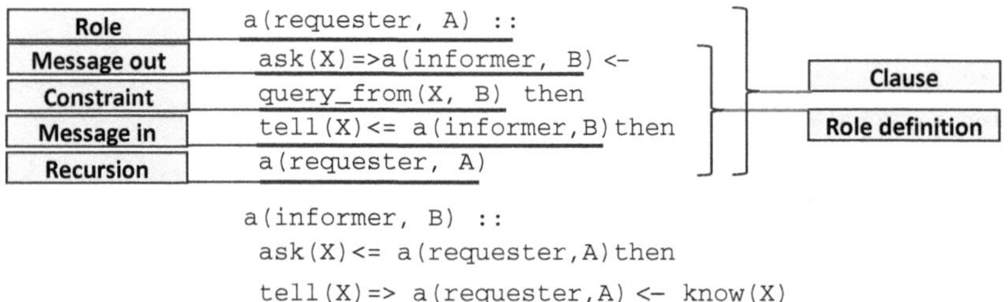


```
a(informer, B) ::
  ask(X)<= a(requester,A)then
  tell(X)=> a(requester,A) <- know(X)
```

Fig. 2. An example of an interaction model with two clauses in LCC

Fig.2 illustrates an example of an interaction model for a simple communication in LCC. There are two roles (clauses) in this interaction model: *requester* and *informer*. In the first clause, a *requester* asks about something from an *informer*, then gets an answer from it and then continues as a *requester*. In the second clause, an *informer* is asked by a *requester* and then it should tell the *requester* if it knows the answer.

3 Probing Attack in Multi-Agent Systems

We redefine the probing attack [15]in conventional network security to be applicable in multi-agent systems. A probing attack in network security is an attack based on injecting traffic into the victim's network and analysing the results [16]. It is a sort of active traffic analysis, which is a popular attack in cryptography [17, 18] and is a basis for other attacks in computer network systems [2].

In our case, an adversary, who plays a role in an interaction model, could infer information not only from the interaction model itself, but also from the local knowledge of other agents. An adversary could control other agents' behaviour in an interaction, by publishing a malicious interaction model. Furthermore, it could access the private local knowledge (e.g. decision rules and policies) of the victim agents by injection of facts to the agent knowledge-base, asking queries and analysing results.

We can define four types of probing attacks on open multi-agent systems: (1) explicit query attack, (2) implicit query attack, (3) injection attack and (4) indirect query. In explicit query probing attack, the idea is to make several direct queries to an agent via messages (Fig. 3-a). It may seem an elementary attack, but there can be sophisticated versions of it, such as gathering provenance information [19, 20] by an attacker or accessing all the information in a semi-open ontology by asking intelligent questions from different parts of it. An example of a semi-open ontology is ontology of a service provider company which is open to customer's questions, but where extensive knowledge of the whole ontology is a commercially confidential asset [9].

In Fig. 3, two simple examples of a proteomics lab interaction model illustrate the first two types of probing attack. This is a modified version of the DNA sequencing interaction model [21] in the OpenKowledge project [22] and it is used for knowledge sharing between researchers and proteomics labs. In the proposed scenario in [21] a query is passed on to each laboratory in a list of proteomics labs and the results are sent back to the researcher to be analysed. It could be a case that proteomics labs may not wish to share all DNA sequencing information with researchers. In Fig. 3 examples, an adversary (in the role of *researcher*) could ask explicit and implicit queries from a proteomics lab agent (*omicslab*) to access commercially important information. In Fig. 3-a, in the *omicslab* clause (lines 9 to 13), when a proteomics lab agent *O* receives an *ask(X)* message, it explicitly sends X, which is a private DNA sequence, to the *researcher*. This could be categorised as an explicit query attack.

```
1.a(researcher(LabList), R) ::
2.  (ask(X)=>a(omicslab,H)<-
3.             LabList=[H|T]    then
4.   tell(X)<=a(omicslab,H)   then
5.   null <- processResult(X, H)
6.   then a( researcher(T), R)
7. ) or
8. null <- LabList = []

9.a(omicslab, O) ::
10. ask(X)<= a(researcher,R) then
11. tell(X)=>a(researcher,R)
12.                      <-know(X)
13. then a(omicslab, O)
```

(a)

```
1.a(researcher(LabList), R) ::
2.  (ask(X)=>a(omicslab, H) <-
3.             LabList=[H|T]   then
4.   tell(Y)<= a(omicslab,H) then
5.   null <- processResult(X,Y,H)
6.   then a( researcher(T), R)
7. ) or
8. null <- LabList = []

9.a(omicslab, O) ::
10. ask(X)<= a(researcher,R)then
11. tell(Y)=>a(researcher,R)<-
12.                     Combine(X,Y)
13. then a(omicslab, O)
```

(b)

Fig. 3. Two examples of explicit and implicit query attacks, in which a malicious researcher could access confidential information of proteomics lab agents. In (a), *omicslab* agent receives an explicit query asking *X* (line 10) and reveals *X* by sending back *tell(X)* message to the researcher (line 11). In (b), an implicit query *Combine(X,Y)* is asked as a constraint in the *omicslab* clause (line 12), receiving the *tell(Y)* message by the researcher agent informs it that the constraint holds by the *omicslab* agent.

The second type of probing attack is asking an implicit query on confidential information. An adversary often might not be interested to ask a query explicitly, for various reasons; e.g. a direct question from confidential information may be forbidden or might attract the attention of the victim. An implicit query could be asked by placing a query as a constraint in LCC, rather than sending a message. In other words, an adversary could not only infer information from a received message, but also from analysing the constraints in an interaction model. An example of confidential information in proteomics lab could be the combination (binding potential) of two publicly known proteins that activate a particular gene. In this example, the relation between two pieces of public information is private. In Fig. 3-b, X and Y are not confidential but a malicious *researcher, R,* could recognise whether proteins X and Y could combine not by asking a direct question, but by putting a *combine(X,Y)* constraint in line 12. When *O* sends the non-confidential *tell(Y)* message to *R* it will indirectly inform *R* that *X* and *Y* could combine together because R knows that *combine(X, Y)* had to be satisfied before the *tell(Y)* message could be sent.

The third type of probing attack happens by injection of some facts into the system and asking queries before and after the injection. Arguably, the whole interaction model that has been designed by an adversary could be considered as injected information for agents using it. But the purpose of the injection is to introduce the constraints in the victim's interaction model. In this type of attack, the assumption is that the injection affects decisions of the victim. This attack is similar to the implicit query attack and in some cases might be considered as compound implicit queries. We illustrate a sample attack in Fig. 4 and Fig. 5 inspired by an example of a probing attack in authorisation languages by Gurevich and Neeman [23].

```
1.  a(vendor, V)::
2.    ask(S)<= a(customer,C) then
3.    null <- (¬want(C,S) ∨ payFor(C,S) )    then      // injection
4.    null <- (¬SupplyFrom(X)   ∨ want(C,S) ) then     // injection
5.    ok => a(customer,C) <- agree(C,S)    then  // implicit query
6.    ...
7.    then a(vendor, V)
```

Fig. 4. A fragment of a selling interaction model shows an example of type three probing attack

Fig. 4 shows one clause of a selling interaction model that could be used for a probing attack by injection. The attack begins when an agent selects a *vendor* role of this malevolent interaction model, which has been created and published by an adversary. The adversary (*C*) plays the role of *customer* and initiates the interaction by sending the *ask(S)* message to the vendor. The goal of the adversary is to discover the confidential fact whether the X company is the supplier of the *vendor (SupplyFrom(X))*. The first two constraints (line 3) tell the *vendor* that the *customer pays* for S or does not *want* S. The next two constraints (line 4) denote (inject) the fact that *X* is not the vendor's *supplier* or the customer *wants* S. In other words, these constraints are added information to the knowledge-base of the *vendor* agent and could shape its decisions. The subsequent implicit query asking if the *vendor* agrees with the deal is sent (line 5) to signal to the attacker that the complex constraint was satisfied. These injections and the agent's response to the query are not still enough for the attacker to infer the validity of *SupplyFrom(X)*. Then the adversary terminates this interaction and initiates two other interactions with the victim (Fig. 5).

Each new interaction model injects only one part of the previous injections and asks the same implicit query. If the answer to the first query is positive (an *ok* message) and to the next two queries are negative, after some analyses (see section 4.4), the adversary could infer the confidential fact that who is the supplier of the *vendor* (*SupplyFrom(X)*).

```
a(vendor2, V)::
 null<-want(C,S) then //injection
 ok=>a(customer,C) <- agree(C,S)
  /* query */     ...
```
(a)

```
a(vendor3, V)::
 null<- payFor(C,S)then //injection
  ok=>a(customer,C) <- agree(C,S)
      /* query */     ...
```
(b)

Fig. 5. Definitions of the vendor roles in two malicious interaction models as parts of a probing attack scenario

Indirect query is the fourth type of probing attack, in which an adversary tries to access confidential information of the victim agent via a third party for reasons similar to the implicit attack. Indirect attack is a modification of the explicit query attack and could also be combined with the other types of probing attacks. A modified fragment of an interaction model in MIAKT project [12], which aims to support multidisciplinary meetings for the diagnosis and management of breast cancers, is illustrated in Fig. 6. The *dataHandler* retrieves a patient's private data based on the request submitted by an authorised domain specialist (Fig. 6-a, line 3), but an illegitimate *nurse* has open access to this without any authorisation check (Fig. 6-b, line 5).

```
1. a(dataHandler,H) ::
2. patient_record(Patient) <=  a(specialist,E) then
3.  inform(Patient) =>a(specialist,E) <- is_authorised(E,ID)and
4.  get_patient_id(Patient,ID) then ...
```
(a)

```
1.  a(specialist,E) ::
2.  patient_record(Patient) =>a(dataHandler,H) then
3.    process(Patient) <- inform(Patient) <=  a(dataHandler,H) then ...
4.  patient_record(Patient) <=  a(nurse, N) then
5.    inform(Patient) => a(nurse, N)  ...
```
(b)

Fig. 6. A fragment of an interaction model to support multidisciplinary meetings for the diagnosis and management of breast cancer.**(a)** the data handler role[12]. **(b)** the specialist role.

4 Attack Detection

We suggest a framework to detect probing attacks, which benefit from electronic institutions to attack MAS. Fig. 7 shows the necessary steps in the detection of malicious interaction models.

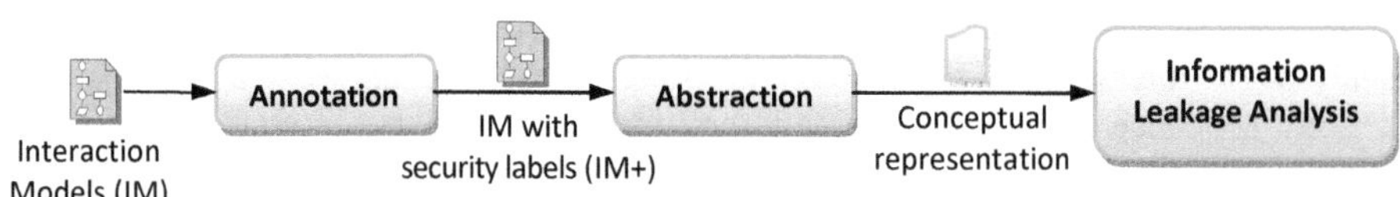

Fig. 7. Different steps to detect possibility of probing attack from interaction models

4.1 Annotation

The first step to analyse secrecy of the interaction models is adding security labels to the existing LCC code. In the original LCC syntax there is no means of assigning security levels to information. Variables, constants and constraints are ultimately the most elementary causes of the described information leak, so when we receive an interaction model, we could annotate it to reflect the confidentiality level of the information. Fig. 8 suggests an added syntax for LCC with two levels of confidential terms: *l* (means low security) and *h* (means high security). The default security level for the terms without labels would be low.

```
Term  := Constant | Variable | P(Term,...) | sTerm
sTerm := Term{lb}
lb := l | h
```

Fig. 8. Adding security labels to the LCC syntax

4.2 Abstraction

The next step in our security analysis is converting the annotated interaction models to simpler logical representations, which is called *conceptual representation*, in order to illustrate only the related parts of the LCC code to the secrecy evaluation. Although LCC resembles a type of logic programming language, the conversion of LCC specifications to logical expressions is not necessarily based on simple interpretation of LCC operators to their equivalent logical operators. What we need for our conceptual representation is a more minimal interpretation of LCC, which reflects information leaks or helps to find knowledge leakage.

The conceptual representation links the notion of electronic institutions with the idea of information flow analysis. It could vary in detection of different types of probing attacks and from various stakeholders' points of view. For example when an adversary has designed and published the interaction model herself / himself, and plays one or more roles in it, she/he might be only interested to analyse clauses related to other roles.

We now introduce two conceptual representations of interaction models for detection of different types of probing attack. They are to some extent similar, but the main differences are derived from the way an adversary exploits the interaction model and what the interaction model could add to the knowledge of an agent. In both representations, if we use non-temporal logic for the conceptual representations, the *then* operator in LCC will be equivalent to a logical conjunction. That is because we analyse the interaction model ahead of time, so we can ignore the effect of the actions' sequence on the information inferred by the adversary. We also interpret the choice operator *or* in LCC as logical disjunction and message passing operators, which are represented by *send/receive*, as a way of finding the query. We can legitimately do this because we are not defining the semantics of the LCC specification but, instead, we are describing the (constraint-based) information that can be inferred to be true if the definition is satisfied (i.e. it has completed in the interaction).

In the first version, the conditional operator (□̃) in LCC is interpreted as a material conditional in logic. For example the *omicslab* clause in Fig. 3-a simply could be represented by two logical expressions as:

```
receive(R, ask(X)),
know(X)→ send(R, tell(X))
```

This represents the conditional nature of the constraints, so in combination with a security type system, it could be used for analysing direct and indirect information flows and consequently for detection of explicit, implicit or indirect query attacks. On the other hand, this representation does not reflect the injecting capability of constraints, so it is not suggested for detecting injection probing attacks.

IN_0 ={**receive(R,ask(X)**}
 	
q_0 ={**Combine(X,Y)**}
(a)
	IN_1 ={
	want(C,S)→ payFor(C,S),
	SupplyFrom(X) → want(C,S)
	}
	q_1 ={**agree(C,S)**}
	(b)

IN_2 = {**want(C,S)**} q_2 ={**agree(C,S)**} (c)	IN_3 = {**payFor(C,S)**} q_3 ={**agree(C,S)**} (d)

Fig. 9. Abstraction examples. *IN* is the conceptual representation of an LCC clause, *q* is a query. **(a)** Abstraction of the implicit query attack in Fig. 3-b. `ask(X)<= a(researcher,R)` is represented by *receive(R,ask(X)),* where *R* is the sender Id, and *ask(X)* is the received message, the constraint *Combine* is interpreted as a query, the sent message in the left hand side of `<-` is not represented, because it does not affect **(b)** Abstraction of the injection attack example in Fig. 4 **(c)** Abstraction of the injection attack example in Fig. 5-a **(d)** Abstraction of the injection attack example in Fig. 5-b.

In the second representation of interaction models, which mainly addresses injection attack detection, constraints are interpreted as queries or injection from the counterpart agent (an adversary). Hence the conditional operator (`<-`) is used just to find the queries and injections and it does not appear in the representation. The sent message in the left of `<-`(if it exists), could be an answer to the query, but it is not represented in this abstraction, because it does not affect our injection attack analysis. The received message's parameters are also considered new information for the receiver agent. If the abstraction contains any injection, it could change the agent's knowledge state, which affects the agent's decisions. The equivalent representation of Fig. 3-b and Fig. 4 would be as shown in Fig. 9. While the main target of this abstraction is detecting injection attacks, it can also represent the implicit query attack as shown in Fig. 9-a. We use the second representation in our secrecy analysis for the rest of this paper.

4.3 Updated LCC Rewrite Rules

In order to integrate the abstraction phase into the LCC interpreter and to detect the attacks against interaction models, we have upgraded the LCC *clause expansion mechanism* [5] for detection of probing attacks by amending the LCC *rewrite rules*. In [5], Robertson defined the following clause expansion mechanism for agents to unpack any LCC interaction model they receive and suggested applying rewrite rules to expand the interaction state:

$$\left(C_i \xrightarrow{M_i, M_{i+1}, S, O_i} C_{i+1}, \ldots, C_{n-1} \xrightarrow{M_{n-1}, M_n, S, O_n} C_n\right)$$

where C_n is an expansion of the original LCC clause C_i in terms of the interaction model S and in response to the set of received messages M_i, O_n is an output message set, M_n is a remaining unprocessed set of messages.

The rewrite rules allow an agent to conform to the interaction model by unpacking clauses, finding the next step and updating the interaction state. The rewrite rules are defined in the LCC interpreter, which should be installed on each agent running LCC codes. For more information about LCC expansion algorithm see [5] and [24]. The updated LCC rewrite rules augmented with security-related information is shown in Fig. 10.

The general format of the new rewrite rules in Fig. 10 is as following:

s(A LCC rewrite rule, Δ, Δ′),

in which s is the notion of the new rewrite rules, Δ is the current security environment and Δ′ is the updated security environment after expanding the rewrite rule. Δ= (R, L, K), where R is the conceptual representation of interaction models and contains the set of injections and queries, L is the mapping between conceptual representation and the confidentiality labels and K is the agents' current state of knowledge.

The LCC rewrite rules are in the form of $X \xrightarrow{M_i, M_o, S, O} Y$, where Y is the expansion of X, M_i is the initial set of messages, O is the output message set, and M_o is the subset of M_i, which is not yet processed and S is the interaction model. As the result of the nine rewrite rules in Fig. 10, one clause of an interaction model is expanded. The first rule starts unpacking a clause by expanding the body of it (B) and the rules (2) to (9) expand different parts of the clause body. Based on the *closed* rules in (10), an interaction rule is decided to be closed. *e_s* rules are to extract the conceptual representation of a term and satisfy the constraints. They have the following format:

e_s (Δ, Δ′, C, X)

where
Δ = security environment before abstraction of C,
Δ′ = security environment after abstraction of C,
C = the constraint to be satisfied,
X = could be either Δ, if C is a pre-condition or Δ′, if C is a post-condition.

extract_rep(Δ, Δ′, C) function returns true and is in charge of the abstraction phase, in which the conceptual representation is extracted from the constraint C[1] and the

[1] The constraints have been converted into the conjunctive normal form (CNF).

security environment Δ is updated into Δ'. The *extract_rep* is also called when we have disjunctive constraints to be able to extract conditional injections too. *satisfied(C,Δ)* is true if C can be satisfied from the current environment Δ. *satisfied(C,Δ')* is true if the updated environment Δ' could fulfil the constraint C.

$$s\left(A :: B \xrightarrow{M_i, M_o, S, O} A :: E, \Delta, \Delta'\right) \quad if\ s\left(B \xrightarrow{M_i, M_o, S, O} E, \Delta, \Delta'\right) \tag{1}$$

$$s\left(A_1\ or\ A_2 \xrightarrow{M_i, M_o, S, O} E, \Delta, \Delta'\right) \quad if\ \neg closed(A_2) \wedge s\left(A_1 \xrightarrow{M_i, M_o, S, O} E, \Delta, \Delta'\right) \tag{2}$$

$$s\left(A_1\ or\ A_2 \xrightarrow{M_i, M_o, S, O} E, \Delta, \Delta'\right) \quad if\ \neg closed(A_1) \wedge s(A_2 \xrightarrow{M_i, M_o, S, O} E, \Delta, \Delta') \tag{3}$$

$$s\left(A_1\ then\ A_2 \xrightarrow{M_i, M_o, S, O} E\ then\ A_2, \Delta, \Delta'\right) \quad if\ s(A_1 \xrightarrow{M_i, M_o, S, O} E, \Delta, \Delta') \tag{4}$$

$$s\left(A_1\ then\ A_2 \xrightarrow{M_i, M_o, S, O} A_1\ then\ E, \Delta, \Delta'\right) \quad if\ closed(A_1) \wedge s(A_2 \xrightarrow{M_i, M_o, S, O} E, \Delta, \Delta') \tag{5}$$

$$s\left(C \leftarrow M \Leftarrow A \xrightarrow{M_i, M_i - \{M \Leftarrow A\}, S, \emptyset} c(M \Leftarrow A), \Delta, \Delta'\right) \ if\ (M \Leftarrow A) \in M_i \wedge e\_s(\Delta, \Delta', C, \Delta') \tag{6}$$

$$s\left(M \Rightarrow A \leftarrow C \xrightarrow{M_i, M_o, S, \{M \Rightarrow A\}} c(M \Rightarrow A), \Delta, \Delta'\right) \quad if\ e\_s(\Pi, \Pi', C, \Delta) \tag{7}$$

$$s\left(null \leftarrow C \xrightarrow{M_i, M_o, S, \emptyset} c(M \Rightarrow A), \Delta, \Delta'\right) \quad if\ e\_s(\Pi, \Pi', C, \Delta) \tag{8}$$

$$s\left(a(R, I) \leftarrow C \xrightarrow{M_i, M_o, S, \emptyset} a(R, I) :: B, \Delta, \Delta'\right) \ if\ closed(P, a(R, I) :: B) \wedge e\_s(\Pi, \Pi', C, \Delta) \tag{9}$$

$$\begin{aligned} &closed\big(c(X)\big) \\ &closed(A\ or\ B) \leftarrow closed(A) \vee closed(B) \\ &closed(A\ then\ B) \leftarrow closed(A) \wedge closed(B) \\ &closed(X :: B) \leftarrow closed(B) \end{aligned} \tag{10}$$

$$e\_s(\Delta, \Delta', C, \Delta) \leftarrow extract\_rep(\Delta, \Delta', C) \wedge satisfied(C, \Delta) \tag{11}$$

$$e\_s(\Delta, \Delta', C, \Delta') \leftarrow extract\_rep(\Delta, \Delta', C) \wedge satisfied(C, \Delta') \tag{12}$$

$$e\_s(\Delta, \Delta', C_1 \wedge C_2, \_) \leftarrow e\_s(\Delta, \Delta', C_1, \_) \wedge e\_s(\Delta, \Delta', C_2, \_) \tag{13}$$

$$e\_s(\Delta, \Delta', C_1 \vee C_2, \_) \leftarrow extract\_rep(\Delta, \Delta', C_1 \vee C_2) \wedge (e\_s(\Delta, \Delta', C_1, \_) \vee e\_s(\Delta, \Delta', C_2, \_)) \tag{14}$$

Fig. 10. The amended LCC rewrite rules, which include security-related information, for expansion of one clause in an interaction model

$$i(S, M_i, S_f, \Delta, \Delta_f) \leftrightarrow \begin{pmatrix} S = S_f \\ \wedge \\ \Delta = \Delta_f \end{pmatrix} \vee \left(\left(\begin{array}{c} S \overset{S}{\supseteq} S_p \quad \wedge \\ s(S_p \xrightarrow{M_i, M_o, S, O} S'_p, \Delta, \Delta') \wedge LA(\Delta', p) \wedge \\ S_p \overset{S}{\cup} S = S' \quad \wedge \\ i(S', M_o, S_f, \Delta, \Delta_f) \end{array} \right) \right) \tag{15}$$

$$S \overset{S}{\supseteq} S_p \leftrightarrow \exists R, B. (S_p \in S \quad \wedge \quad S_p = a(R, I) :: B) \tag{16}$$

Fig. 11. Revised definition of a trace through an LCC interaction model *S*

In [24] the behaviour of agents coordinated through LCC definitions is defined in terms of traces produced via application of rewrites to LCC clauses. Fig. 11 extends this definition to include security constraints. Here, *S* is the state of an interaction, M_i is the initial set of messages, *p* is a unique identifier for a peer. $i(S, M_i, S_f, \Delta, \Delta')$ is true when the sequence of interactions and an initial set of messages M_i change the initial state of the interaction model *S* and security environment Δ to the state S_f and the security environment Δ'. $S \overset{S}{\supseteq} S_p$ (16) selects a clause S_p from the interaction state *S*. $S_p \overset{S}{\cup} S$ merges specific clause S_p to *S* and generate a new interaction state S'. *LA* is responsible for the information leakage analysis, described in section 4.4. If it detects an attack, it will prevent expanding the rest of the interaction model and will generate an alert.

4.4 Information Leakage Analysis

After the conceptual representation of interaction models, in which injections and queries are defined, we can analyse them to detect an injection probing attack. A probing attack happens when a malicious agent could infer anything about its counterpart's local knowledge. We use Becker's inference system[13] to detect probing attacks from interaction models' conceptual representations.

Becker has introduced an inference system for *detectability*[2] [25] of a specific property in Datalog-based policy languages. Although this inference system has been created for credential-based authorisation policies with some modifications it could also be used to detect probing attacks on multi-agent systems. We want to know when an adversary injects expressions into the agent's private knowledge-base and asks a query, what else the adversary could infer from the knowledge-base. To answer this question we use the inference system in Fig. 12, which is called by the *LA* function introduced in Fig. 11.

In this inference system, as described in section 4.3, $\Delta = \{R, L, K\}$ and *R* is the set of conceptual representations of different clauses, in which an agent is playing a role. $R=\{(IN_i, q_i)\ldots\}$, where IN_i is a set of ground injections in clause *i* and q_i is its

[2] Detectability (or non-opacity) is an information flow property that shows the ability to infer a specific predicate from a set of rules.

corresponding query. The inference system assumes that the injection is ground and the query is monotonic (without negation). *K* is the agent's confidential local knowledge set, which is the basis of the agent's decisions and is not visible by the adversary from outside. The injections' set *IN* is also assumed to influence the judgements of the agent in the current interaction. The axiom (V) says that if *IN'* contains *IN* ($IN' \succcurlyeq IN$), all facts that are entailed from $IN \cup K$, could also be entailed from $IN' \cup K$. In case of ground *K*, the *containment* relation ($\succcurlyeq$) is decidable. (VI) is similar to (V) and is for negative queries. (VIII) is the most important part of the inference system and tells us what can be inferred from the knowledge set *K* when *IN* is injected to it by an adversary.

$$\text{(I)}\ \frac{q \text{ is monotonic, } IN \text{ is ground, } q \text{ holds after injection of } IN \text{ to } K}{(R, L, K), IN \vdash q} \qquad \text{(II)}\ \frac{\Delta, IN \vdash q,\ q \Rightarrow q'}{\Delta, IN\ \vdash q}$$

$$\text{(III)}\ \frac{K \cup IN \vdash q,\ (IN, q) \in R}{(R, L, K), IN \vdash q} \qquad \text{(IV)}\ \frac{K \cup IN \nvdash q,\ (IN, q) \in R}{(R, L, K), IN \vdash \neg q}$$

$$\text{(V)}\ \frac{\Delta, IN \vdash q,\ IN' \succcurlyeq IN,\ q \text{ is monotonic}, IN' \text{is ground}}{\Delta, IN' \vdash q} \qquad \text{(VI)}\ \frac{\Delta, IN \vdash q,\ IN' \preccurlyeq IN\ \neg q \text{ is monotonic},\ IN' \text{is ground}}{\Delta, IN' \vdash q}$$

$$\text{(VII)}\ \frac{\Delta, IN \vdash q_1,\ \Delta, IN \vdash q_2}{\Delta, IN \vdash q_1 \wedge q_2} \qquad \text{(VIII)}\ \frac{\Delta,\ K \cup IN \vdash q}{\Delta, K \vdash q \vee \bigvee_{a \in IN} fired(IN, head(a))}$$

Fig. 12. The adapted inference system of Becker [13] to detect information leaks as a part of our attack detection framework

The *fired(I,f)* operator [13] in (VIII) is

$$\neg f \wedge \bigvee_{\alpha \in S} \bigwedge_{x \in \alpha} x$$

where *S* is a set of explanations α of why any ground atom f is inferred from the injection set *I* (i.e. $I \cup \alpha \vdash f$) and it could be computed by the standard abduction method [26]. The intuition behind the *fired* operator is that when an adversary injects some expressions (*IN*) into the agent's knowledge-base *K* and receives a result (i.e. $K \cup IN \vdash q$), either q holds in *K*, or at least one of the expressions (e.g. *f*) in *IN* has the main role in proving q, so *f* is fired in the context of K [13].

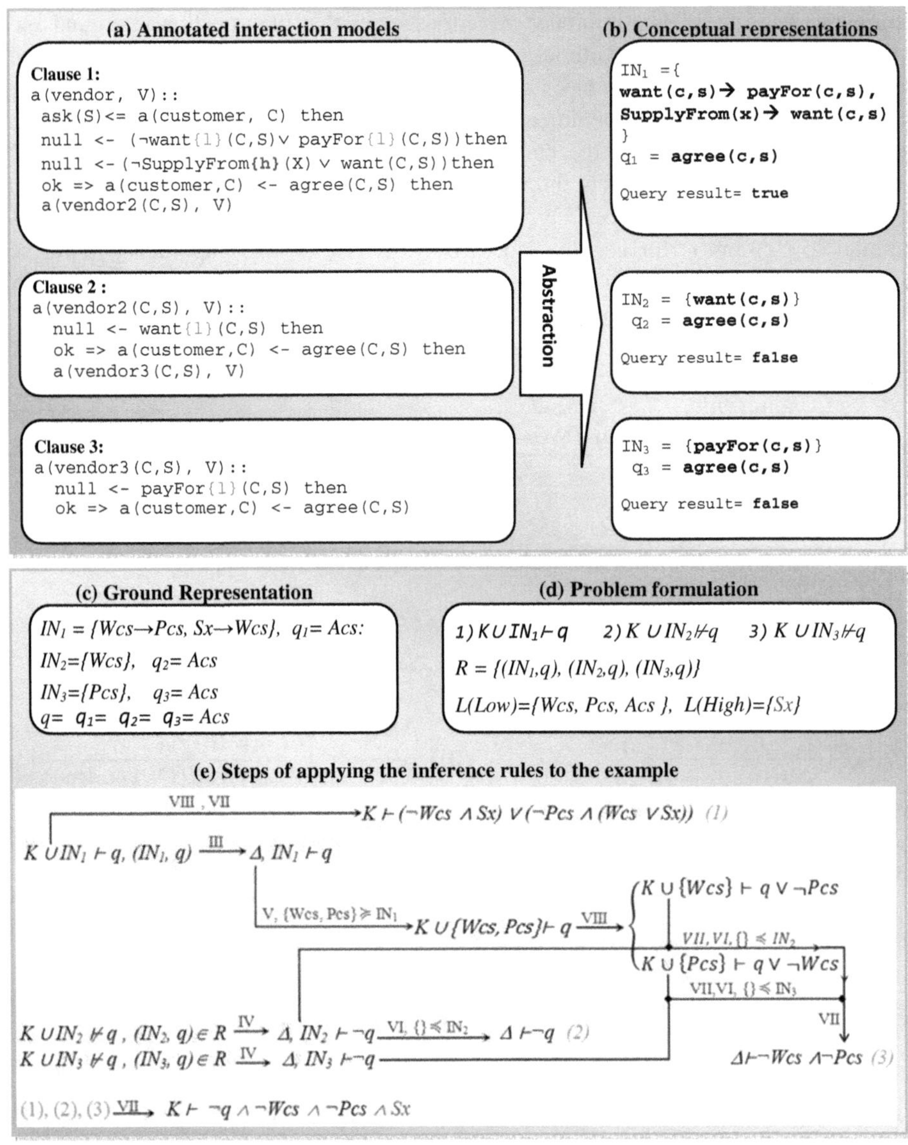

Fig. 13. An example of using the inference system to detect the possibility of probing attack. Finally, it shows what an adversary could infer from the local knowledge (K) of the victim agent using the three introduced clauses.

4.5 Example

To illustrate the detection mechanism of malicious interaction models, we formulate an injection attack in Fig. 13 similar to the scenario in Fig. 4 and Fig. 5. The first step is annotation of the interaction model with security labels; in our case labels indicate the security level of a piece of information on an ordinal scale (high and low) and the default for non-labelled terms would be low. The second step is abstraction, in which the conceptual representation of each clause is generated. Following the abstraction, we must convert the injections and queries to ground expressions to be able to use this inference system. Finding a ground substitution for these expressions does not cause loss of generality. Injections and queries in an interaction model are showed as $K \cup IN_i \vdash q$, which means q holds after injection of IN_i to the knowledge state K. It is assumed that the adversary's query is successful the first time and unsuccessful the second and third times.

The sequence of inference rules in Fig. 13 (e) shows what the adversary could infer from the local knowledge of the victim agent. As a result of this analysis, we know the adversary could find the following facts from the target agent's local knowledge:

$$\neg\text{agree}(c,s) \wedge \neg\ \text{want}(c,s) \wedge \neg\text{payFor}(c,s) \wedge \text{SupplyFrom}(x).$$

All the inferred facts might be important but in this example, SupplyFrom(x), which reveals high level private information about the supplier of the target vendor, is detected as information leakage. The detection happens when the third clause of Fig. 13 is interpreted by the LCC interpreter, so it stops execution of the clause and generates an alert.

5 Discussion

Two reasons that security problems might lead to probing attacks in languages like LCC are (1) no distinguished notion of private and public data in the LCC code and (2) no mechanism for information leakage control in an interaction. Two countermeasures to these problems are adding some access control features in LCC and secrecy analysis of interaction models. The annotation phase in the proposed framework adds security labels to LCC terms and the inference module analyses vulnerabilities of the interaction models against injection attacks.

This solution exploits *detectability*, which is a popular tool in information flow analysis which is the main techniques for studying confidentiality[27]. Hence, the suggested attack detection mechanism is promising enough to preserve the secrecy of interaction models against injection probing attacks. Becker's inference system is sound and for ground finite detectability is fully decidable, but it's completeness is still an open problem [13]. For our analysis, the injections and the query have to be ground expressions. Nevertheless, finding a ground substitution for the conceptual representation of the interaction models might not cause loss of generality in practice. It is because the detection happens in run-time, so variables have been replaced with constants, before the ground substitution phase.

In order to detect injection attacks, all clauses related to a specific peer should be analysed together, although LCC can be interpreted and executed by agents in distributed peer to peer networks and each clause of an interaction model might be run separately. That is the reason of sending the identifier of a peer to the secrecy analysis module *LA* in Fig. 11. For the same purpose, the attack detection system is defined as a part of the LCC interpreter, which is installed on each peer.

If we wanted to prevent the injection attack, it would have been necessary to simulate the interactions that a peer undertakes and to know the held constraints in advance. But there is no centralised control point in choreography systems, so we can not prevent probing attacks before they happen and we may only detect them during run time.

It is important to remember that the suggested detection framework is intended to detect only one type of probing attack, i.e. injection attack. To detect other probing attacks, we suggest replacing the abstraction and the information leakage analysis modules with a secure type analysis module, in which every well-typed LCC interaction model is secure. Another advantage of using a security type system is that it can detect indirect information flows in interaction models and it is not depend on single execution of an interaction, so it can be used in advance to prevent probing attacks.

6 Conclusion

In this paper, we have introduced probing attacks on multi-agent systems governed by electronic institutions and developed a secrecy analysis framework for the LCC interaction models to detect probing attacks. We have proposed four types of probing attacks, namely, explicit query, implicit query, injection and indirect query attacks on choreography systems using LCC interaction models.

The three main steps of the attack detection system are *annotation*, *abstraction*, and *information leakage analysis*. In the *annotation* phase, we label LCC interaction models to reflect the confidentiality level (high or low) of each term. For each interaction model, the *abstraction* generates a logical representation that helps to find information leaks. In the *information leakage analysis* phase, we have adapted Becker's inference system, which shows the possibility of private information disclosure by an adversary. The inference system tells us whether an adversary could infer some facts from the local knowledge of an agent, just by injecting sets of ground statements and queries. The suggested attack detection system is deployed on each agent as a part of the LCC interpreter. Hence, we have updated the LCC rewrite rules in the LCC interpreter to do the abstraction and information leakage analysis.

To generalise our work to other electronic institution languages besides LCC, we could adapt the abstraction module for each language. We are now working on a security type system for LCC to be able to detect and prevent other types of probing attacks.

References

1. Artikis, A., Sergot, M., Pitt, J.: Specifying Norm-Governed Computational Societies. ACM Transactions on Computational Logic 10(1), 1–42 (2009)
2. Esteva, M., De La Cruz, D., Rosell, B., et al.: Engineering open multi-agent systems as electronic institutions. In: Procedings of the National Conference on Artificial Intelligence (AAA 2004), pp. 1010–1011. AAAI Press (2004)

3. Joseph, S., de Pinninck, A.P., Robertson, D., et al.: OpenKnowledge Deliverable 1.1: Interaction Model Language Definition (2006)
4. Robertson, D.: Multi-agent Coordination as Distributed Logic Programming. In: Demoen, B., Lifschitz, V. (eds.) ICLP 2004. LNCS, vol. 3132, pp. 416–430. Springer, Heidelberg (2004)
5. Robertson, D.: A Lightweight Coordination Calculus for Agent Systems. In: Leite, J., Omicini, A., Torroni, P., Yolum, p. (eds.) DALT 2004. LNCS (LNAI), vol. 3476, pp. 183–197. Springer, Heidelberg (2005)
6. Van't Noordende, G.J., Overeinder, B.J., Timmer, R.J., et al.: Constructing secure mobile agent systems using the agent operating system. International Journal of Intelligent Information and Database Systems 3(4), 363–381 (2009)
7. Endsuleit, R., Wagner, A.: Possible attacks on and countermeasures for secure multi-agent computation. In: Arabnia, H.R., Aissi, S., Mun, Y. (eds.) SAM 2004, pp. 221–227. CSREA Press (2004)
8. Venkatesan, S., Chellappan, C.: Protection of Mobile Agent Platform through Attack Identification Scanner (AIS) by Malicious Identification Police (MIP). In: First International Conference on Emerging Trends in Engineering and Technology, pp. 1228–1231. IEEE (2008)
9. Bijani, S., Robertson, D.: A Review of Attacks and Security Approaches in Open Multi-agent Systems. Artificial Intelligence Review (2012)
10. Xiao, L., Lewis, P., Dasmahapatra, S.: Secure Interaction Models for the HealthAgents System. In: Harrison, M.D., Sujan, M.-A. (eds.) SAFECOMP 2008. LNCS, vol. 5219, pp. 167–180. Springer, Heidelberg (2008)
11. Xiao, L., Dasmahapatra, S., Lewis, P., et al.: The design and implementation of a novel security model for HealthAgents. Knowledge Engineering Review 26(2) (2011)
12. Hu, B., Dasmahapatra, S., Lewis, P., et al.: Facilitating Knowledge Management in Pervasive Health Care Systems. Networked Knowledge-Networked Media 221, 285–304 (2009)
13. Becker, M.Y.: Information Flow in Credential Systems. In: 23rd IEEE Computer Security Foundations Symposium (CSF), pp. 171–185. IEEE (2010)
14. Milner, R., Parrow, J., Walker, D.: A Calculus of Mobile Processes.1. Information and Computation 100(1), 1–40 (1992)
15. Anderson, R., Kuhn, M.: Tamper Resistance: A Cautionary Note. In: Proceedings of the Second USENIX Workshop on Electronic Commerce, vol. 2, pp. 1–11. USENIX Association (1996)
16. Zheng, J., Hu, M.-Z.: Intrusion Detection of DoS/DDoS and Probing Attacks for Web Services. In: Fan, W., Wu, Z., Yang, J. (eds.) WAIM 2005. LNCS, vol. 3739, pp. 333–344. Springer, Heidelberg (2005)
17. Ishai, Y., Sahai, A., Wagner, D.: Private Circuits: Securing Hardware against Probing Attacks. In: Boneh, D. (ed.) CRYPTO 2003. LNCS, vol. 2729, pp. 463–481. Springer, Heidelberg (2003)
18. Schmidt, J.-M., Kim, C.: A Probing Attack on AES. In: Chung, K.-I., Sohn, K., Yung, M. (eds.) WISA 2008. LNCS, vol. 5379, pp. 256–265. Springer, Heidelberg (2009)
19. Xu, S., Ni, Q., Bertino, E., et al.: A characterization of the problem of secure provenance management. In: IEEE International Conference on Intelligence and Security Informatics, ISI 2009, pp. 310–314. IEEE (2009)
20. Braun, U., Shinnar, A., Seltzer, M.: Securing provenance. In: Proceedings of the 3rd Conference on Hot Topics in Security, pp. 1–5. USENIX Association (2008)
21. Abian, J., Atencia, M., Besana, P., et al.: OpenKnowledge Deliverable 6.3: Bioinformatics Interaction Models (2008)

22. Siebes, R., Dupplaw, D., Kotoulas, S., et al.: The openknowledge system: an interaction-centered approach to knowledge sharing. In: Proceedings of the 15th International Conference on Cooperative Information Systems (CoopIS), pp. 381–390 (2007)
23. Gurevich, Y., Neeman, I.: DKAL: Distributed-knowledge authorization language. In: IEEE 21st Computer Security Foundations Symposium, CSF 2008, pp. 149–162. IEEE (2008)
24. Robertson, D., Barker, A., Besana, P., et al.: Models of interaction as a grounding for peer to peer knowledge sharing. In: Advances in Web Semantics I, pp. 81–129 (2009)
25. Bryans, J.W., Koutny, M., Mazare, L., et al.: Opacity generalised to transition systems. International Journal of Information Security 7(6), 421–435 (2008)
26. Kakas, A.C., Kowalski, R.A., Toni, F.: The Role of Abduction in Logic Programming. In: Gabbay, D.M., Hogger, C.J., Robinson, J.A. (eds.) Handbook of Logic in Artificial Intelligence and Logic Programming: Logic Programming 5, pp. 235–324. Oxford University Press, USA (1998)
27. Gorrieri, R., Martinelli, F., Matteucci, I.: Towards information flow properties for distributed systems. Electronic Notes in Theoretical Computer Science 236, 65–84 (2009)

Detecting Conflicts in Commitments

Akın Günay and Pınar Yolum

Department of Computer Engineering,
Boğaziçi University,
34342, Bebek, İstanbul, Turkey
{akin.gunay,pinar.yolum}@boun.edu.tr

Abstract. Commitments are being used widely to specify interaction among autonomous agents in multiagent systems. While various formalizations for a commitment and its life cycle exist, there has been little work that studies commitments in relation to each other. However, in many situations, the content and state of one commitment may render another commitment useless or even worse create conflicts. This paper studies commitments in relation to each other. Following and extending an earlier formalization by Chesani *et al.*, we identify key conflict relations among commitments. The conflict detection can be used to detect violation of commitments before the actual violation occurs during agent interaction (run-time) and this knowledge can be used to guide an agent to avoid the violation. It can also be used during creation of multiagent contracts to identify conflicts in the contracts (compile-time). We implement our method in $\mathcal{REC}$ and present a case study to demonstrate the benefit of our method.

1 Introduction

A commitment is a contract from one agent to another to bring about a certain property [2, 11]. For instance a merchant and a customer may have a contract, in which the customer agrees to pay to the merchant in return of the delivery of a good. This contract can be represented as a commitment, in which the merchant will be committed to the customer to deliver a good, if it is paid. In this commitment, the merchant is the debtor, the customer is the creditor, delivery of the good is the property and payment is the condition of the commitment.

Commitments are dynamic entities and they evolve over time according to the occurrence of events in the environment they exist. To represent the dynamic nature of a commitment, the commitment is associated with a state and transitions between states are defined over a set of operations. These states and operations are called the life cycle of a commitment. Previous work has studied the life cycle of individual commitments in detail [5, 10, 12–14]. However, individual life cycle of a commitment provides limited information to manage and monitor commitments in a multiagent system.

Example 1. Consider the two commitments: The first commitment is between a merchant and a customer, which states, if the customer pays for some goods,

C. Sakama et al. (Eds.): DALT 2011, LNAI 7169, pp. 51–66, 2012.

then the merchant will be committed to deliver the goods within the next day. The second commitment is between the merchant and a delivery company, which states, if the merchant pays for the delivery of some goods, then the delivery company will be committed to deliver these goods to the customer within three to five days.

If we examine the commitments in Example 1 individually according to the life cycle of a commitment, then we do not detect any problem, since both commitments are valid. However if we examine the two commitments together, then it is obvious that the first commitment is going to be violated. This is because the merchant commits to the customer to deliver the goods in the next day, but the commitment with the delivery company cannot deliver before three days. This example demonstrates that if we examine commitments in a multiagent system together, instead of examining them individually, we can detect possible problems as early as the commitments created.

The above example demonstrates the benefit of examining commitments together in order to detect possible problems in advance at run-time. However, the same idea can also be used in an offline manner to detect inconsistencies in multiagent contracts. A multiagent contract is simply a set of related commitments. A major issue in a contract is the consistency between the commitments of the contract. If there are inconsistencies between commitments, then one commitment may not be satisfied without violating other commitment(s), which causes a participating agent to find itself in a problematic situation. In order to avoid such situations we should examine the commitments in a contract together and eliminate the inconsistencies before creating the contract.

In this paper, we present a method that examines commitments in a multiagent system together in order to capture commitment pairs such that one commitment cannot be satisfied without violating the other commitment. The major benefit of our approach is capturing such situations in advance before a commitment is actually violated. Hence, it makes it possible to take early action to avoid future problems. We use an extended version of event calculus formalization of commitments proposed by Chesani *et al.* [3]. We extend this formalization by introducing the axioms for conditional commitments, which are essential to fully model commitments. On top of this formalization, we identify and develop a set of axioms to reason about inconsistencies between commitments. To achieve this, we define a *conflict* relation between commitments. The conflict relation indicates that a commitment cannot be satisfied without violating another. Our formalism and approach to capture inconsistencies in contracts is executable in $\mathcal{REC}$ [3], which is a tool for reasoning based on reactive event calculus.

Our major contributions in this paper are (1) extending the previous event calculus formalization of commitments by introducing conditional commitments; (2) introducing new axioms to define a conflict relation between commitments; (3) use of conflicts of commitments to detect violation of a commitment in advance before the commitment is actually violated.

The rest of the paper is structured as follows. Section 2 reviews commitments and describes the extended formal model of commitments in event calculus.

Section 3 describes the conflict relations of commitments and how they can be used to capture inconsistencies in contracts. Section 4 examines our approach over a running example. Finally, Section 5 concludes the paper with further discussion.

2 Background: Commitments

A commitment is made from one agent to another to bring about a certain property [2, 11]. By participating in a commitment, the participating agents put themselves under the obligation to satisfy the requirements of the commitment. A commitment is represented as $C(x, y, q, p)$, which states that the *debtor* agent x will be committed to the *creditor* agent y to bring about the *property* p, if the *condition* q is satisfied.

In order to represent real world situations more precisely, the condition and the property of a commitment may be associated with temporal quantifiers, which defines when and how the condition and the property must be satisfied. In general there are two types of temporal quantifiers [3, 7]. Existential temporal quantifier states that the associated property must be satisfied at least at one moment within a given interval of moments. Universal temporal quantifier states that the associated property must be satisfied at all moments within a given interval of moments.

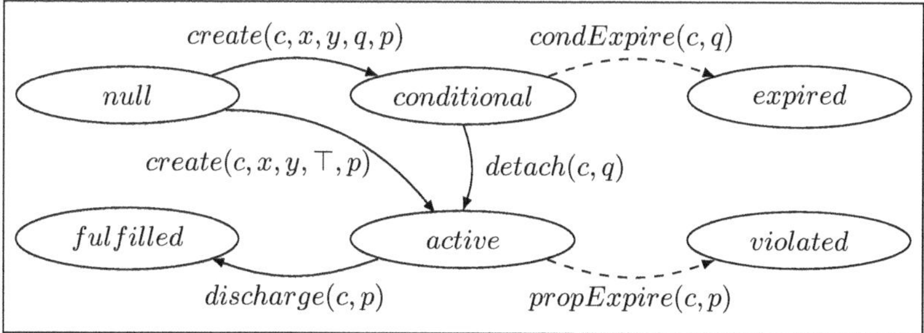

Fig. 1. Life cycle of a commitment

A commitment is a dynamic entity and has a life cycle. Each commitment has a state that evolves over time. The state of a commitment changes according to a set of operations that can be performed by the participating agents of the commitment. The state of a commitment also changes, when the condition or the property of the commitment is not satisfied according to the associated temporal quantifier. In this paper we use the commitment life cycle that we present in Figure 1. In this life cycle we skip operations such as delegate and cancel, which are used in previous work, for simplicity.

The following operations can be performed on a commitment.

- *create*(c, x, y, q, p): Creates a new commitment c, in which x is the debtor, y is the creditor, q is the condition and p is the property of the commitment. This operation can only be performed by the debtor x.
- *detach*(c, q): Detaches the condition q from the commitment c. This operation can only be performed by the creditor y.
- *discharge*(c, p): Discharges the commitment c, when the property p is satisfied. This operation can only be performed by the debtor x.

condExpire(c, q) and *propExpire*(c, p) are meta operations that show that the condition q and property p of the commitment c are violated according to the associated temporal quantifier, respectively. A commitment can be in one of the following states.

- *null*: A dummy state, which is assigned to a commitment before its creation.
- *conditional*: The condition of the commitment is not satisfied yet. This is like an offer and neither the debtor nor the creditor is under the obligation of the commitment.
- *expired*: The condition of the commitment is violated considering to the associated temporal quantifier. Hence, the commitment expires. This usually corresponds to the rejection of an offer.
- *active*: The debtor is under the obligation of the commitment to satisfy the property of the commitment. Otherwise, the debtor may be punished depending on the properties of the underlying environment.
- *fulfilled*: The property of the commitment is satisfied and the debtor fulfilled its commitment. The debtor is no more under the obligation of the commitment.
- *violated*: The property of the commitment is not satisfied and the debtor violates its commitment.

2.1 Event Calculus

Event calculus is a formalism to reason about events and their effects. An *event* in event calculus initiates or terminates a *fluent*. A fluent is a property whose value is subject to change over time. A fluent starts to hold after an event that initiates it and ceases to hold after an event that terminates it. Event calculus was introduced by Kowalski and Sergot [6] and extended by Shanahan [9].

In the following, $\mathcal{E}$ is a sort of events (variables $E, E_1, E_2, ...$), $\mathcal{F}$ is a sort of fluents (variables $F, F_1, F_2, ...$) and $\mathcal{T}$ is a sort for integer time moments (variables $T, T_1, T_2, ...$), which are ordered by the $<$ relation that is transitive and asymmetric. Variables are universally quantified, unless otherwise specified.

The event calculus predicates are as follows [9].

- *initiates*(E, F, T): Fluent F starts to hold after event E at time T.
- *terminates*(E, F, T): Fluent F ceases to hold after event E at time T.
- *initially*(F): Fluent F holds from time 0.

- $happens(E, T)$: Event E occurs at time T.
- $holdsAt(F, T)$: Fluent F holds at time T.
- $clipped(F, T_1, T_2)$: Fluent F is terminated between times T_1 and T_2.

In the following we present the axiomatisation of the event calculus predicates.

Axiom 1

$$holdsAt(F, T) \leftarrow \\ \quad initially(F) \wedge \neg clipped(F, 0, T) \qquad \blacksquare$$

Axiom 1 states that the fluent F holds at time T, if it held at time 0 and has not been terminated between 0 and T.

Axiom 2

$$holdsAt(F, T_2) \leftarrow \\ \quad happens(E, T_1) \wedge initiates(E, F, T_1) \wedge \neg clipped(F, T_1, T_2) \wedge T_1 < T_2 \qquad \blacksquare$$

Axiom 2 states that the fluent F holds at time T, if the fluent F is initiated by an event E at some time T_1 before T_2 and the fluent F has not been terminated between T_1 and T_2.

Axiom 3

$$clipped(F, T_1, T_2) \leftrightarrow \\ \quad \exists E, T[happens(E, T) \wedge terminates(E, F, T) \wedge T_1 < T < T_2] \qquad \blacksquare$$

Axiom 3 states that fluent F is clipped between T_1 and T_2, if and only if there is an event E happens between T_1 and T_2 and terminates the fluent F .

2.2 Formalizing Commitments in Event Calculus

In the rest of this section, we present the event calculus axioms that represent the life cycle of a commitment. These axioms extend the axioms introduced by Chesani *et al.* [3] by introducing the conditional commitment, which is not present in the axioms of Chesani *et al.*. The conditional commitment is essential to represent a complete life cycle of a commitment.

In the following, we use $\mathcal{A}$ as a sort of agents (variables $A, A_1, A_2, ...$), $\mathcal{P}$ as the set of properties (variables $P, P_1, ..., Q, Q_1, ...$), $\mathcal{C}$ as the set of commitments (variables $C, C_1, C_2, ...$) and $\mathcal{S}$ as the set of commitment states. We represent an existentially quantified moment interval as $e(T_1, T_2)$, a universally quantified moment interval as $u(T_1, T_2)$ and a property as $prop(\mathcal{Q}(T_1, T_2), F)$, in which $\mathcal{Q} = \{e, u\}$. We represent a commitment as $comm(A_1, A_2, Q, P)$. The state of a commitment is represented by the fluent $status(C, S)$. We also use predicates $conditional(C, T)$, $expired(C, T)$, $active(C, T)$, $violated(C, T)$ and $fulfilled(C, T)$ to represent that at moment T the commitment C is in conditional, expired, active, violated and fulfilled state, respectively.

Axiom 4 (Creating active commitment)
The *create*(E, A, C, T) operation performed by the debtor A through the occurrence of event E at moment T creates the commitment C in active state.

$$initiates(E, status(comm(A_1, A_2, \top, P), active), T) \leftarrow \\ create(E, A_1, comm(A_1, A_2, \top, P), T)$$ ∎

Axiom 5 (Creating conditional commitment)
The *condCreate*(E, A, C, T) operation performed by the debtor A through the occurrence of event E at moment T creates the commitment C in conditional state.

$$initiates(E, status(comm(A_1, A_2, Q, P), conditional), T) \leftarrow \\ condCreate(E, A_1, comm(A_1, A_2, Q, P), T)$$ ∎

Axiom 6 (Expiration of conditional commitment)
The state of a commitment changes from conditional to expired, when the condition of the commitment is not detached by the creditor within the corresponding moment interval.

$$initiates(E, status(comm(A_1, A_2, Q, P), expired), T) \leftarrow \\ condExpire(E, comm(A_1, A_2, Q, P), T)$$

$$terminates(E, status(comm(A_1, A_2, Q, P), conditional), T) \leftarrow \\ condExpire(E, comm(A_1, A_2, Q, P), T)$$

A commitment in conditional state with an existentially quantified condition expires, when the commitment is still in conditional state after the corresponding moment interval.

$$condExpire(E, comm(A_1, A_2, prop(e(T_1, T_2), F), P), T) \leftarrow \\ conditional(comm(A_1, A_2, prop(e(T_1, T_2), F), P), T) \wedge T > T_2$$

A commitment in conditional state with a universally quantified condition expires, when the condition does not hold at any moment within the corresponding moment interval.

$$condExpire(E, comm(A_1, A_2, prop(u(T_1, T_2), F), P), T) \leftarrow \\ conditional(comm(A_1, A_2, property(u(T_1, T_2), F), P), T) \wedge \\ \neg holdsAt(F, T) \wedge T_1 \leq T \wedge T \leq T_2$$ ∎

Axiom 7 (Detaching conditional commitment)
The state of a commitment changes from conditional to active, when the commitment is detached by the creditor through the occurrence of event E at moment T.

$$initiates(E, status(comm(A_1, A_2, Q, P), active), T) \leftarrow \\ detach(E, A_2, comm(A_1, A_2, Q, P), T)$$

$$terminates(E, status(comm(A_1, A_2, Q, P), conditional), T) \leftarrow \\ detach(E, A_2, comm(A_1, A_2, Q, P), T)$$

A commitment in conditional state with an existentially quantified condition is detached, when the event E initiates the fluent F of the condition within the corresponding moment interval.

$$detach(E, A_2, comm(A_1, A_2, prop(e(T_1, T_2), F), P), T) \leftarrow \\ conditional(comm(A_1, A_2, prop(e(T_1, T_2), F), P), T) \wedge \\ initiates(E, F, T) \wedge T_1 \leq T \wedge T \leq T_2$$

A commitment in conditional state with a universally quantified condition is detached, when the commitment is still in conditional state after the end of the corresponding moment interval of the condition.

$$detach(E, A_2, comm(A_1, A_2, prop(u(T_1, T_2), F), P), T) \leftarrow \\ conditional(comm(A_1, A_2, prop(u(T_1, T_2), F), P), T) \wedge T > T_2$$ ∎

Axiom 8 (Violating active commitment)
The state of a commitment changes from active to violated, when the property of the commitment is not discharged by the debtor within the corresponding time interval.

$$initiates(E, status(comm(A_1, A_2, Q, P), violated), T) \leftarrow \\ propExpire(E, comm(A_1, A_2, Q, P), T)$$

$$terminates(E, status(comm(A_1, A_2, Q, P), active), T) \leftarrow \\ propExpire(E, comm(A_1, A_2, Q, P), T)$$

A commitment in active state with an existentially quantified property expires, when the commitment is still in active state after the corresponding moment interval.

$$propExpire(E, comm(A_1, A_2, Q, prop(e(T_1, T_2), F)), T) \leftarrow \\ active(comm(A_1, A_2, Q, prop(e(T_1, T_2), F)), T) \wedge T > T_2$$

A commitment in conditional state with a universally quantified property expires, when the property does not hold at any moment within the corresponding moment interval.

$$propExpire(E, comm(A_1, A_2, Q, prop(u(T_1, T_2), F)), T) \leftarrow \\ active(comm(A_1, A_2, Q, prop(u(T_1, T_2), F)), T) \\ \neg holdsAt(F, T) \wedge T_1 \leq T \wedge T \leq T_2$$ ∎

Axiom 9 (Discharging active commitment)
The state of a commitment changes from active to fulfilled, when the commitment is discharged by the debtor through the occurrence of event E at moment T.

$$initiates(E, status(comm(A_1, A_2, Q, P), fulfilled), T) \leftarrow \\ discharge(E, A_1, comm(A_1, A_2, Q, P), T)$$

$$terminates(E, status(comm(A_1, A_2, Q, P), active), T) \leftarrow \\ discharge(E, A_1, comm(A_1, A_2, Q, P), T)$$

A commitment in active state with an existentially quantified property is discharged, when the event E initiates the fluent F of the property within the corresponding moment interval.

$$discharge(E, A_1, comm(A_1, A_2, Q, prop(e(T_1, T_2), F)), T) \leftarrow \\ active(comm(A_1, A_2, Q, prop(e(T_1, T_2), F)), T) \wedge \\ initiates(E, F, T) \wedge T_1 \leq T \wedge T \leq T_2$$

A commitment in active state with a universally quantified property is discharged, when the commitment is still in active state after the end of the corresponding moment interval of property.

$$discharge(E, A_1, comm(A_1, A_2, Q, prop(u(T_1, T_2), F), T) \leftarrow \\ active(comm(A_1, A_2, Q, prop(u(T_1, T_2), F)), T) \wedge T > T_2$$ ∎

3 Conflicting Commitments

Our aim in this paper is to develop a method to capture commitment pairs, such that one of the commitments cannot be satisfied without violating the other commitment. We call such commitment pairs as conflicting commitments. Since satisfaction and violation of a commitment is determined according to the satisfaction and violation of its committed property, in order to capture conflicting commitments, we should first define conflicting properties. Similar to the conflicting commitments, two properties conflict with each other if one of the properties cannot be satisfied without violating the other. The idea of our method is, if properties of two commitments conflict with each other, then the commitments also conflict with each other.

3.1 Conflicting Properties

In order to define a conflict between two properties we have to know the meaning of the fluents involved by these properties in the intended domain of the underlying multiagent system. This is necessary since without such a domain knowledge, fluents are meaningless. In order to formalize this situation, we use a *fluent conflict* relation. Two fluents conflict with each other if it is not possible to hold both fluents at the same time in a given domain.

Definition 1. *Fluents F_1 and F_2 in a given domain $\mathcal{D}$ are in a fluent conflict, if it is not possible to hold both fluents at the same moment in the domain $\mathcal{D}$. The predicate $fluentConf(F_1, F_2, \mathcal{D})$ indicates the fluent conflict between the fluents F_1 and F_2 in domain $\mathcal{D}$.*

Example 2. Consider the fluent *carRented*(C, P), which means the car C is rented to the person P. Now consider the same fluent with two different set of grounded values, *carRented(herbie, sally)* and *carRented(herbie, linus)*. The first fluent states that the car *herbie* is rented to *sally* and the second fluent states that the car *herbie* is rented to *linus*. As a domain knowledge, we know that the same car cannot be rented to two different person at the same time. Hence, we also know *carRented(herbie, sally)* and *carRented(herbie, linus)* cannot hold at the same moment. As result these two fluents conflict with each other.

The above case can be represented as the following rule in domain D:

$$fluentConf(carRented(C, P_1), carRented(C, P_2), D) \leftarrow \\ isCar(C) \wedge isPerson(P_1) \wedge isPerson(P_2) \wedge P_1 \neq P_2$$

In the rest of the paper we assume that the domain dependent fluent conflict knowledge is already present.

Definition 2. *Properties* P_1 *and* P_2 *are in a property conflict relation if it is not possible to satisfy one property without violating the other. The predicate* $propConf(P_1, P_2)$ *indicates a conflict between properties* P_1 *and* P_2.

Occurrence of a property conflict depends on the existence of a fluent conflict between the fluents of the properties as we discussed above and the temporal quantifiers of the properties. There are three possible cases considering temporal quantifiers of the properties as we present below.

Existential-Existential. A property conflict relation between two existentially quantified properties occurs if and only if fluents of these properties are in fluent conflict relation and both properties must be satisfied at a common moment.

Axiom 10

$$propConf(prop(e, (T_1, T_2), F_1), prop(e, (T_3, T_4), F_2) \leftarrow \\ fluentConf(F_1, F_2, D) \wedge T_1 = T_2 = T_3 = T_4$$

Example 3. Consider the properties *prop*$(e(1, 1), isRented(herbie, sally))$ and *prop*$(e(1, 1), isRented(herbie, linus))$. The first property is satisfied if the car *herbie* is rented by *sally* exactly at moment 1 and the second property is satisfied if the car *herbie* is rented by *linus* exactly at moment 1. As domain knowledge we know that the fluents *isRented(herbie, sally)* and *isRented(herbie, linus)* have a fluent conflict, which means the car *herbie* cannot be rented both by *sally* and *linus* at moment 1. Thus, it is not possible to satisfy one of these properties without violating the other, therefore these two properties are in property conflict.

Note that, in order to have a property conflict in the case of existentially quantified properties, the moment intervals of the properties must refer exactly to the same moment. If the moment interval is not just on a moment, it is possible to satisfy both properties, even if the fluents of the properties have a fluent conflict.

Existential-Universal. A property conflict between an existentially and a universally quantified property occurs if there is a fluent conflict between the fluents of the properties and the moment interval of the universally quantified property covers the moment interval of the existentially quantified property.

Axiom 11

$$\begin{aligned}&propConf(prop(e(T_1,T_2),F_1),prop(u(T_3,T_4),F_2) \leftarrow\\&\quad fluentConf(F_1,F_2,D) \wedge T_3 \leq T_1 \wedge T_2 \leq T_4\end{aligned}$$ ∎

Example 4. Consider the properties *prop*($e(1,3)$, *isRented*(*herbie*, *sally*)) and *prop*($u(1,5)$, *isRented*(*herbie*, *linus*)). The first property is satisfied if the car *herbie* is rented by *sally* at least at one moment between 1 and 3 and the second property is satisfied if the car *herbie* is rented by *linus* at all moments between 1 and 5. As domain knowledge we know that the fluents *isRented*(*herbie*, *sally*) and *isRented*(*herbie*, *linus*) have a fluent conflict, which means the car *herbie* cannot be rented both by *sally* and *linus* between moments 1 and 3. If *herbie* is rented to *sally* at any moment between 1 and 3 to satisfy the first property, then it is not possible to satisfy the second property. If *herbie* is rented to *linus* at all moment between 1 and 5 to satisfy the second property, then it is not possible to satisfy the first property. Thus, it is not possible to satisfy one of these properties without violating the other and these two properties are in property conflict.

Universal-Universal. A property conflict between two universally quantified properties occurs if there is a fluent conflict between the fluents of the properties and the moment intervals of the properties overlap with each other.

Axiom 12

$$\begin{aligned}&propConf(prop(u(T_1,T_2),F_1),prop(u(T_3,T_4),F_2)) \leftarrow\\&\quad fluentConf(D,F_1,F_2) \wedge\\&\quad [T_1 \leq T_3 \wedge T_3 \leq T_2 \vee T_3 \leq T_1 \wedge T_1 \leq T_4]\end{aligned}$$ ∎

Example 5. Consider the properties *prop*($u(1,5)$, *isRented*(*herbie*, *sally*)) and *prop*($u(3,7)$, *isRented*(*herbie*, *linus*)). The first property is satisfied if the car *herbie* is rented by *sally* at all moments between 1 and 5 and the second property is satisfied if the car *herbie* is rented by *linus* at all moments between 3 and 7. As domain knowledge we know that the fluents *isRented*(*herbie*, *sally*) and *isRented*(*herbie*, *linus*) have a fluent conflict, which means the car *herbie* cannot be rented both by *sally* and *linus* between moments 3 and 5. If *herbie* is rented to *sally* at all moments between 1 and 5 to satisfy the first property, then it is not possible to satisfy the second property. If *herbie* is rented to *linus* at all moment between 3 and 7 to satisfy the second property, then it is not possible to satisfy the first property. Thus, it is not possible to satisfy one of these properties without violating the other and these two properties are in property conflict.

3.2 Conflict Relations between Commitments

Now we define the first type of conflict relation between two commitments using the property conflict relation that we defined before. A *commitment conflict* relation may occur between two active commitments, which indicates that one of the commitments cannot be satisfied without violating the other.

Definition 3. *Given the two commitments C_1 and C_2 with properties P_1 and P_2, respectively, there is a commitment conflict between commitments C_1 and C_2, if the properties P_1 and P_2 have a property conflict and commitments C_1 and C_2 are in active state. The fluent $commConf(C_1, C_2)$ indicates a conflict between commitments C_1 and C_2.*

Axiom 13 (Commitment conflict)

$$\begin{aligned}&initiates(E, commConf(comm(\_,\_,Q_1,P_1), comm(\_,\_,Q_2,P_2)), T) \leftarrow \\ &\quad active(comm(\_,\_,Q_1,P_1),T) \wedge active(comm(\_,\_,Q_2,P_2),T) \wedge \\ &\quad propConf(P_1,P_2)\end{aligned}$$ ∎

Example 6. Consider the commitments $comm(charlie, sally, \top, prop(u(1,5), isRented(herbie, sally)))$ and $comm(charlie, linus, \top, prop(u(3,7), isRented(herbie, linus)))$. The first commitment states that *charlie* is committed to *sally* to rent *herbie* at all moments between 1 and 5 and the second commitment states that *charlie* is committed to *linus* to rent *herbie* at all moments between 3 and 7. We know that there is a property conflict between the properties of these two commitments. Hence it is not possible to satisfy both properties. As result, it is also not possible to satisfy one commitment without violating the other. If *charlie* rents *herbie* to *sally* and satisfies his commitment to *sally*, then he violates his commitment to *linus*. On the other hand, if *charlie* rents *herbie* to *linus* and satisfies his commitment to *linus*, then he violates his commitment to *sally*.

Note that, the debtors and the creditors are actually irrelevant while capturing commitment conflicts. The only relevant factors are the property conflict between the properties of the commitments and the states of the commitments.

The commitment conflict relation that we discuss above points out to a definite violation of at least one commitment. This happens, since both commitments are in active state. However, this is not the case if at least one of the commitments are not in active but conditional state. In this case, occurrence of a commitment conflict and violation of the commitment depends on the satisfaction of the condition(s) of the commitment(s). In the following we define another relation, which we call *conditional commitment conflict* relation between commitments to reflect such situations.

Definition 4. *Given the two commitments C_1 and C_2 with conditions Q_1 and Q_2, and properties P_1 and P_2, respectively, there is a conditional commitment conflict between commitments C_1 and C_2 if the properties P_1 and P_2 have a property conflict and at least one of the commitments C_1 or C_2 is in conditional* *state, if not in active state. The fluent* $condCommConf(C_1, C_2)$ *indicates a conditional commitment conflict between commitments* C_1 *and* C_2*.*

Axiom 14 defines the conditional commitment conflict, where one commitment is in active state and the other commitment is in conditional state. Note that, if the condition of the commitment in conditional state is satisfied, then the conditional conflict relation between the commitments is terminated and the commitment conflict relation is initiated.

Axiom 14 (Conditional commitment conflict (active-conditional))

$$\begin{aligned}&initiates(E, condCommConf(comm(\_,\_,Q_1,P_1), comm(\_,\_,Q_2,P_2)), T) \leftarrow\\&\quad active(comm(\_,\_,Q_1,P_1),T) \wedge conditional(comm(\_,\_,Q_2,P_2),T) \wedge\\&\quad propConf(P_1,P_2)\end{aligned}$$

Axiom 15 defines the conditional commitment conflict, where both commitments are in conditional state. Note that, if one of the conditions is satisfied, then Axiom 14 applies.

Axiom 15 (Conditional commitment conflict (conditional-conditional))

$$\begin{aligned}&initiates(E, condCommConf(comm(\_,\_,Q_1,P_1), comm(\_,\_,Q_2,P_2)), T) \leftarrow\\&\quad conditional(comm(\_,\_,Q_1,P_1),T) \wedge\\&\quad conditional(comm(\_,\_,Q_2,P_2),T) \wedge\\&\quad propConf(P_1,P_2)\end{aligned}$$

Example 7. Consider the commitments *comm(charlie, sally, prop(e(1, 3), isPaid(sally)), prop(u(3, 5), isRented(herbie, sally)))* and *comm(charlie, linus , ⊤, prop(u(3, 7), isRented(herbie, linus)))*. The first commitment is in conditional state, which means that *charlie* will be committed to *sally* to rent *herbie* at all moments between 3 and 5, if *sally* pays the rent between moments 1 and 3 and the second commitment is in active state, which means that *charlie* is committed to *linus* rent *herbie* at all moments between 3 and 7. We know that there is a property conflict between the properties of these two commitments. In this case, occurrence of a commitment conflict depends on the satisfaction of the condition of the first commitment. If *sally* does not pay, then the first commitment expires and the conflict is resolved automatically.

4 A Commitment Conflict Scenario

We present a scenario to demonstrate how the conflict relations that we define can be used to capture violation of a commitment in a multiagent system, before the violation actually occurs. We also implement this scenario in the REC tool and we present the trace of the execution.

Scenario Description. There are two customers Sally and Linus and a car rental agent Charlie. Charlie has a commitment in conditional state to Sally, which states, if Sally pays the rent between days one and three, then Charlie will be committed to Sally to rent a car to her between days four and seven. Charlie has also a commitment in conditional state to Linus, which states, if Linus uses a promotion ticket between days one and five, then Charlie will be committed to Linus to rent a car to him for days six and seven for a cheaper price. We also know that Charlie has just one car, namely Herbie, available for rent for the next seven days.

In this scenario, it is obvious that Charlie will get into trouble if both Sally and Linus satisfy the conditions of their own commitments. If this happens, Charlie will have active commitments to both of them to rent a car at the same dates. However, Charlie has only one car to rent at that dates, hence he cannot satisfy one of these commitments without violating the other. This situation cannot be captured at run time by considering these two commitments individually, at least until one of the commitments is actually violated. However, if we consider these commitments together, we can capture that there is a potential problem, immediately when the two commitments are created.

Let us first define the fluents, the events and effects of the events on the fluents in our scenario.

Fluents:

- $rentPaid(C, Car, A)$: The customer C paid the rent for the car Car to the agency A.
- $promeUsed(C, Car, A)$: The customer C used a promotion ticket for the car Car to the agency A.
- $rented(Car, C)$: The car Car is rented to the customer C.

Events:

- $payRent(C, Car, A)$: The customer C pays the rent for the car Car to the agency A.
- $usePromo(C, Car, A)$: The customer C gives the promotion ticket for the car Car to the agency A.
- $rent(A, Car, C)$: The agency A rents the car Car to the customer C.

Effects of events on fluents:

- $initiates(payRent(C, Car, A), rentPaid(C, Car, A), T)$
- $initiates(usePromo(C, Car, A), promoUsed(C, Car, A), T)$
- $initiates(rent(A, Car, C), rented(Car, C), T)$

Finally we define the creation of commitments as result of the event as follows.

$$
\begin{aligned}
&ccreate(offer(A, Car, C)), A, comm(A, C,\\
&\qquad prop(e(T, T_2), rentPaid(C, Car, A)),\\
&\qquad prop(u(T_3, T_4), rented(Car, C))), T) \leftarrow\\
&\qquad T_2 \ is\ T + 2 \wedge T_3 \ is\ T + 3 \wedge T_4 \ is\ T_3 + 3
\end{aligned}
$$

$$ccreate(promote(A, Car, C)), A, comm(A, C,$$
$$prop(e(T, T_2), promoUsed(C, Car, A)),$$
$$prop(u(T_3, T_4), rented(Car, C))), T) \leftarrow$$
$$T_2 \ is \ T + 4 \wedge T_3 \ is \ T + 5 \wedge T_4 \ is \ T_3 + 1$$

Assume that the domain dependent fluent conflicts are already defined and following list of happens statement shows the execution of the system.

$$happens(offer(charlie, herbie, sally), 1)$$
$$happens(promote(charlie, herbie, linus), 1)$$
$$happens(payRent(sally, herbie, charlie), 2)$$
$$happens(rent(charlie, herbie, sally), 3)$$
$$happens(usePromo(linus, herbie, charlie), 4)$$

Let us trace the execution. At moment 1, *charlie* creates two conditional commitments as described in the scenario. Let us call the commitment between *charlie* and *sally* as C_S and the commitment between *charlie* and *linus* as C_L. The property of the commitment C_S is $prop(u(4,7), rented(herbie, sally))$ and the property of the commitment C_L is $prop(u(6,7), rented(herbie, linus))$. Assuming that there is a fluent conflict between the two grounded *rented* fluent, by using the Axiom 12 we can conclude that there is a property conflict between the properties of the commitment C_S and C_L. Detection of this property conflict further causes the condition of the Axiom 15 to hold, which allows us to conclude that there is a conditional commitment conflict between the commitments C_S and C_L. Hence, we immediately capture that depending on the satisfaction of the conditions of these two commitments C_S and C_L, one of these commitments cannot be satisfied without violating the other. At moment 2, *sally* pays the rent and satisfies the condition of her own commitment C_S and the state of C_S changes to active. At that moment using the Axiom 14, we can deduce that we have still a conditional commitment conflict, which depends on the satisfaction of the condition of the commitment C_L. At moment 3, *charlie* rents *herbie* to *sally* to satisfy the commitment C_S. Finally, at moment 4 by using the promotion ticket, *linus* satisfies the condition of the commitment C_L and the state of this commitment changes to active. Accordingly the condition of the Axiom 13 holds and we conclude that there is a commitment conflict. At that moment, we definitely know that at least one of the commitments C_S and C_L is going to be violated. Note that, if we examine the commitments using only the life cycle axioms, we cannot capture the violation of one of these commitments not before moment 6.

5 Discussion

In this paper we introduce the conflict relation between two commitments. A conflict relation indicates one of the commitments in this relation cannot be satisfied without violating the other commitment. To formalize this conflict relation we first extend the existing event calculus formalization of the commitments with conditional commitments and then introduce a set of new axioms to capture conflicts between commitments. We implement our axioms using the REC tool and evaluate them on a multiagent scenario. In our future work we plan to apply our method to capture inconsistencies in multiagent contracts [4]. We also left detection of conflicts between more than two commitments and handling of conflicting commitments as future work.

The first formalization of commitments in event calculus is introduced by Yolum and Singh [14]. In their formalization they do not use an explicit state definition for commitments. They discuss how a multiagent protocol can be represented in a flexible way by using the event calculus formalization of commitments and they also show how agents can reason about commitments on the execution of the protocol. In a series of papers Torroni and his colleagues develop another event calculus based monitoring framework for commitments, which uses SCIFF abductive logic programming proof-procedure [1, 3]. Their framework is capable of efficiently monitoring evolution of commitments in a multiagent system at run-time. We use their framework as a basis for our work. We extend their commitment formalization with conditional commitments and on top of this formalization we build our axioms to define conflict relation of commitments.

Singh discusses semantics of dialectical and practical commitments [12]. In his work, Singh provides a unified temporal logic based semantics for dialectical and practical commitments. Our main motivation in this paper is to deal with practical commitments and we do not discuss dialectical commitments. Singh also provides some reasoning postulates related to the ones we discuss here. These are named consistency and strong consistency, which states an agent cannot commit to false and an agent cannot commit to a negation of previously committed property, respectively. Especially, the strong consistency postulate corresponds to our commitment conflict relation. However, the postulates introduced by Singh acts as a constraint and restrict existence of such commitments. We do not put any restrictions on commitments, instead our aim is to just detect such situations and let dealing with the situation to the underlying multiagent system.

Mallya *et al.* discuss resolvability of commitments [8]. They use a variant of CTL to formalize commitments and provide a set of definitions about when a commitment is resolvable using the same temporal quantifiers for properties of commitments. Their discussion concentrates on the resolvability of individual commitments. In our work we assume that all commitments are individually resolvable as defined by Mallya *et al.*. However, our work can be used in order to capture resolvability of multiple commitments, considering individual resolvability.

Acknowledgment. This research is partially supported by Boğaziçi University Research Fund under grant BAP5694, and the Turkish State Planning Organization (DPT) under the TAM Project, number 2007K120610. Akın Günay is partially supported by TÜBİTAK National PhD Scholarship (2211).

References

1. Alberti, M., Chesani, F., Gavanelli, M., Lamma, E., Mello, P., Torroni, P.: Verifiable agent interaction in abductive logic programming: The sciff framework. ACM Transactions on Computational Logic 9, 1–43 (2008)
2. Castelfranchi, C.: Commitments: From Individual Intentions to Groups and Organizations. In: Lesser, V.R., Gasser, L. (eds.) ICMAS, pp. 41–48. The MIT Press (1995)
3. Chesani, F., Mello, P., Montali, M., Torroni, P.: Commitment Tracking via the Reactive Event Calculus. In: Proceedings of the 21st International Joint Conference on Artifical Intelligence, pp. 91–96. Morgan Kaufmann Publishers Inc. (2009)
4. Desai, N., Narendra, N.C., Singh, M.P.: Checking Correctness of Business Contracts via Commitments. In: Proceedings of the 7th International Joint Conference on Autonomous Agents and Multiagent Systems, AAMAS 2008, vol. 2, pp. 787–794 (2008)
5. Fornara, N., Colombetti, M.: Operational Specification of a Commitment-Based Agent Communication Language. In: Proceedings of the First International Joint Conference on Autonomous Agents and Multiagent Systems, AAMAS 2002, pp. 536–542. ACM (2002)
6. Kowalski, R., Sergot, M.: A Logic-based Calculus of Events. New Generation Computing 4, 67–95 (1986)
7. Mallya, A.U., Huhns, M.N.: Commitments Among Agents. IEEE Internet Computing 7, 90–93 (2003)
8. Mallya, A.U., Yolum, P., Singh, M.P.: Resolving Commitments Among Autonomous Agents. In: Dignum, F.P.M. (ed.) ACL 2003. LNCS (LNAI), vol. 2922, pp. 166–182. Springer, Heidelberg (2004)
9. Shanahan, M.: The Event Calculus Explained. In: Veloso, M.M., Wooldridge, M.J. (eds.) Artificial Intelligence Today. LNCS (LNAI), vol. 1600, pp. 409–430. Springer, Heidelberg (1999)
10. Singh, M.P.: Agent Communication Languages: Rethinking the Principles. Computer 31(12), 40–47 (1998)
11. Singh, M.P.: An Ontology for Commitments in Multiagent Systems. Artificial Intelligence and Law 7(1), 97–113 (1999)
12. Singh, M.P.: Semantical Considerations on Dialectical and Practical Commitments. In: Proceedings of the 23rd International Conference on Artificial Intelligence, AAAI 2008, pp. 176–181. AAAI Press (2008)
13. Winikoff, M., Liu, W., Harland, J.: Enhancing Commitment Machines. In: Leite, J., Omicini, A., Torroni, P., Yolum, p. (eds.) DALT 2004. LNCS (LNAI), vol. 3476, pp. 198–220. Springer, Heidelberg (2005)
14. Yolum, P., Singh, M.P.: Flexible Protocol Specification and Execution: Applying Event Calculus Planning using Commitments. In: Proceedings of the First International Joint Conference on Autonomous Agents and Multiagent Systems, AAMAS 2002, pp. 527–534. ACM (2002)

Formalizing Commitments Using Action Languages

Tran Cao Son[1], Enrico Pontelli[1], and Chiaki Sakama[2]

[1] Dept. Computer Science, New Mexico State University
{tson,epontell}@cs.nmsu.edu
[2] Computer and Comm. Sciences, Wakayama Univ.
sakama@sys.wakayama-u.ac.jp

Abstract. This paper investigates the use of high-level action languages for representing and reasoning about commitments in multi-agent domains. We introduce the language $\mathcal{L}^{mt}$, an extension of the language $\mathcal{L}$, with new features motivated by the problem of representing and reasoning about commitments. The paper demonstrates how features and properties of commitments can be described in this action language. We show how $\mathcal{L}^{mt}$ can handle both simple commitment actions as well as complex commitment protocols. Furthermore, the semantics of $\mathcal{L}^{mt}$ provides a uniform solution to different problems in reasoning about commitments such as the problem of (*i*) verifying whether an agent fails (or succeeds) to deliver on its commitments; (*ii*) identifying pending commitments; and (*iii*) suggesting ways to satisfy pending commitments.

1 Introduction and Motivation

Commitments are an integral part of societies of agents. Modeling commitments has been an intensive topic of research in autonomous agents. The focus has often been on the development of ontologies for commitments [6,15], on the identification of requirements for formalisms to represent commitments [13], and the development of formalisms for specifying and verifying protocols or tracking commitments [7,19,11].

Commitments are strongly related to agents' behavior and capabilities, and they are often associated with time constraints, such as a specific time (or time interval) in the future. For example, a customer will not pay for the promised goods if the goods have not been delivered; a client will have to wait for her cheque if the insurance agent does not keep her promise of entering her claim into the system; or an on-line shopper needs to pay for the order within 10 minutes after clicking the 'Check Out' button. Thus, any formalization of *commitments* should be considered in conjunction with a formalization of *actions* and *changes*, which allows us to reason about narratives in presence of (quantitative) time constraints, actions with durations, etc.

Action languages (e.g., $\mathcal{A}$, $\mathcal{B}$, and $\mathcal{C}$ [10]), with their English like syntax and simple transition function based semantics, provide an easy and compact way for describing dynamic systems. Unlike event calculus —an action description formalism often used in the literature for reasoning about commitments—action languages can elegantly deal with indirect effects of actions and static laws. Furthermore, off-the-shelf implementations of various action languages are available. Research has provided various avenues to extend the basic action languages with advanced features, such as resources, deadlines, and preferences. Existing action languages, on the other hand, do not provide

C. Sakama et al. (Eds.): DALT 2011, LNAI 7169, pp. 67–83, 2012.

means for expressing statements like *"I will make some sandwiches"* or *"I will come at 7pm."* Both statements are about achieving a certain state of the world without specifying how. The first statement does not indicate a specific time in the future while the second does. Moreover, with a few exceptions, action languages have been developed mostly for single-agent environments. Action languages have been successfully used in specifying and reasoning about narratives (e.g., [2,4]). Some attempts to use action languages in formalizing commitments have been made [8,9]. However, these attempts do not consider time constraints and actions with durations.

In this paper we answer the question of whether action languages, like $\mathcal{B}$ or $\mathcal{L}$, can be enriched with adequate features to enable the representation of domains where agents can interact through commitments, maintaining the desirable features of having a clear semantics and a declarative representation. In particular, we develop an action language, called $\mathcal{L}^{mt}$, to perform this activity. $\mathcal{L}^{mt}$, an extension of the action language $\mathcal{L}$ [2,3,4], is a language for multi-agent domains with features related to time, observations, and delayed effects. The main reason behinds the selection of $\mathcal{L}$ for our work lies in that $\mathcal{L}$ allows for the reasoning about narratives which is necessary for reasoning about commitments while other languages such as $\mathcal{A}$, $\mathcal{B}$, and $\mathcal{C}$ do not. We show that several tasks related to reasoning with commitments, such as identifying satisfied, pending, and unsatisfied commitments, can be expressed as *queries* in $\mathcal{L}^{mt}$. Furthermore, the problem of finding a way to satisfy pending commitments can be directly addressed using planning. The language also provides a natural means for specifying, verifying, and reasoning about protocols among agents.

2 The Language $\mathcal{L}^{mt}$

In this section, we extend the language is an extension of the language $\mathcal{L}$ [3,4] to consider concurrency, actions with durations, time constraints and multi-agency. We first define the language $\mathcal{L}^m$ for concurrency and multi-agency. To deal with time constraints and action with durations, we extend $\mathcal{L}^m$ and define $\mathcal{L}^{mt}$.

2.1 Adding Concurrency and Multi-agency to $\mathcal{B}$: The Action Language $\mathcal{L}^m$

The signature of the language is $\langle \mathcal{AG}, \{\mathcal{F}_i, \mathcal{A}_i\}_{i \in \mathcal{AG}} \rangle$ where $\mathcal{AG}$ is a (finite) set of agent identifiers and $\mathcal{F}_i$ and $\mathcal{A}_i$ are the sets of *fluents* and the set of *actions* of the agent i, respectively. We assume that $\mathcal{A}_i \cap \mathcal{A}_j = \emptyset$ for any two distinct $i, j \in \mathcal{AG}$. Observe also that $\bigcap_{i \in S} \mathcal{F}_i$ may be not empty for some $S \subseteq \mathcal{AG}$. This represents the fact that fluents in $\bigcap_{i \in S} \mathcal{F}_i$ are relevant to all the agents in S. A *fluent literal* (or *literal*) is either a fluent or a fluent preceded by $\neg$. Given a literal ℓ, we denote with $\bar{\ell}$ its complement. A *fluent formula* is a propositional formula constructed from literals. A *multi-agent domain specification* is a set of axioms of the following forms:

$$a \textbf{ causes } \ell \textbf{ if } \psi \quad (1) \qquad\qquad \textbf{impossible } A \textbf{ if } \psi \quad (3)$$

$$\varphi \textbf{ if } \psi \quad (2) \qquad\qquad \textbf{initially } \ell \quad (4)$$

where $a \in \bigcup_{i \in \mathcal{AG}} \mathcal{A}_i$ is an action, ℓ is a fluent literal, ψ and φ are sets of fluent literals (interpreted as conjunctions), and $A \subseteq \bigcup_{i \in \mathcal{AG}} \mathcal{A}_i$ is a set of actions.

Axioms of type (1), (2), and (3) are referred to as *dynamic laws*, *static laws* (or *state constraints*), and *non-executability laws*, respectively. Intuitively, a dynamic law describes the direct effects of execution of one action (possibly concurrently to other actions), i.e., it says that the execution of a, under the condition that ψ is true, causes ℓ to be true. A static law describes integrity constraints on states of the world. It states that whenever ψ is true then φ must be true but does not require that if ψ is false then φ must be true. In this sense, a static law of the form (2) differs from a logical implication $\psi \Rightarrow \varphi$. Statements of the type (3) encode conditions that prevent the (concurrent) execution of groups of actions, i.e., it states that the set of actions A cannot be simultaneously executed. Statements of type (4) are employed to describe the initial state of the world.

Let $D = \bigcup_{i \in \mathcal{AG}} D_i$ be the domain description defined over the set of fluents $\bigcup_{i \in \mathcal{AG}} \mathcal{F}_i$ and the set of actions $\bigcup_{i \in \mathcal{AG}} \mathcal{A}_i$. An *action snapshot* is a set $\{a_i\}_{i \in \mathcal{AG}}$ where $a_i \in \mathcal{A}_i \cup \{\texttt{noop}\}$. Intuitively, each action snapshot A encodes a set of actions that the agents in $\mathcal{AG}$ concurrently execute in a state where, $a_i = \texttt{noop} \in A$ indicates that the agent i does not participate in A. The semantics of the multi-agent domain D is defined by the transition function Φ_D, which maps a snapshot of actions and a state to a set of states. Intuitively, given an action snapshot A and a state s, the transition function Φ_D defines the set of states that may be reached after executing A in state s. If $\Phi_D(A, s)$ is the empty set, then A is not executable in s.

An *interpretation* I of the fluents in D is a maximal consistent set of fluent literals drawn from $\mathcal{F}$. A fluent f is said to be true (resp. false) in I iff $f \in I$ (resp. $\neg f \in I$). The truth value of a fluent formula in I is defined recursively over the propositional connectives in the usual way. For example, $f \wedge q$ is true in I iff f is true in I and q is true in I. We say that I satisfies φ ($I \models \varphi$) if φ is true in I.

Let I be a set of fluent literals. We say that I is closed under D if for every rule (φ **if** ψ) in D, if $I \models \psi$ then $I \models \varphi$. By $Cl_D(I)$ we denote the smallest superset of I which is closed under D. A *state* of D is an interpretation that is closed under the set of static causal laws of D.

A set of actions B is *prohibited (not executable)* in a state s if there exists an executability condition of the form (3) in D such that $A \subseteq B$ and $s \models \psi$.

The *effect of an action snapshot* A in a state s of D is the set of formulae $e_A(s) = \{\ell \mid D \text{ contains a law } a \textbf{ causes } \ell \textbf{ if } \psi,\ a \in A, \text{ and } s \models \psi\}$.

Given the domain description D, if A is prohibited in s, then $\Phi_D(A, s) = \emptyset$, otherwise $\Phi_D(A, s) = \{s' \mid s' = Cl_D((s \cap s') \cup e_A(s)) \textit{ and } s' \textit{ is a state}\}$. The function Φ_D is extended to define $\widehat{\Phi_D}$ for reasoning about the effects of sequences of action snapshots as follows. For a state s and a sequence of action snapshots $\alpha = [A_1, \ldots, A_n]$, let $\alpha_{n-1} = [A_1, \ldots, A_{n-1}]$, we define

$$\widehat{\Phi_D}(\alpha, s) = \begin{cases} \{s\} & \text{if } n = 0 \\ \emptyset & \text{if } \widehat{\Phi_D}(\alpha_{n-1}, s) = \emptyset \vee \exists s'.[s' \in \widehat{\Phi_D}(\alpha_{n-1}, s) \wedge \Phi_D(A_n, s') = \emptyset] \\ \bigcup_{s' \in \widehat{\Phi_D}(\alpha_{n-1}, s)} \Phi_D(A_n, s') & \text{otherwise} \end{cases}$$

An *initial state* is a state s_0 such that, for each statement of type (4) in D we have that $s_0 \models \ell$. We will assume from now on that there exists at least one initial state. A trajectory is a sequence $s_0 \beta_0 s_1 \beta_1 \ldots \beta_{n-1} s_n$ such that each β_j is a snapshot, s_0 is an initial state, and $s_i \in \Phi_D(s_{i-1}, \beta_{i-1})$ for $1 \leq i \leq n$.

We allow *queries* to be composed, of the form: φ **after** α, where φ is a fluent formula and α is a sequence of action snapshots. A query q is true w.r.t. an initial state s_0, denoted $s_0 \models q$, if $\widehat{\Phi_D}(\alpha, s_0) \neq \emptyset$ and $\forall s \in \widehat{\Phi_D}(\alpha, s_0)$ we have that $s \models \varphi$. A query q is entailed by D ($D \models q$) if for each initial state s_0 of D we have $s_0 \models q$.

2.2 Considering Time: The Action Language $\mathcal{L}^{mt}$

The language proposed so far does not allow for the specification of durative actions. In particular, we wish to be able to model actions with delayed effects and actions whose effects can be overridden by the execution of another action. For example, pumping gasoline into the tank causes the tank to be full after 5 minutes; drilling a hole in the tank takes only 1 minute and will cause the tank never to be full. The execution of drilling 1 minute after initiating the pumping action will cause the tank to never become full. Thus, the execution of the action drill makes the tank no longer full and this effect cannot be reversed by other actions. To address the first issue, we introduce the notion of *annotated fluents*, i.e., fluents associated to relative time points, and use annotated fluents in axioms of the form (1)-(3). To deal with the second issue, we introduce the notions of *irreversible* and *reversible* processes. Note that axioms of the form (4) described the initial state of the world and thus will not be changed.

The signature of $\mathcal{L}^{mt}$ extends the signature of $\mathcal{L}^{m}$ with a countable set of *process names* $\mathcal{P}$. An *annotated literal* is of the form ℓ^t, where ℓ is a fluent literal and $t > 0$ is an integer, representing a future point in time. We also allow annotations of the form $\ell^{\vee[t_1,t_2]}$, denoting $\ell^{t_1} \vee \cdots \vee \ell^{t_2}$ for $t_1 \leq t_2$. *Annotated formulae* are propositional formulae that use annotated literals. Given a fluent formula φ (i.e., where fluents are not annotated), φ^t ($\varphi^{\vee[t_1,t_2]}$) is the annotated formula obtained by replacing each literal ℓ in φ with the annotated literal ℓ^t ($\ell^{\vee[t_1,t_2]}$). An annotated formula is *single time* if it is of the form $\varphi^{\vee[t_1,t_2]}$ for some non-annotated formula φ. An annotated formula is *actual* if no literal in the formula is annotated. For an annotated formula φ, φ^{+t} is the formula obtained by replacing each ℓ^r in φ with ℓ^{r+t}.

A multi-agent domain specification is a collection of laws of the form (1)-(3) and laws of following forms:

$$\varphi \textbf{ starts } \mathit{process\_id} \ [\ \textbf{reversible} \mid \textbf{irreversible}\ ]\ \ell^{\hat{t}} \tag{5}$$

$$\varphi \textbf{ stops } \mathit{process\_id} \tag{6}$$

$$a \textbf{ starts } \mathit{process\_id} \ [\ \textbf{reversible} \mid \textbf{irreversible}\ ]\ \ell^{\hat{r}} \textbf{ if } \varphi \tag{7}$$

$$a \textbf{ stops } \mathit{process\_id} \textbf{ if } \varphi \tag{8}$$

where the φ's are sets of fluent literals, $a \in \cup_{i \in \mathcal{AG}} \mathcal{A}_i$, $\ell^{\hat{t}}$ and $\ell^{\hat{r}}$ are time annotated literals, of the form $\vee[t_1, t_2]$ with $1 \leq t_1 \leq t_2$ and $\vee[r_1, r_2]$ with $0 \leq r_1 \leq r_2$,[1] and *process_id* belongs to $\mathcal{P}$. The main novelty is the introduction of the notion of *process*. A process is associated to a delayed effect, denoted by $\ell^{\hat{t}}$, and the time interval $\hat{t}$ indicates when the process will produce its effect. A process can be started by an action

[1] For simplicity, we do not consider $\wedge[t_1, t_2]$. This is because a law with the annotation $\wedge[t_1, t_2]$ can be replaced by a set of laws whose annotation is $\vee[t_i, t_i]$ for $t_1 \leq t_i \leq t_2$.

or a property. Each **reversible** process can be interrupted by a **stops** action/condition before materializing its effects, while **irreversible** processes cannot be interrupted.

The notion of a state in an $\mathcal{L}^{mt}$ domain D is similar to a state in $\mathcal{L}$ domain, in that it is an interpretation of the fluents in D and needs to satisfy the constraints imposed by static laws in D. In presence of processes, a state of the world needs to account for changes that will occur only in the future, when a process reaches its completion. For example, an action $sendPayment$ may state that the action starts a process named *payment_process* whose effect is to make $paid$ true 3, 4, or 5 units of time after the execution of the action. For this reason, we introduce the notion of an *extended state* as a triple (s, IR, RE) where s is a state and IR and RE are sets of pairs of future effects, each of the form $(x : \hat{\ell^t})$, where x is a process name and $\hat{\ell^t}$ is an annotated literal. s encodes the *current* state of the world, while IR and RE contain the irreversible and reversible processes, respectively. (s, IR, RE) is *complete* if $IR = \emptyset$ and $ER = \emptyset$.

In presence of future effects encoded by the processes, the world changes due to (*i*) the completion of a process; or (*ii*) action occurrences. Let us consider an extended state $(s, \{(x : p^1)\}, \emptyset)$ with $(x : p^1)$ as a process whose effect is p. Intuitively, if nothing happens, we would expect that p would be true in the world state one unit of time from the current time. This results in the new extended state of the world $(s \setminus \{\neg p\} \cup \{p\}, \emptyset, \emptyset)$. If instead we perform in the initial extended state an action a, whose effect is to make q true in the next moment of time, then the next state will be $(s \setminus \{\neg p, \neg q\} \cup \{p, q\}, \emptyset, \emptyset)$. Thus, in order to define the semantics of $\mathcal{L}^{mt}$ domains, we need two steps. First, we specify an update function, which computes the extended state which is t units of time from the current state assuming that no action occurs during this time span. Second, we define the transition function that takes into consideration the action occurrences.

The *update* of an extended state (s, IR, RE) is used to move forward by one time step; the time of the annotated fluents is decreased by one. Fluents that have become actual are used to update the state—in such a case we need to ensure that irreversible changes prevail over reversible ones. Formally, for $\hat{s} = (s, IR, RE)$, the set of literals that should be used in updating s in the next moment of time is

$$\tau(\hat{s}) = \{\ell \mid (x : \ell^1) \in IR\} \cup \{\ell \mid (x : \ell^1) \in RE \text{ such that } \nexists (z : \bar{\ell}^1) \in IR\}.$$

For a state s, the set of processes started and stopped by s in the next moment of time is $IR_1(s) = \{(process\_id : \hat{\ell^t}) \mid$ there exists a law of the form (5) with the option **irreversible** such that $s \models \varphi\}$, $RE_1(s) = \{(process\_id : \hat{\ell^t}) \mid$ there exists a law of the form (5) with the option **reversible** such that $s \models \varphi\}$, and $P_2(s) = \{process\_id \mid$ there exists a law of the form (6) such that $s \models \varphi\}$. For a set of process names N and a set of future effects X, let $X \setminus N = X \setminus \{(x : \ell^t) \mid x \in N, (x : \ell^t) \in X\})$.

The update of $\hat{s}$ by one unit of time is a set of extended states defined as follows:

$$update(\hat{s}) = \{(s', I(IR, s'), R(ER, s') \mid s' = Cl_D(\tau(\hat{s}) \cup (s \cap s')) \text{ and } s' \text{ is a state}\}$$

where, $I(IR, s') = (IR - 1) \cup IR_1(s')$ and $R(ER, s') = ((RE - 1) \cup RE_1(s')) \setminus P_2(s')$, and for a set of future effects X, we have $X - d = \{(x : \ell^{t-d}) \mid (x : \ell^t) \in X\}$. Intuitively, s' is a state that satisfies the effects that need to be true one unit from the current state. For $t > 0$, let $\hat{s} + t = \bigcup_{\hat{u} \in update(\hat{s}+t-1)} update(\hat{u})$ where $\hat{s} + 0 = \hat{s}$.

Given an extended state $\hat{s} = (s, IR, ER)$ and an annotated literal ℓ^t, we say that ℓ^t holds in $\hat{s}$, denoted $\hat{s} \models \ell^t$, if, for $t = 0$, $\hat{s} \models \ell^t$ if $s \models \ell$, and, for $t > 0$, $\hat{s} \models \ell^t$ if $\hat{u} \models \ell$ for every $\hat{u} \in \hat{s} + t$.

Let us now consider the case where an action snapshot $A = \{a_i\}_{i \in \mathcal{AG}}$ is executed in the extended state $\hat{s}$. Intuitively, there are two possible types of effects: the direct effect of the actions ($e_A(s)$) and the processes that are created by the actions. We know that $e_A(s)$ must be satisfied in the next time point. The effects of the processes starting by A in s, denoted by $procs_A(s)$, is a set of pairs (IR', RE') where:

- For each (a_i **starts** p_{id} **irreversible** $\ell^{\vee[t_1,t_2]}$ **if** φ) in D, with $a_i \in A$ and $s \models \varphi$, we have that IR' contains $(p_{id} : \ell^t)$ for some t s.t. $t_1 \leq t \leq t_2$;
- For each (a_i **starts** p_{id} **reversible** $\ell^{\vee[t_1,t_2]}$ **if** φ) in D, with $a_i \in A$, and $s \models \varphi$, we have that RE' contains $(p_{id} : \ell^t)$ for some t s.t. $t_1 \leq t \leq t_2$.

In addition, the set of processes stopped by A in s is defined as $stop_A(s) = \{p_{id} \mid (\ a_i$ **stops** p_{id} **if** $\varphi\ ) \in D, s \models \varphi\}$. Intuitively, each (IR', RE') encodes a possible set of effects that the snapshot A can create given the current state of the world is s. $stop_A(s)$ is the set of processes that need to be stopped.

We are now ready to define transition function Φ^t_D for $\mathcal{L}^{mt}$ domains which maps extended states and action snapshots to sets of extended states. We assume that $\top$ is a special process name in $\mathcal{P}$ that does not appear in any laws of D. For a set of literals L, we define $\oplus(L) = \{(\top : \ell^1) \mid \ell \in L\}$. Given an extended state $\hat{s} = (s, IR, RE)$, a fluent literal ℓ holds in $\hat{s}$ if ℓ holds in s. The notion of executability of a set of actions can be carried over to $\mathcal{L}^{mt}$ domains without changes as it only considers the current state of the world. The transition function Φ^t_D is:

$$\Phi^t_D(A, \hat{s}) = \bigcup_{(I,R) \in procs_A(s)} update((s, IR \cup I \cup \oplus(e_A(s)), (RE \cup R) \setminus stop_A(s))$$

if A is executable in s, and $\Phi^t_D(\hat{s}, A) = \emptyset$ otherwise. Intuitively, $\Phi^t_D(\hat{s}, A)$ encodes the possible trajectories of the world given that A is executed in $\hat{s}$. We extend Φ^t_D to $\widehat{\Phi^t_D}$ which operates on sequences of action snapshots in the same way as done for Φ_D.

In presence of time, we might be interested in the states of the world given that A is executed t units of time from the current state of the world. We overload Φ^t_D and define

$$\Phi^t_D(\hat{s}, A, t) = \widehat{\Phi^t_D}(\hat{s}, [\underbrace{\{\texttt{noop}\}_{i \in \mathcal{AG}}, \ldots, \{\texttt{noop}\}_{i \in \mathcal{AG}}}_{t}] \circ [\, A\,])$$

We also write $\Phi^t_D(\hat{s}, A, t) + t_1$ to denote

$$\Phi^t_D(\hat{s}, A, t) + t_1 = \bigcup_{\hat{s'} \in \Phi^t_D(\hat{s}, A, t)} \widehat{\Phi^t_D}(\hat{s'}, [\underbrace{\{\texttt{noop}\}_{i \in \mathcal{AG}}, \ldots, \{\texttt{noop}\}_{i \in \mathcal{AG}}}_{t_1}])$$

Intuitively, a member of $\Phi^t_D(\hat{s}, A, t) + t_1$ is a possible extended state after t_1 time steps from the execution of A, which in turn was executed t time steps from $\hat{s}$.

Let us define a *timed action snapshot* to be a pair (A, t) where A is an action snapshot and t is a time reference. $\widehat{\Phi^t_D}$ can also be extended to a transition function that operates on sequences of timed action snapshots $\alpha = [(A_1, t_1), \ldots, (A_n, t_n)]$ where $t_1 < t_2 < \ldots < t_n$ and A_i's are action snapshots as follows:

- For $n = 0$: $\widehat{\Phi^t_D}(\hat{s}, \alpha) = \hat{s}$; and
- For $n > 0$: $\widehat{\Phi^t_D}(\hat{s}, \alpha) = \bigcup_{\hat{u} \in \Phi^t_D(\hat{s}, A_1, t_1)} \widehat{\Phi^t_D}(\hat{u}, \beta)$
  where $\beta = [(A_2, t_2 - t_1), \ldots, (A_n, t_n - t_1)]$ if $\widehat{\Phi^t_D}(\hat{u}, \beta) \neq \emptyset$ for every $\hat{u} \in \Phi^t_D$ $(\hat{s}, A_1, t_1)$; otherwise, $\widehat{\Phi^t_D}(\hat{s}, \alpha) = \emptyset$.

For a state s and a sequence of timed action snapshot α, $\widehat{\Phi^t_D}(s,\alpha) = \widehat{\Phi^t_D}((s,\emptyset,\emptyset),\alpha)$.

Example 1. Let us consider a slight modification of the popular Netbill example [13]. Let us assume that every action takes one day to complete but the action of sending the payment might take 3 to 5 days for its effects to materialize. Also, as long as the payment has not been made, the customer can still cancel the payment. We envision $\mathcal{AG} = \{merchant, customer\}$. Both the *merchant* and the *customer* use the set of fluents $\mathcal{F} = \{request, paid, goods, receipt, quote, accept\}$; the agents use the sets of actions:

$$\mathcal{A}_{merc} = \{sendQuote, sendGoods, sendReceipt\}$$
$$\mathcal{A}_{cust} = \{sendRequest, sendAccept, sendPayment\}$$

The domain specification D_n consists of the following axioms ($\mathcal{P} = \{pmt\}$):

Customer	Merchant
sendRequest **causes** *request*	*sendGoods* **causes** *goods*
sendAccept **causes** *accept*	*sendReceipt* **causes** *receipt*
sendPayment **starts** *pmt* **reversible** $paid^{\vee[3,5]}$	*sendQuote* **causes** *quote*
cancelPayment **stops** *pmt*	**impossible** $\{sendReceipt\}$ **if** $\neg paid$
impossible $\{sendAccept\}$ **if** $\neg quote$	**impossible** $\{sendGoods\}$ **if** $\neg accept$
impossible $\{cancelPayment\}$ **if** *paid*	

The last two laws state that the *Merchant* cannot execute the action *sendReceipt* if $\neg paid$ is true (the *Customer* has not paid yet); he cannot execute the action *sendGoods* if $\neg accept$ is true (the *Customer* has not accepted the offer). On the other hand, the *Customer* cannot execute the action *sendAccept* if he has not received the quote.

Let $s_0 = \{request, quote, accept, \neg paid, \neg receipt, \neg goods\}$, and $\alpha_1 = \{\texttt{noop}, sendGoods\}$. α_1 is executable in s_0 and $\Phi^t_{D_n}((s_0,\emptyset,\emptyset),\alpha_1) = \{(s'_0,\emptyset,\emptyset)\}$, where

$$s'_0 = \{request, quote, accept, \neg paid, \neg receipt, goods\}.$$

Let $\hat{u} = (s'_0,\emptyset,\emptyset)$ and $\alpha_2 = \{sendPayment, \texttt{noop}\}$. It is easy to see that

$$\Phi^t_D(\hat{u},\alpha_2) = \{update((s'_0,\emptyset,\{(pmt : paid^i)\})) \mid i = 3,4,5\}$$

Thus, $\Phi^t_D(\hat{u},\alpha_2) + 3 = \{(u',\emptyset,\emptyset)\} \cup \{update((s'_0,\emptyset,\{(pmt : paid^i)\})) \mid i = 1,2\}$ where $u' = \{request, quote, accept, paid, \neg receipt, goods\}$. We can see that $\Phi^t_D(\hat{u},\alpha_2) + 5 = \{(u',\emptyset,\emptyset)\}$. □

3 Basic Commitments in $\mathcal{L}^{mt}$

We demonstrate that $\mathcal{L}^{mt}$ is adequate to encode commitments and their manipulation. Commitments are encoded as a new class of fluents and are manipulated by *commitment actions*. Due to the lack of space, we present our study on unconditional commitments [15]. Detailed treatment for conditional commitments can be found in [18].

A *commitment* is of the form $c(x,y,\varphi,t_1,t_2)$, where $x,y \in \mathcal{AG}$, $0 < t_1 \leq t_2$, and φ is formula. This states that the debtor x agrees to establish φ between t_1 and t_2 for the creditor y. For example, the statement "A commits to visit B in three hours," conveys the commitment $c(A,B,arrived,3,3)$. A commitment where we do not care when the property is made true can be expressed using a disjunctive annotation.

Observe that we can think of commitment fluents as propositions, i.e., $c(x,y,\varphi)$ is a syntactic sugar for $c\_x\_y\_name(\varphi)$ where $name(\varphi)$ is a propositional variable representing the name of the formula φ. We assume that the various propositions $c(x,y,\varphi)$

are in $\bigcap_{i \in \mathcal{AG}} \mathcal{F}_i$. We also assume that, to enable communication, if $c(x, y, \varphi)$ is a commitment fluent, then φ is a fluent formula which uses fluents from $\mathcal{F}_x \cap \mathcal{F}_y$. The following operations are used to manipulate commitments:

- *Creation:* $create(x, y, \varphi, t_1, t_2)$ describes the fact that agent x creates a commitment towards agent y in the period between t_1 and t_2. We assume that each created commitment is associated to a unique identifier;
- *Discharge:* $discharge(x, y, \varphi)$ indicates that agent x discharges a commitment towards agent y (by satisfying the request);
- *Release:* $release(x, y, \varphi)$ indicates that agent y releases x from its obligation;
- *Assignment:* $assign(x, y, k, \varphi, t_1, t_2)$ indicates that agent y transfers the commitment to a different creditor (with a new time frame);
- *Delegation:* $delegate(x, y, k, \varphi, t_1, t_2)$ indicates that agent x delegates the commitment to another debtor (with a new time frame);
- *Cancel:* $cancel(x, y, \varphi, \psi, t_1, t_2)$ indicates that x modifies the terms of the commitment (by canceling the previous one and generating a new one).

These manipulations of commitments are the consequence of actions performed by the agents or conditions occurring in the state of the world. We consider two types of enabling statements, called *trigger statements*, for commitment manipulation

$$[a \mid \varphi] \ \textbf{triggers} \ c\_activity$$

where φ is a fluent formula, $a \in \mathcal{A}$, and $c\_activity$ is one of the activities (or commitment actions). They indicate that the commitment activity $c\_activity$ should be executed whenever φ holds or a is executed. An example of the first type of statement is

$$paid \ \textbf{triggers} \ create(m, c, receipt, 1, 3) \tag{9}$$

which encodes the fact that the merchant agrees to send the customer the receipt between 1 and 3 units of time since receiving the payment. The statement

$$sendAccept \ \textbf{triggers} \ create(c, m, paid, 1, 5) \tag{10}$$

states that the customer agrees to pay for the goods between 1 to 5 units of time after sending the acceptance notification. A more complicated trigger statement is the following, taken from an example in [7],

$$broken \ \textbf{triggers} \ create(s, c, (broken \Rightarrow paid\_10), k, k)$$

for $k \geq 3$, which represents the agreement between the service provider (s) and a customer (c) that, if the printer is broken, the service provider needs to fix it within three days or faces the consequence of paying \$10 each day the printer is not fixed.

A *domain with commitments* is a pair (D, C) where D is a domain specification in $\mathcal{L}^{mt}$ and C is a collection of trigger statements. Intuitively, a domain with commitments is an action theory enriched with a set of (social or contractual) agreements between agents in the domain which are expressed by the set of trigger statements. For example, let D_n be the domain in Example 1 and C_1 be the set consisting of the two statements (9) and (10), we have that (D_n, C_1) is a domain with commitments.

In the following, we will define the semantics of a domain with commitments (D, C) by translating it into a $\mathcal{L}^{mt}$ domain D' where D' consists of D and a collection of dynamic laws and static laws originating from C. In the following, we will associate with the commitment $c(x, y, \varphi)$ an unique process identifier, $id(x, y, \varphi)$, which indicates that x commits to create φ for y.

- Let

$$a \textbf{ triggers } c\_activity$$

be an action trigger in C. We consider the following cases:

◦ if $c\_activity = create(x, y, \varphi, t_1, t_2)$, then the laws

$$a \textbf{ causes } c(x, y, \varphi) \text{ and}$$
$$a \textbf{ starts } id(x, y, \varphi) \textbf{ reversible } done(x, y, \varphi)^{\vee[t_1, t_2]}$$

are added to D'. The dynamic law records the fact that the commitment $c(x, y, \varphi)$ has been made by the execution of the action a. The second law starts a process which indicates that the commitment must be satisfied between t_1 and t_2. The fluent $done(x, y, \varphi)$ is introduced to record that there is an active commitment from x towards y to achieve φ. The annotation $\vee[t_1, t_2]$ indicates that this commitment must be completed between the interval $[t_1, t_2]$. Observe that the creation of a commitment $c(x, y, \varphi)$ will also start the process $id(x, y, \varphi)$.

◦ if $c\_activity = discharge(x, y, \varphi)$ then D' contains

$$a \textbf{ causes } \neg c(x, y, \varphi) \textbf{ if } c(x, y, \varphi),$$
$$a \textbf{ causes } \varphi \textbf{ if } c(x, y, \varphi), \text{ and}$$
$$a \textbf{ stops } id(x, y, \varphi) \textbf{ if } c(x, y, \varphi).$$

The action a triggers the discharge of the commitment $c(x, y, \varphi)$ by satisfying it. Therefore, it is translated into a dynamic law that states that the commitment no longer exists and that φ is achieved. It will also stop the process $id(x, y, \varphi)$ which is associated with $c(x, y, \varphi)$.

◦ if $c\_activity = release(x, y, \varphi)$ then the laws

$$a \textbf{ stops } id(x, y, \varphi) \textbf{ if } c(x, y, \varphi) \text{ and}$$
$$a \textbf{ causes } \neg c(x, y, \varphi) \textbf{ if } c(x, y, \varphi)$$

belongs to D'. The action stops the commitment process and records that the commitment has been removed.

◦ if $c\_activity = assign(x, y, k, \varphi, t_1, t_2)$ then D' contains

$$a \textbf{ causes } \neg c(x, y, \varphi) \textbf{ if } c(x, y, \varphi),$$
$$a \textbf{ causes } c(x, k, \varphi),$$
$$a \textbf{ stops } id(x, y, \varphi) \textbf{ if } c(x, y, \varphi), \text{ and}$$
$$a \textbf{ starts } id(x, k, \varphi) \textbf{ reversible } done(x, k, \varphi)^{\vee[t_1, t_2]}.$$

The law takes the responsible of achieving φ for y from x and assigns it to k. The two dynamic laws indicate this. The next two laws state that the action stops the commitment process $id(x, y, \varphi)$ and starts the commitment process $id(x, k, \varphi)$.

- if $c\_activity = delegate(x, y, k, \varphi, t_1, t_2)$ then D' contains

$$a \textbf{ stops } id(x, y, \varphi) \textbf{ if } c(x, y, \varphi),$$
$$a \textbf{ causes } \neg c(x, y, \varphi) \textbf{ if } c(x, y, \varphi),$$
$$a \textbf{ causes } c(k, y, \varphi), \text{ and}$$
$$a \textbf{ starts } id(k, y, \varphi) \textbf{ reversible } done(k, y, \varphi)^{\vee[t_1, t_2]}.$$

This is similar to the case of $release$, only with different debtor.

- if $c\_activity = cancel(x, y, \varphi, \psi, t_1, t_2)$ then D' contains

$$a \textbf{ stops } id(x, y, \varphi) \textbf{ if } c(x, y, \varphi),$$
$$a \textbf{ causes } \neg c(x, y, \varphi) \textbf{ if } c(x, y, \varphi),$$
$$a \textbf{ causes } c(x, y, \psi), \text{ and}$$
$$a \textbf{ starts } id(x, y, \psi) \textbf{ reversible } done(x, y, \psi)^{\vee[t_1, t_2]}.$$

The action stops the commitment process $id(x, y, \varphi)$ which means that the commitment $c(x, y, \varphi)$ no longer exists. It also starts a new commitment process $id(x, y, \psi)$ which is supposed to fullfils the commitment $c(x, y, \varphi)$.

- Let

$$\psi \textbf{ triggers } c\_activity,$$

be a fluent trigger in C. The translation of a fluent trigger into statements in $\mathcal{L}^{mt}$ is similar to the translation of an action trigger and is obtained from the corresponding action trigger one by:

  - replacing a dynamic law of the form (a **causes** φ **if** λ) with (φ **if** λ, ψ);
  - replacing a law of the form (a **starts** p_{id} [**reversible** | **irreversible**] φ **if** λ) with the law (ψ **starts** p_{id} [**reversible** | **irreversible**] φ **if** λ); and
  - replacing a law of the form (a **stops** p_{id} **if** λ) with the law (ψ **stops** p_{id} **if** λ).

We further need to include some additional static laws: if $c(x, y, \varphi)$ is present and φ is true, then the commitment can be released: $\neg c(x, y, \varphi)$ **if** $\varphi, done(x, y, \varphi)$.

Let $\mathcal{M} = (D, C)$ be a domain with commitments. We denote with $\tau(C)$ the collection of axioms generated from the translation process mentioned above; with a slight abuse of notation, we denote $\tau(\mathcal{M}) = D \cup \tau(C)$. By definition, the domain $\tau(\mathcal{M})$ defines a transition function $\Phi^t_{\tau(\mathcal{M})}$ which determines the possible evolutions of the world given a state and the sequence of timed action snapshots $[(\alpha_1, t_1), \ldots, (\alpha_n, t_n)]$. The function $\Phi^t_{\tau(\mathcal{M})}$ can be used to specify the transition function for $\mathcal{M}$, i.e., the transition function $\Phi_{\mathcal{M}}$ for $\mathcal{M}$ is defined to be the function $\Phi^t_{\tau(\mathcal{M})}$. Observe that each state of $\tau(\mathcal{M})$ consists of fluent literals in D and commitments which appear in $\tau(C)$. In the definition of $\Phi^t_{\tau(\mathcal{M})}$, this is treated as any normal fluent. The presence of $c(x, y, \varphi)$ in a state indicates that the commitment $c(x, y, \varphi)$ has been made. $done(x, y, \varphi)$ encodes the fact that the commitment $c(x, y, \varphi)$ needs to be realized by the debtor.

Example 2. Consider the domain with commitments $\mathcal{M}_1 = (D_n, C_2)$, where D_n is the domain description described in Example 1 and C_2 is the set of statements consisting of (9), (10), and the following statements

$$request \textbf{ triggers } create(m, c, quote, 1, 1)$$

and

$$accept \textbf{ triggers } create(m, c, goods, 1, 1).$$

So, the set of fluents in $\tau(\mathcal{M}_1)$, denoted by $\mathcal{F}_1$, consists of $\mathcal{F}$ (the set of fluents of D_1) and the commitment fluents such as $c(m, c, receipt)$, $c(c, m, paid)$, $c(m, c, quote)$, and $c(m, c, goods)$, and fluents of the form $done(x, y, \varphi)$ which are introduced by the translation from $\mathcal{M}_1$ to $\tau(\mathcal{M}_1)$. Let $s_0 = \{\neg f \mid f \in \mathcal{F}_1\}$, we have that

$$\Phi^t_{\tau(\mathcal{M}_1)}(s_0, \{sendRequest\}) = \{[s_0, u, v]\}$$

where $u = s_0 \setminus \{\overline{request, c(m, c, quote)}\} \cup \{request, c(m, c, quote)\}$ and $v = u \setminus \{\overline{done(m, c, quote)}\} \cup \{done(m, c, quote)\}$. The presence of $c(m, c, quote)$ and $done(m, c, quote)$ in u and v is due to the laws $c(x, y, quote)$ **if** $request$ and

$$request \textbf{ starts } c(x, y, quote) \quad \textbf{reversible } \; done(x, y, \varphi)^1$$

respectively, both are the result of the translation to laws in $\tau(\mathcal{M}_1)$ of the statement

$$request \textbf{ triggers } create(m, c, quote, 1, 1).$$ □

Let $\mathcal{M} = (D, C)$ be a domain with commitments and $\gamma = [s_0, \ldots, s_n]$ be a sequence of states in $\tau(\mathcal{M})$. Let $c(x, y, \varphi)$ be a commitment fluent appearing in γ. We say that $c(x, y, \varphi)$ is

- *satisfied* in γ if $s_n \models \neg c(x, y, \varphi)$;
- *violated* in γ if $s_n \models c(x, y, \varphi) \wedge done(x, y, \varphi)$; or
- *pending* in γ if $s_n \models c(x, y, \varphi)$ and $s_n \not\models done(x, y, \varphi)$.

The reasoning about commitments given the execution of a sequence of action snapshots can then be defined as follows. Let $\mathcal{M} = (D, C)$ be a domain with commitments, s_0 be a state in D, and $A = [(\alpha_1, t_1), \ldots, (\alpha_n, t_n)]$ be a sequence of timed action snapshots. We say that a commitment $c(x, y, \varphi)$ is *factual* during the execution of A in s if there exists a sequence of states $\gamma = [s_0, \ldots, s_m]$ in $\widehat{\Phi^t}_{\tau(\mathcal{M})}(s_0, A)$ and $c(x, y, \varphi)$ appears in γ. A factual commitment $c(x, y, \varphi)$ is

- *satisfied* after the execution of A in s_0 if it is satisfied in every sequence of states belonging to $\widehat{\Phi^t}_{\tau(\mathcal{M})}(s_0, A)$.
- *strongly violated* after the execution of A in s_0 if it is violated in every sequence of states belonging to $\widehat{\Phi^t}_{\tau(\mathcal{M})}(s_0, A)$.
- *weakly violated* after the execution of A in s_0 if it is violated in some sequence of states belonging to $\widehat{\Phi^t}_{\tau(\mathcal{M})}(s_0, A)$.
- *pending* after the execution of A in s_0 if it is not violated in any sequence of states and not satisfied in some sequences of states belonging to $\widehat{\Phi^t}_{\tau(\mathcal{M})}(s_0, A)$.

Example 3. Consider the domain $\mathcal{M}_1$ and the state s_0 in Ex. 2. We have that $c(m, c, quote)$ is violated after the execution of $sendRequest$ at s_0, since $\Phi^t_{\tau(\mathcal{M}_1)}(s_0, \{sendRequest\}) = \{[s_0, u, v]\}$. It is easy to verify that for $A = [(sendRequest, 0), (sendQuote, 1)]$, $\Phi^t_{\tau(\mathcal{M}_1)}(s_0, A) = \{[s_0, u, v']\}$ where $v' = u \setminus \{\neg done(m, c, quote), \neg quote, c(m, c, quote)\} \cup \{done(m, c, quote), quote, \neg c(m, c, quote)\}$. This implies that the commitment $c(m, c, quote)$ is satisfied after the execution of A in s_0. □

4 Observations and Narratives

4.1 Observation Language

We consider an extension of the action language by enabling the representation of *observations*. We extend the signature of the language $\mathcal{L}^{mt}$ with a set of *situation constants* **S**, containing two special constants, s_0 and s_c, denoting the initial situation and the current situation. Observations are axioms of the forms:

$$\varphi \ \textbf{at} \ \mathsf{s} \quad (11) \qquad \mathsf{s} \ \textbf{at} \ t \quad (13)$$

$$\alpha \ \textbf{occurs\_at} \ \mathsf{s} \quad (12) \qquad \alpha \ \textbf{between} \ \mathsf{s}_1, \mathsf{s}_2 \quad (14) \qquad \mathsf{s}_1 \prec \mathsf{s}_2 \quad (15)$$

where φ is a fluent formula, α is a (possibly empty) sequence of timed action snapshots, and $\mathsf{s}, \mathsf{s}_1, \mathsf{s}_2$ are situation constants which differ from s_c. Axioms of the forms (11) and (15) are called *fluent facts* and *precedence facts*, respectively. (11) states that φ is true in the situation s. (15) says that s_1 occurs before s_2. Axioms of the forms (12) and (14) are referred to as *occurrence facts*. (12) indicates that α starts its execution in the situation s. On the other hand, (14) states that α starts and completes its execution in s_1 and s_2, respectively. Axioms of the form (13) link situations to time points.

A *narrative of a multi-agent system* (a *narrative*, for short) is a pair (D, Γ) where D is a domain description and Γ is a set of observations of the form (11)-(15) such that $\{\mathsf{s}_0 \prec \mathsf{s}, \ \mathsf{s} \prec \mathsf{s}_c \mid \mathsf{s} \in \mathbf{S}\} \subseteq \Gamma$.

Observations are interpreted with respect to a domain description. While a domain description defines a transition function that characterizes what states *may* be reached when an action is executed in a state, a narrative consisting of a domain description together with a set of observations defines the possible situation histories of the system. This characterization is achieved by two functions, Σ and Ψ. While Σ maps situation constants to sequences of sets of actions, Ψ picks one among the various transitions given by $\Phi_D(A, s)$ and maps sequences of sets of actions to a unique state.

More formally, let (D, Γ) be a narrative. A *causal interpretation* of (D, Γ) is a partial function Ψ from action snapshots sequences to extended states, whose domain is nonempty and prefix-closed.[2] By $Dom(\Psi)$ we denote the domain of a causal interpretation Ψ. Notice that $[] \in Dom(\Psi)$ for every causal interpretation Ψ. A *causal model* of D is a causal interpretation Ψ such that $\Psi([])$ is an extended state of D and, for every $\alpha \circ [A] \in Dom(\Psi)$, $\Psi(\alpha \circ [A]) \in \Phi_D(A, \Psi(\alpha))$.

A *situation assignment* of **S** with respect to D is a mapping Σ from **S** into the set of sequences of action snapshots of D that satisfy the following properties: $\Sigma(\mathsf{s}_0) = []$ and, for every $\mathsf{s} \in \mathbf{S}$, $\Sigma(\mathsf{s})$ is a prefix of $\Sigma(\mathsf{s}_c)$.

An *interpretation* M of (D, Γ) is a triple (Ψ, Σ, Δ), where Ψ is a causal model of D, Σ is a situation assignment of **S** such that and $\Sigma(\mathsf{s}_c)$ belongs to the domain of Ψ, and Δ is a *time assignment* which maps prefixes of $\Sigma(\mathsf{s}_c)$ to the set of non-negative numbers, with the following restrictions: $\Delta([\,]) = 0$ and $\Delta(\beta) \le \Delta(\gamma)$ for every $\beta \sqsubseteq \gamma \sqsubseteq \Sigma(\mathsf{s}_c)$. Additionally, for every α, β s.t. $\beta \circ \alpha \sqsubseteq \Sigma(\mathsf{s}_c)$, $\Psi(\beta \circ \alpha)$ belongs to $\widehat{\Phi^t_D}(\Psi([\,]), (\beta, 0) \circ (\alpha, \Delta(\beta)))$.

[2] A set X of action sequences is prefix-closed if for every sequence $\alpha \in X$, every prefix of α is also in X. The symbol $\circ$ denotes list concatenation.

For an interpretation $M = (\Psi, \Sigma, \Delta)$ of (D, Γ):

(i) α **occurs_at** s is true in M if the sequence $\Sigma(\mathsf{s}) \circ \alpha$ is a prefix of $\Sigma(\mathsf{s_c})$;
(ii) α **between** $\mathsf{s}_1, \mathsf{s}_2$ is true in M if $\Sigma(\mathsf{s}_1) \circ \alpha = \Sigma(\mathsf{s}_2)$;
(iii) φ **at** s is true in M if φ holds in $\Psi(\Sigma(\mathsf{s}))$;
(iv) $\mathsf{s}_1 \prec \mathsf{s}_2$ is true in M if $\Sigma(\mathsf{s}_1)$ is a prefix of $\Sigma(\mathsf{s}_2)$;
(v) s **at** t is true in M if $\Delta(\Sigma(\mathsf{s})) = t$.

Given two sequences of sets of actions $\alpha = [A_1, \ldots, A_n]$ and $\alpha' = [B_1, \ldots, B_m]$, we say that α is a subsequence of α', denoted by $\alpha \ll \alpha'$, if α can be obtained from α' by (*i*) deleting some B_i from α'; and (*ii*) replacing some action $a \in \mathbf{A}$ in the remaining B_i by `noop`. An interpretation $M = (\Psi, \Sigma, \Delta)$ is a *model* of a narrative (D, Γ) if all facts in Γ are true in M, and there is no other interpretation $M' = (\Psi, \Sigma', \Delta')$ such that M' satisfies condition (i) above and $\Sigma'(\mathsf{s_c})$ is a subsequence of $\Sigma(\mathsf{s_c})$. These models are minimal, as they exclude extraneous actions. A narrative is *consistent* if it has a model.

We can also envision an extension of the query language by allowing queries of the form φ **after** α **at** s, where the testing of the entailment starts from the states in $\Psi(\Sigma(\mathsf{s}))$. In the presence of time, given a narrative (D, Γ) and a fluent formula φ, we are also interested in knowing whether φ^t is true (resp. false) in a situation s for some $t_1 \leq t \leq t_2$. This is expressed using a query of the form

$$\varphi^{\vee[t_1,t_2]} \ \textbf{at} \ \mathsf{s} \tag{16}$$

We say that a query q of form (16) holds w.r.t. (D, Γ) (i.e., $(D, \Gamma) \models q$) if, for every model $M = (\Psi, \Sigma, \Delta)$ of (D, Γ), there exists $t_1 \leq t \leq t_2$ s.t. φ is true in $\Psi(\Sigma(\mathsf{s})) + t$.

4.2 Narratives and Commitments

A *narrative with commitments* is a triple (D, Γ, C) where (D, C) is a domain with commitments and Γ is a collection of observations. The semantics of a narrative with commitments (D, Γ, C) is defined by (*i*) translating it to the narrative $(\tau(\mathcal{M}), \Gamma)$ in $\mathcal{L}^{mt}$ where $\mathcal{M} = (D, C)$; and (*ii*) specifying models of $(\tau(\mathcal{M}), \Gamma)$ to be models of (D, Γ, C). To save space, we omit the specific details on the semantics of narratives with commitments. Let $N = (D, \Gamma, C)$ be a narrative and M be a model of N. We say that a commitment $c(x, y, \varphi)$ is:

- *satisfied* by M if $M \models \neg c(x, y, \varphi)$ **at** $\mathsf{s_c}$.
- *violated* by M if $M \models (done(c, y, \varphi) \wedge c(x, y, \varphi))$ **at** $\mathsf{s_c}$.
- *pending* w.r.t. M if $M \models \neg done(c, y, \varphi) \wedge c(x, y, \varphi)$ **at** $\mathsf{s_c}$.

Given a narrative N, we will say that a commitment is satisfied if it is satisfied in all models of N; it is strongly violated if it is violated in all models of N; and it is weakly violated if it is violated in some models of N.

Example 4. Consider the narrative $N_1 = (D_n, \Gamma, C_2)$ where $\mathcal{M}_1 = (D_n, C_2)$ is the domain description in Ex. 2 and Γ consists of the precedence facts $\mathsf{s}_0 \prec \mathsf{s}_1 \prec \mathsf{s}_2 \prec \mathsf{s}_3 \prec \mathsf{s_c}$ and the following observations:

$$\neg paid \wedge \neg accept \wedge \neg quote \wedge \neg goods \ \textbf{at} \ \mathsf{s}_0$$

$$sendRequest \ \textbf{occurs\_at} \ \mathsf{s}_0 \quad \text{and} \quad sendAccept \ \textbf{occurs\_at} \ \mathsf{s}_2$$

where $\mathsf{s}_0, \mathsf{s}_1, \mathsf{s}_2, \mathsf{s}_3, \mathsf{s_c}$ are situation constants.

A model $M = (\Psi, \Sigma, \Delta)$ for this narrative can be built as follows:

- The sequences of actions leading to the various situations are $\Sigma(\mathsf{s}_0)$=[ ], $\Sigma(\mathsf{s}_1)$=[$\{sendRequest\}$], $\Sigma(\mathsf{s}_2)$=[$\{sendRequest\}, \{sendQuote\}$], and $\Sigma(\mathsf{s}_3)$=$\Sigma(\mathsf{s}_c)$=[$\{sendRequest\}, \{sendQuote\}, \{sendAccept\}$].
- $\Psi([\,])$ is the state where all fluents are false and $\Psi(\mathsf{s}_i) = \widehat{\Phi^t}_{\mathcal{M}_1}(\Sigma(\mathsf{s}_i), \Psi([\,]))$.
- The time assignment for situation constants is given by $\Delta(\mathsf{s}_i) = i$ for each i and $\Delta(\mathsf{s}_c) = 3$. This is because each action only takes one unit of time to accomplish.

The presence of the action $sendQuote$ can be explained by the fact that $quote$ is the precondition for $sendAccept$. We can show that M is a model of the narrative N_1.

The minimality condition of models of a narrative also allows us to prove that, for every model $(\Psi', \Sigma', \Delta')$ of $\mathcal{M}_1$, the situation assignment Σ' is identical to Σ and $\Psi'([\,])$ must satisfy $\{\neg paid, \neg accept, \neg quote, \neg goods\}$. This allows us to conclude that $N_1 \models (\neg paid$ **at** s) for s $\in$ **S** and $N_1 \models c(c, m, paid) \wedge \neg done(c, m, paid)$ **at** s_c. We can show that the commitment $c(m, c, quote)$ is satisfied, the commitment $c(c, m, paid)$ is pending, and there are no violated commitments. □

5 Complex Commitments and Protocols

A basic commitment represents a promise made by an agent to another one, but without specifying a precise procedure to accomplish the commitment. Basic commitments also do not describe complex dependencies among "promises".

A *protocol* is a pair (P_{id}, P) where P_{id} is a unique identifier and P is of the form:

1. a set $\{a_i\}_{i \in \mathcal{AG}}$, where $a_i \in \mathcal{A}_i \cup \{any\}$;
2. $?\varphi$ where φ is a formula;
3. $p_1; \ldots; p_n$ where p_i's are protocols;
4. $p_1 | \ldots | p_n$ where p_i's are protocols;
5. **if** φ **then** p_1 **else** p_2 where p_1, p_2 are protocols and φ is a formula;
6. **while** φ **do** p where p is a protocol and φ is a formula;
7. $p_1 < p_2$ where p_1 and p_2 are protocols.

Intuitively, Case (1) describes a request for execution of certain specific actions by certain agents (*any* indicates that we do not care about what that agent is doing); Case (2) is a test action, which tests for the condition φ in the world state; Case (3) sequentially composes protocols, i.e., it requires first to meet the requirements of p_1, then those of p_2, etc.; Case (4) requires any of the protocols $p_1, \ldots, p_n$ to be satisfied, i.e., it represents a non-deterministic choice; Cases (5) and (6) are the usual conditional selection and iteration over protocols; Case (7) is a partial ordering among protocols, indicating that p_1 must be completed sometime before the execution of p_2. According to this definition, (p_0, *sendGoods* < *sendPayment* < *sendReceipt*) is a protocol.

The language can be extended to allow statements that trigger complex commitments, analogously to the case of basic commitments:

$$[a \mid \varphi] \ \textbf{triggers} \ \textit{complex commitment}$$

A narrative can be extended with the following type of observation:

$$P_{id} \ \textbf{at} \ \mathsf{s} \tag{17}$$

where P_{id} is a protocol identifier. This observation states that the protocol referred to by P_{id} has started execution at situation s. A narrative is a triple (D, Γ, C) where Γ can contain also protocol observations.

For a trajectory $h = s_0\alpha_1 s_1 \ldots \alpha_k s_k$, s_0 is called the start of h and is denoted by $start(h)$. $h[i,j]$ denotes the sub-trajectory $s_i\alpha_{i+1}\ldots\alpha_j s_j$. For every state s, $traj(s)$ denotes a set of trajectories whose start state is s. Given a protocol P and a trajectory $h = s_0\alpha_1 \ldots \alpha_k s_k$, we say that h is an *instance* of (P_{id}, P) if

- If $P = \{a_i\}_{i\in\mathcal{AG}}$ then $k = 1$ and, if $\alpha_1 = \{a_i^1\}_{i\in\mathcal{AG}}$, then for each $a_i \neq$ *any* we have $a_i = a_i^1$.
- If $P = \varphi$ then $k = 0$ and $s_0 \models \varphi$.
- If $P = p_1; \ldots; p_n$ then there exists some sequence of indices $i_0 = 0 \leq i_1 \leq \ldots \leq i_n \leq i_{n+1} = k$ such that $h[i_{i_t}, i_{i_{t+1}}]$ is an instance of p_t.
- If $P = p_1 | \ldots | p_n$ then there exists some $1 \leq i \leq n$ such that h is an instance of p_i.
- If $P =$ **if** φ **then** p_1 **else** p_2 and $s_0 \models \varphi$ then h is an instance of P if it is an instance of p_1; otherwise, h must be an instance of p_2.
- If $P =$ **while** φ **do** p and $s_0 \not\models \varphi$ then h is an instance of P if $k = 0$; otherwise, there is an index $0{\leq}i{\leq}k$ s.t. $h[0,i]$ is an instance of p and $h[i,k]$ is an instance of P.
- If $P = p_1 < p_2$ then there exists $0 \leq i \leq j \leq k$ such that $h[0,i]$ is an instance of p_1 and $h[j,k]$ is an instance of p_2.

$(P_{id}, P) \models h$ denotes that h is an instance of (P_{id}, P).

We will now complete the definition of a model of a narrative with protocols. The notion of interpretation and the entailment relation between interpretations and observations, except for the observations of type (17), are defined as in the previous section. For an interpretation $M = (\Psi, \Sigma, \Delta)$ of a narrative (D, Γ, C) and a protocol observation $(P_{id}$ **at** s$) \in C$, we say that $M \models (P_{id}$ **at** s$)$ if there exists some instance $s_0\alpha_1 s_1 \ldots \alpha_k s_k$ of (P_{id}, P) where: $s_0 = \Psi(\Sigma(\mathsf{s}))$, $\Sigma(\mathsf{s}) \circ [\alpha_1, \ldots, \alpha_k]$ is a prefix of $\Sigma(\mathsf{s_c})$;[3] and For every $1 \leq j \leq k$, $\Psi(\Sigma(\mathsf{s}) \circ [\alpha_1, \ldots, \alpha_j]) = s_j$. The remaining definitions related to narratives can be used unchanged for narratives with protocols.

Example 5. Let $N_2 = (D_n, \Gamma, C_2)$ where D_n is defined as in Exp. 4, C_2 is defined as in Exp. 4 with the addition of the protocol $(p_0,$ *sendGoods* $<$ *sendPayment* $<$ *sendReceipt*$)$ and Γ consists of the precedence facts $\mathsf{s_0} \prec \mathsf{s_c}$ and the single observation p_0 **at** $\mathsf{s_0}$. Observe that any instance of p_0 contains the actions *sendGoods*, *sendPayment*, and *sendReceipt*, in this order. The executability condition of *sendGoods* implies that *accept* has to be true at the time it is executed. Together with the minimality condition of models of N_2, we have that for every model $M = (\Psi, \Sigma, \Delta)$ of N_2, $\Psi(\mathsf{s_0}) \models$ *accept*. We construct one model as follows:

- $\Sigma(\mathsf{s_0}) = [\,]$ and $\Sigma(\mathsf{s_c}) = [\{\mathit{sendGoods}\}, \{\mathit{sendPayment}\}, \{\mathit{sendReceipt}\}]$;
- $\Psi(\mathsf{s_0}) = s_0$ where *accept* $\in s_0$, and $\Psi(\mathsf{s_c}) \in \widehat{\Phi^t_{\tau(\mathcal{M}_2)}}(s_0, \Sigma(\mathsf{s_c}))$;
- $\Delta(\mathsf{s_0}) = 0$ and $\Delta(\mathsf{s_c}) = 3$.

Observe that we can also infer that, in the above model, the customer must have paid right after he/she received the goods (at time 1), since (*i*) *paid* must be true for *sendReceipt* to be executed; and (*ii*) *sendReceipt* is executed at time 2. □

[3] We use $\circ$ to denote concatenation of lists.

6 Related Works

Our proposal is related to several works on reasoning with commitments. The main differences between our work and previous works lie in our use of an action language and in our formulation of various problems as a query in our language; this also allows the use of planning to satisfy pending commitments. The treatment of commitments and the ontology for commitments adopted in this paper is largely inspired by [13,15]. Space limitations allow us to highlight only some representative cases.

With respect to [19], our formalization of basic commitments embedded in a domain with commitments and in a narrative of a multi-agent system allows also for a protocol specification that subsumes that of [19]. Similar differences are present w.r.t. [11], which builds on dynamic temporal logic.

Our approach has some relations to [7]; using a reactive event calculus, they provide a notion similar to narratives. Besides being different from each other in the use of an action language, our approach considers protocols and [7] does not. The same authors, in [16], propose a new language for modeling commitments in which existential quantifier of time points are used. The use of disjunctive time specification in annotating fluent formulas in our work allows us to avoid the issues raised in [12,16].

[8,9] also makes use of an action language in dealing with commitments and protocols. While we focus on formalizing commitments, the works [8,9] use C+ in specifying protocols. A protocol in our definition is similar to a protocol defined in [8,9] in that it restricts the evolution of the system to a certain sets of trajectories. In this sense, our definition of protocols provides the machineries for off-line verification of properties of protocols [17]. By introducing the observation of the from "P_{id} **at** s" we allow for the possible executions of a protocol in different states and hence different contexts. However, we do not have the notion of a transformer as in [8] and the ability to handle nested commitments as in [9].

The use of complex protocols in commitments has also been explored in [1].

The language $\mathcal{L}^{mt}$ is an evolution of a classical action languages, drawing features like static causal laws from $\mathcal{B}$ [10], narrative and observations from $\mathcal{L}$ [3,4], and time and deadlines from $\mathcal{ADC}$ [5]. To the best of our knowledge, $\mathcal{L}^{mt}$ is the first action language with all these features, *embedded in the context of modeling multi-agent domains*. $\mathcal{L}^{mt}$ has similarities to the language PDDL 2.1 in that it can describe systems with durative actions and delayed effects. $\mathcal{L}^{mt}$ has a transition function based semantics and considers observations, ir/reversible processes and multiple agents, while PDDL 2.1 does not. It should also be mentioned that $\mathcal{L}^{mt}$ differs from the event calculus in that it allows representing and reasoning with static causal laws and considers ir/reversible fluents while event calculus does not. These are also the differences between $\mathcal{L}^{mt}$ and situation calculus based approaches to dealing with duration [14].

7 Discussion and Conclusion

In this paper, we show how various problems in reasoning about commitments can be described by a suitable instantiation of commitment actions in the language $\mathcal{L}^{mt}$. In particular, we show how the problem of verifying commitments or identifying pending commitments can be posed as queries to a narrative with commitments. We show how the language can also be easily extended to consider commitment protocols.

Since our framework provides a way to identify pending, violated, and satisfiable commitments given a narrative (D, Γ, C), a natural question that arises is what should the agents do to satisfy the pending commitments. The semantics of domains with commitments suggests that we can view the problem of identifying a possible course of actions for the agents to satisfy the pending commitments as an instance of the planning problem and thus can be solved by planning techniques. An investigation of the application of multi-agent planning techniques in generating plans to satisfy pending commitments is one of our main goals in this research in the near future.

References

1. Baldoni, M., Baroglio, C., Marengo, E.: Commitment-Based Protocols with Behavioral Rules and Correctness Properties of MAS. In: Omicini, A., Sardina, S., Vasconcelos, W. (eds.) DALT 2010. LNCS, vol. 6619, pp. 60–77. Springer, Heidelberg (2011)
2. Balduccini, M., Gelfond, M.: Diagnostic Reasoning with A-Prolog. TPLP 3(4,5) (2003)
3. Baral, C., Gelfond, M., Provetti, A.: Representing Actions: Laws, Observations and Hypothesis. JLP 31(1-3) (1997)
4. Baral, C., McIlraith, S., Son, T.C.: Formulating diagnostic problem solving using an action language with narratives and sensing. In: KR, pp. 311–322 (2000)
5. Baral, C., Son, T.C., Tuan, L.C.: A transition function based characterization of actions with delayed and continuous effects. In: KR, pp. 291–302 (2002)
6. Castelfranchi, C.: Commitments: From individual intentions to groups and organizations. In: Int. Conf. on Multiagent Systems, pp. 41–48. The MIT Press (1995)
7. Chesani, F., Mello, P., Montali, M., Torroni, P.: Commitment tracking via the reactive event calculus. In: IJCAI (2009)
8. Chopra, A.K., Singh, M.P.: Contextualizing commitment protocol. In: AAMAS, pp. 1345–1352. ACM (2006)
9. Desai, N., Chopra, A.K., Singh, M.P.: Representing and reasoning about commitments in business processes. In: AAAI, pp. 1328–1333 (2007)
10. Gelfond, M., Lifschitz, V.: Action languages. ETAI 3(6) (1998)
11. Giordano, L., Martelli, A., Schwind, C.: Specifying and Verifying Interaction Protocols in a Temporal Action Logic. Journal App. Logic 5(2) (2007)
12. Mallya, A., Yolum, P., Singh, M.P.: Resolving Commitments among Autonomous Agents. In: Dignum, F.P.M. (ed.) ACL 2003. LNCS (LNAI), vol. 2922, pp. 166–182. Springer, Heidelberg (2004)
13. Mallya, A., Huhns, M.: Commitments among agents. IEEE Internet Comp. 7(4) (2003)
14. Reiter, R.: Knowledge in Actions. MIT Press (2001)
15. Singh, M.P.: An ontology for commitments in multiagent systems. Artif. Int. Law 7(1) (1999)
16. Torroni, P., Chesani, F., Mello, P., Montali, M.: Social Commitments in Time: Satisfied or Compensated. In: Baldoni, M., Bentahar, J., van Riemsdijk, M.B., Lloyd, J. (eds.) DALT 2009. LNCS, vol. 5948, pp. 228–243. Springer, Heidelberg (2010)
17. Torroni, P., et al.: Modelling interactions via commitments and expectations. In: Handbook of Research on Multi-Agent Systems, pp. 263–284. IGI Global (2009)
18. Son, T.C., Pontelli, E., Sakama, C.: Formalizing Commitments Using Action Languages. Technical Report. NMSU-2010, `http://www.cs.nmsu.edu/~tson/papers/techrep1001.pdf`
19. Yolum, P., Singh, M.P.: Flexible protocol specification and execution: applying event calculus planning using commitments. In: AAMAS, pp. 527–534. ACM (2002)

Lightweight Coordination Calculus for Agent Systems: Retrospective and Prospective

David Robertson

Informatics, University of Edinburgh, UK

Abstract. The Lightweight Coordination Calculus was presented in a paper to DALT 2004 as a method for specifying a class of social norms for multi-agent systems. This was intended for use in the engineering of a range of applications but at the time the original paper was written this was an aspiration and we had little experience of actual use of the method. In this paper I summarise how experience with this approach has developed in the seven years from 2004 to date.

1 Introduction: Original Aims of the Lightweight Coordination Calculus

The Lightweight Coordination Calculus (LCC) was first presented at DALT [1] and at ICLP [2] in 2004. The aim of these papers, and of the DALT paper particularly, was to provide a means by which declarative programming might apply directly to the problem of coordinating agents that had not previously worked together. This sort of problem had been tackled previously but the primary means of attack had been either to standardise agent ontologies or standardise on performatives for agent illocutions. The former is difficult to scale to large and open systems because of problems in making sure that agents actually use language in comparable ways (and being able to check that they have). The latter is difficult to scale to complex social interactions in which a standard set of performatives leaves too much to the interpretation locally of agents. It appears to be very difficult in practice to build agents independently but with enough innate commonality to reliably perform complex social interactions. Work on institutions in the multi-agent community was, in 2004, already providing a partial answer to this problem by providing systems for specifying the desired interactions, separately from the agents involved. The practical aim of LCC was to turn this into a programming problem by viewing interactions between agents as executable specifications that could be communicated between agents that wished to coordinate. The theoretical aim of LCC was to form a bridge to multi-agent institutions from more abstract work on languages for communicating processes, then use this to bring techniques from formal reasoning into electronic institutions. A more detailed overview of the broader aims of LCC appears in [3].

2 Relating LCC to Other Languages: Translators and Meta Interpreters

One of the most frequent questions asked about LCC was how it related to other languages. This question was hard to answer definitively because a wide variety of

C. Sakama et al. (Eds.): DALT 2011, LNAI 7169, pp. 84–89, 2012.

languages are in use for coordination between systems, inside and outside of the multi-agent community. Several translators were written from such languages to LCC. Li built translators to LCC from service orchestration languages such as the Business Process Execution Language for Web Services BPEL4WS [4] (an XML-based language for describing workflow amongst Web services). Sierra's group at IIIA, Barcelona, added a translation facility to the ISLANDER electronic institution specification system [5]. A translator is the most obvious bridge between languages but languages like these are quite complex so the translators themselves are non-trivial to build. An alternative solution is to use LCC to specify an interpreter for another language, similarly to the way in which one traditionally uses a declarative language to define interpreters for other languages. Although it is unusual to think of a protocol language, like LCC, as an interpreter this works well in practice because the structure of LCC is suited to the task, as demonstrated by Li [6,7]. By bringing LCC into contact with other systems it became possible to explore more extensively how it could apply more broadly, particularly for Web service choreography [8].

3 Protocol Brittleness: Ontologies, Constraints and Adaptation

A strength of LCC is its ability to be used as, effectively, a programming language that coordinates agents. This is also a weakness, however, because the autonomy expected of agents often demands flexibility in interaction. If LCC protocols are too brittle then the interaction simply fails. One way to tackle this is, of course, to write LCC specifications that are more sophisticated but that creates work for LCC "programmers" so various routes for adding various forms of more generic flexibility have been explored. A principal cause of brittleness is ontology mismatch - agents that could cooperate but fail because each describes its world in different ways. Mechanisms were invented for assisting in mapping local agent ontologies to terms in LCC specifications [9] and for using statistical information on the correlations between LCC terms to infer ontology mappings [10,11]. A second cause of brittleness in LCC was the inability to commit precisely to a constraint without committing to specific values for variables - this gave brittleness to interactions that required progressive refinement of the constraint space. Mechanisms were invented to add finite domain constraints to LCC-based systems, thus allowing one form of constraint representation and providing for constraint relaxation [12]. A third cause of brittleness was that agents originally had no control over the structure of LCC specifications - they could only choose whether or not to participate in a particular LCC-supported interaction, with no option to adapt the rules of interaction as they participated. This is a particular issue in argumentation systems, where the course of future interaction may be influenced strongly by the structure of arguments used previously within the same interaction. Mechanisms based on protocol synthesis were invented to produce these forms of interaction in a class of argumentation systems [13]. Later, LCC was used as a prototypical low level language for the protocol level of the Argument Interchange Format [14] which is a general purpose framework for describing argumentation systems.

4 Community Formation: Discovery, Group Formation and Trust

LCC is, deliberately, neutral to the manner in which it is used to coordinate agents. Nevertheless, in practice agent coordination that is sustainable over time has to occur in environments that support the interactions between agents and this requires mechanisms for helping agents to discover agents that are likely to be compatible; to form appropriate groups to achieve tasks and to establish trust. A range of methods have been developed to address aspects of this problem. At one end of the range, there are statistical methods for recommending compatible groups of agents based on previous successful/unsuccessful interactions [15]. These sorts of methods give crude measures of compatibility but have the advantage of requiring only simple statistical data on the history of interactions and no adaptation of the agents themselves. At the other end of the range are methods that check deontic specifications of agents (their permissions, obligations, etc) in real time against the LCC interaction specifications in which they are involved [16]. These allow more subtle control at the interface between agents and their interactions but at the cost of additional representation of deontic specifications for agents and of the inference machinery needed to perform the checking.

5 Application Areas

Although originally developed with multi-agent systems in mind, LCC has been used in a wide variety of contexts. In proteomics it has been used to share data on protein structure between protein data bases [17] and, in subsequent research, between research labs in Spain's ProteoRed network. In astrophysics, LCC has been used as a high level, executable specification language for data intensive experiments [18]. In crisis management, LCC has been used in simulation experiments comparing methods of centralised and peer to peer response to emergency flooding situations in the Trentino region of Italy [19]. In healthcare, LCC provided the basis for peer to peer sharing of healthcare workflows based on the ProForma system of medical protocol specification - this formed the basis for the Safe and Sound initiative (`www.clinicalfutures.org`) [20,21]. In computer games, LCC has been used as a language for specifying coordination between game agents in Unreal Tournament [22]. In service environments, LCC has been used in the development of market systems for confederations of services [23]. The common theme across all of these applications is the need for a compact language for specifying desired interactions plus a relatively straightforward way to make these easy to share and connect to local systems (whether these are autonomous agents or more traditional services).

6 Work in Progress

In the seven years since the DALT 2004 paper the world has changed considerably. Personal devices have become more sophisticated, more capable of data intensive processing and are much more ubiquitous. Social use of computation is also much more extensive and intimate than ever before. This has created many more potential applications for agents and in particular the coordination of agents. Potentially, these could operate across very large sectors of the population to harness individual sensing and problem solving for problems that hitherto resisted attack. We have already seen examples of this in the numerous social computing and crowdsourcing applications familiar to many. We are also experiencing the social effects of commercial interest in this area (through Facebook and other major companies) and the resulting conflicts over anonymity, privacy and ownership of information. Most of these issues are at least one step removed from declarative agent languages but they do increase the need for such languages and the need for scale and (perhaps) openness of operation places additional demands on specifications for agent interaction. Given this, future developments of LCC focus on community formation (driven from interaction data); security (in the context of electronic institution sharing in open systems); and the ability to synthesise/adapt specifications locally without breaking the coherence of interactions. These issues are not new but we lack methods that apply at current global scale. Further discussion of these issues will appear in [24].

Acknowledgements. This work was initially supported under the Advanced Knowledge Technologies (AKT) Interdisciplinary Research Collaboration (`www.aktors.org`), which is sponsored by the UK Engineering and Physical Sciences Research Council (EPSRC). Development of the OpenKnowledge system (`www.openk.org`) was supported by the European Union Framework 7 programme. Continuing work is supported by an EPSRC e-Science Platform grant. I am grateful for the discussions and inspiration provided by many other researchers on the AKT, OpenKnowledge and e-Science initiatives, as well as those on the other related efforts described in this paper.

References

1. Robertson, D.: A Lightweight Coordination Calculus for Agent Systems. In: Leite, J., Omicini, A., Torroni, P., Yolum, p. (eds.) DALT 2004. LNCS (LNAI), vol. 3476, pp. 183–197. Springer, Heidelberg (2005)
2. Robertson, D.: Multi-agent Coordination as Distributed Logic Programming. In: Demoen, B., Lifschitz, V. (eds.) ICLP 2004. LNCS, vol. 3132, pp. 416–430. Springer, Heidelberg (2004)
3. Robertson, D., Walton, C., Barker, A., Besana, P., Chen-Burger, Y., Hassan, F., Lambert, D., Li, G., McGinnis, J., Osman, N., Bundy, A., McNeill, F., van Harmelen, F., Sierra, C., Giunchiglia, F.: Models of interaction as a grounding for peer to peer knowledge sharing. In: Chang, E., Dillon, T., Meersman, R., Sycara, K. (eds.) Advances in Web Semantics I. LNCS, vol. 4891. Springer, Heidelberg (2008)
4. Andrews, A., Curbera, F., Dholakia, H., Goland, Y., Klein, J., Leymann, F., Liu, K., Roller, D., Smith, D., Thatte, S., Trickovic, I., Weerawarana, S.: Business process execution language for web services, version 1.1 (2003), `http://www-106.ibm.com/developerworks/webservices/library/ws-bpel`

5. Esteva, M., de la Cruz, D., Sierra, C.: Islander: an electronic institutions editor. In: Proceedings of the 1st International Joint Conference on Autonomous Agents and Multi Agent Systems, pp. 1045–1052 (2002)
6. Li, G., Robertson, D., Chen-Burger, J.: Using a multi-agent platform for pure decentralised business workflows. Journal of Web Intelligence and Agent Systems 6 (2008)
7. Li, G., Robertson, D., Chen-Burger, J.: A novel approach for enacting distributed business workflow on a peer-to-peer platform. In: IEEE Conference on e-Business Engineering, Beijing, China (2005)
8. Barker, A., Walton, C., Robertson, D.: Choreographing web services. IEEE Transactions on Services Computing 2 (2009)
9. Giunchiglia, F., McNeill, F., Yatskevich, M., Pane, J., Besana, P., Shvaiko, P.: Approximate, structure-preserving semantic matching. In: 7th International Conference on Ontologies, Databases and Applications of Semantics (2008)
10. Besana, P., Robertson, D.: How Service Choreography Statistics Reduce the Ontology Mapping Problem. In: Aberer, K., Choi, K.-S., Noy, N., Allemang, D., Lee, K.-I., Nixon, L.J.B., Golbeck, J., Mika, P., Maynard, D., Mizoguchi, R., Schreiber, G., Cudré-Mauroux, P. (eds.) ASWC 2007 and ISWC 2007. LNCS, vol. 4825, pp. 44–57. Springer, Heidelberg (2007)
11. Schorlemmer, M., Kalfoglou, Y., Atencia, M.: A formal foundation for ontology-alignment interaction models. International Journal on Semantic Web and Information Systems 3 (2007)
12. Hassan, F., Robertson, D.: A constraint relaxation approach for over-constrained agent interaction. In: 11th Pacific Rim International Workshop on Multi-Agent Systems, Kuala Lumpur, Malasia (2008)
13. McGinnis, J., Robertson, D.: Realizing Agent Dialogues with Distributed Protocols. In: van Eijk, R.M., Huget, M.-P., Dignum, F.P.M. (eds.) AC 2004. LNCS (LNAI), vol. 3396, pp. 106–119. Springer, Heidelberg (2005)
14. Chesnevar, C., McGinnis, J., Modgil, S., Rahwan, I., Reed, C., Simari, G., South, M., Vreeswijk, G., Willmott, S.: Towards an argument interchange format. The Knowledge Engineering Review 21 (2006)
15. Lambert, D., Robertson, D.: Matchmaking Multi-Party Interactions Using Historical Performance Data. In: 4th International Joint Conference on Autonomous Agents and Multi-Agent Systems, Utrecht, The Netherlands (2005)
16. Osman, N., Robertson, D.: Dynamic Verification of Trust in Distributed Open Systems. In: 20th International Joint Conference on Artificial Intelligence, Hyderabad, India (2007)
17. Quan, X., Walton, C., Gerloff, D., Sharman, J., Robertson, D.: Peer-to-peer experimentation in protein structure prediction: an architecture, experiment and initial results. In: International Workshop on Distributed, High-Performance and Grid Computing in Computational Biology, Eilat, Israel (2007)
18. Barker, A., Mann, R.: Integration of multiagent systems to AstroGrid. In: Proceedings of Astronomical Data Analysis Software and Systems XV. European Space Astronomy Centre, Spain (2005)
19. Marchese, M., Vaccari, L., Trecarichi, G., Osman, N., McNeill, F.: Interaction models to support peer coordination in crisis management. In: 5th International Conference on Information Systems for Crisis Response and Management, Washington, DC (2008)
20. Besana, P., Patkar, D., Barker, A., Robertson, D., Glasspool, D.: Sharing choreographies in openknowledge: A novel approach to interoperability. Journal of Software 4, 833–842 (2009)
21. Fox, J., Glasspool, D., Patkar, V., Austin, M., Black, E., South, M., Robertson, D., Vincent, C.: Delivering clinical decision support services: There is nothing as practical as a good theory. Journal of Biomedical Informatics 43, 831–843 (2010)

22. Graham, P.: Multi-agent coordination in complex virtual environments. PhD thesis, Informatics, University of Edinburgh (2011)
23. Guo, L., Darlington, J., Fuchs, B.: Towards an Open, Self-Adaptive and P2P Based e-Market Infrastructure. In: Proceedings of the IEEE International Conference on e-Business Engineering, Macao, China (2009)
24. Robertson, D., Giunchiglia, F.: Programming the social computer. Royal Society Philosophical Transactions A (special issue: Web Science: A New Frontier) (in press)

The Evolution of Interoperability

Amit K. Chopra[1] and Munindar P. Singh[2]

[1] University of Trento, Italy
chopra@disi.unitn.it
[2] North Carolina State University, USA
singh@ncsu.edu

1 History

This note is a retrospective review of our 2006 paper [1] on the properties of protocols, especially interoperability.

A bit of history is in order. By 2006, the importance of a social semantics for protocols was well-established in the multiagent systems community. Further, commitments had emerged as a preeminent abstraction for capturing the semantics. The big advantage was that specifying the meaning of protocol messages in terms of the commitments among agents enabled the agents to act flexibly.

Informally, the notion of flexibility derives from reasoning about the legal executions from a global perspective: if the set of legal executions of a protocol is a subset of those of another, then the latter is more flexible. For example, all other things being equal, a protocol that enables merchants and customers to exchange goods and payment in any order is more flexible than one that only supports payment before goods. Specifying protocols in terms of commitments promotes flexibility because compliance with a protocol amounts to fulfilling one's commitments. This in principle frees a protocol designer from the necessity of specifying the order of messages.

Flexibility is, of course, highly desirable for engineering multiagent systems. It ties in well with qualities that are commonly ascribed to agents—proactivity, opportunism, intelligent exception-handling, and so on. Flexibility is good from the business perspective: the more flexibly one can act the greater are the opportunities for engaging others in business. For example, by adopting a protocol that enables payment and goods to be exchanged in any order, a merchant can also engage customers who are unwilling to make their payments before the delivery of goods.

2 Distributed Enactment

Let us revisit the above assumption that increased flexibility offers expanded possibilities for engaging others. Note that protocols are enacted by agents in distributed settings. In such settings, it is difficult to ensure that the agents operate in lockstep with one another. Specifically, the agents may send and receive messages as they please without being made to block for another agent. This phenomenon is commonly referred to as *asynchrony*. About the only constraint we can rely upon is that the receipt of a message is causally later than its sending. Asynchrony makes interoperation challenging. And

C. Sakama et al. (Eds.): DALT 2011, LNAI 7169, pp. 90–94, 2012.

without interoperability, there can be no meaningful engagement. As a result, increased flexibility might not improve the opportunities for engagement in practice.

For concreteness, let us assume reliable, noncreative, order-preserving, point-to-point messaging. Even so, unexpected things could happen during enactment. Consider two agents who have adopted roles in some protocol. Even in acting according to the protocol, their messages to each other could cross in transit. For example, consider that a merchant's cancellation of an offer it had made earlier to some customer crosses in transit the customer's payment for the offered items. We naturally ask: what is the state of this interaction? Should the customer's payment entitle it to the items offered or should the payment be considered as having been made too late? Answering this question is important to enabling meaningful engagement. In scenarios involving more than two agents, the problem is exacerbated by the fact that an agent would in general lack knowledge of the messages exchanged by agents other than itself.

Perhaps the most commonly adopted solution today is to assume synchronous communication, which means that when an agent sends a message, it waits to take its next step until it receives an acknowledgment for the message it has sent. Synchronous communication is ill-suited to distributed settings since it creates delays corresponding to message roundtrips, and effectively makes one party dependent upon progress by another. Another common solution is to specify protocols so that if agents were to follow them, then the scenario of their messages crossing would not even arise. This is achieved quite simply by specifying protocols in terms of a progression of interaction state and ensuring that in each state, only one agent can send a message (the recipient would eventually block pending receipt of the message). In essence, the agents would enact protocols in close to lockstep synchrony.

Returning to our example, the problem scenario of the cancellation and the payment crossing could be handled as follows. The merchant would not be allowed to cancel offers. If it could, it could do so only in some limited period of time (a *make up your mind* period) before the sending of payment is enabled. Some protocols may be more flexible and allow cancellations at any time. However, in that case, when payment and cancellation cross, the situation for all practical purposes must be handled offline from the system that the protocol represents. (Assigning priorities to the agents can help decide which of two or more conflicting messages "wins". However, such priorities alone cannot synchronize the agents because the agents may since have progressed further.) So, for all practical purposes, it would seem we are stuck with lockstep synchrony in protocols. That does not leave the agents much flexibility. Much research in distributed systems arises from relaxing synchronous enactment in one way or another [11].

It was the thinking leading up to our 2006 paper [1] that made the tension between flexibility and interoperability clear to us. In the paper, we defined the notion of conformance with protocols based on commitments. This notion afforded designers much flexibility in building agent implementations. We defined interoperability following the more traditional manner of distributed systems research (based on the absence of *deadlocks*). We noted that a conformant agent may be noninteroperable with other agents. (In subsequent work not dealing with commitments [2], we revised conformance to be an interoperability preserving relation.) Winikoff [3] also noted the challenge of interoperability with protocols.

Recall that the motivation behind commitment protocols was to enable agents to interact as flexibly as possible. *An agent can do or communicate anything anytime; it is compliant as long as it fulfills its commitments.* However, without reconciling flexibility with interoperability, none of the flexibility could be realized in practice. Since 2006, reconciling flexibility with interoperability has become an important research direction.

3 Commitment-Level Interoperability

We have since made substantial progress on this issue. The key for us was to think in terms of interoperability conceptually. Interoperability is about the assumptions that agents make of each other. When the assumptions are compatible, the agents are interoperable. Traditionally, the assumptions have taken an operational form: they specify the order in which each agent expects to observe messages. A protocol is a global specification of assumptions: we can derive from it the assumptions relevant to any single participant. Traditionally, protocols for distributed systems have been specified operationally (for instance, as a finite state machine).

What made the difference in our work was the realization that for commitment protocols, the assumptions among the agents are the commitments themselves, not the orderings of the messages they exchange. Reconstructing the above problem scenario in terms of commitments, the problem is that the customer would infer that the merchant is, on account of the payment, committed to sending the items offered, whereas the merchant, on account of the cancellation, would infer that it is not. In other words, they would have an incompatible view of the state of the interaction, and their engagement would break down.

The foregoing motivates *alignment* as a definition of interoperability expressed in terms of commitments that we formalized in 2008 [5] and 2009 [4].

We informally state this definition below. We use the notation $\mathsf{C}(x, y, r, u)$ to mean that agent x commits to agent y that if condition r holds, it will bring about condition u. In this definition, the local perspective of an agent refers to the sequence of messages it has observed, including those it has sent and those it has received; a system execution is essentially a snapshot in time: it refers to a set of local perspectives, one for each agent. The meaning of "relevant" in this informal definition is beyond the scope of this paper.

Definition 1. *A multiagent system is aligned (interoperable) if and only if, for every relevant system execution, for every pair of agents (x, y) in the system:*

- *if the local perspective of y entails a commitment of the form $\mathsf{C}(x, y, r, u)$, then the local perspective of x entails it too.*

Essentially what Definition 1 states is an invariant on (relevant) system executions. An interesting observation from the perspective of accommodating flexibility is that the above definition does not refer to the sending or receiving of messages by any agent whatsoever. This lack of consideration on message transmission represents the beginning of freedom from synchronous executions, which facilitates the reconciliation of flexibility with interoperability.

In 2008, we proposed that commitment protocol specifications specify only meanings of messages, not the orders in which agents should exchange messages—another step in our argument [5]. This was in contrast to earlier work, that relied on ordering and occurrence constraints on messages in order to talk of interoperability. Even previous declarative approaches, such as our own [6], sought to capture some aspect of ordering and occurrence. The step to eliminate all such operational considerations when talking about meaning was a major step in the development of multiagent protocols.

In 2009, we proposed the computational rules by agents can reason about their commitments locally [4]. These rules ensure that the invariant that Definition 1 refers to holds regardless of the particular meanings of the messages and independent of the particular decision-making strategies of the agents. In 2010, we presented an architecture in which the computational rules constitute a middleware—logically speaking, the final step of our argument [7].

In reality, the actual thinking and research evolved far more haphazardly than the steps above might indicate. The main point though is this: we wanted highly flexible protocols. So we specified protocols in terms of message meanings. However, meaning-based specifications make interoperability challenging. So we formulated a set of computational rules that guarantee interoperability. The rules form the basis of a middleware that the agents run upon. From the application (agent) perspective, the middleware offers the guarantee of interoperability; its implementation is, however, transparent to agents—just as reliable message queues offer guarantees about message delivery, but are transparent to applications that use them.

4 Conclusions

The knowledge flow between distributed systems research and multiagent systems research has largely been in one direction: toward multiagent systems research. Distributed open systems have informed multiagent systems research since the very beginning [8–10]. The flow need not be one way though. We, as a community of researchers in multiagent systems, place a high value on accommodating the autonomy of agents. Therefore, we value flexibility in protocol enactment. We value social abstractions. These criteria are not central to traditional distributed systems research, but are clearly central to practical distributed systems applications. If we formulate problems keeping our own values in sight, there is a significant potential for influencing the building of large distributed systems that are comprised of multiple autonomous parties [12]. Dealing with multiple autonomous parties is the need of the moment in areas such as health care, e-governance, and interorganizational business processes. A recent collection of manifestos [13] lays out interesting research directions in protocols and multiagent systems.

Acknowledgments. We thank Michael Winikoff for his helpful comments. Amit Chopra's contribution was partially supported by a Marie Curie Trentino Cofund award. Munindar Singh's contribution was partially supported by National Science Foundation under Grant #0910868.

References

1. Chopra, A.K., Singh, M.P.: Producing Compliant Interactions: Conformance, Coverage, and Interoperability. In: Baldoni, M., Endriss, U. (eds.) DALT 2006. LNCS (LNAI), vol. 4327, pp. 1–15. Springer, Heidelberg (2006)
2. Baldoni, M., Baroglio, C., Chopra, A.K., Desai, N., Patti, V., Singh, M.P.: Choice, interoperability, and conformance in interaction protocols and service choreographies. In: Proceedings of the 9th International Conference on Autonomous Agents and Multiagent Systems, pp. 843–850. IFAAMAS (2009)
3. Winikoff, M.: Implementing commitment-based interactions. In: Proceedings of the 6th International Joint Conference on Autonomous Agents and Multiagent Systems, pp. 868–875. IFAAMAS (2007)
4. Chopra, A.K., Singh, M.P.: Multiagent commitment alignment. In: Proceedings of the Eighth International Conference on Autonomous Agents and Multiagent Systems, pp. 937–944. IFAAMAS (2009)
5. Chopra, A.K., Singh, M.P.: Constitutive interoperability. In: Proceedings of the Seventh International Conference on Autonomous Agents and Multiagent Systems, pp. 797–804. IFAAMAS (2008)
6. Chopra, A.K., Singh, M.P.: Contextualizing commitment protocols. In: Proceedings of the Fifth International Joint Conference on Autonomous Agents and Multiagent Systems, pp. 1345–1352. ACM Press (2006)
7. Chopra, A.K., Singh, M.P.: Elements of a Business-Level Architecture for Multiagent Systems. In: Braubach, L., Briot, J.-P., Thangarajah, J. (eds.) ProMAS 2009. LNCS, vol. 5919, pp. 15–30. Springer, Heidelberg (2010)
8. Huhns, M.N. (ed.): Distributed Artificial Intelligence. Pitman/Morgan Kaufmann, London (1987)
9. Gasser, L., Huhns, M.N. (eds.): Distributed Artificial Intelligence, vol. II. Pitman/Morgan Kaufmann, London (1989)
10. Hewitt, C.: Open information systems semantics for distributed artificial intelligence. Artificial Intelligence 47(1-3), 79–106 (1991)
11. Honda, K., Yoshida, N., Carbone, M.: Multiparty asynchronous session types. In: Proceedings of the 35th ACM SIGPLAN-SIGACT Symposium on Principles of Programming Languages (POPL), pp. 273–284 (2008)
12. Chopra, A.K.: Social computing: Principles, platforms, and applications. In: Proceedings of the 1st Workshop on Requirements Engineering for Social Computing (2011)
13. Chopra, A.K., Artikis, A., Bentahar, J., Colombetti, M., Dignum, F., Fornara, N., Jones, A.J.I., Singh, M.P., Yolum, P.: Research directions in agent communication. ACM Transactions on Intelligent Systems and Technologies (2011)

1000 Years of Coo-BDI*

Viviana Mascardi and Davide Ancona

DISI - Università di Genova
Via Dodecaneso 35, 16146, Genova, Italy
{viviana.mascardi,davide.ancona}@unige.it

Abstract. The idea of extending the BDI architecture with cooperativity started shaping in 2003 when two independent proposals to support cooperation in a BDI setting were presented at DALT. One proposal, Coo-BDI, extended the BDI architecture by allowing agents to cooperate by exchanging and sharing plans in a quite flexible way; the other extended the BDI operational semantics for introducing speech-act based communication, including primitives for plan exchange. Besides allowing a natural and seamless integration with speech-act based communication for BDI languages, the intuitions behind Coo-BDI have proved to be promising and attractive enough to give rise to new investigations. In this retrospective review we discuss papers that were influenced by Coo-BDI and we outline other potential developments for future research.

1 Life after Coo-BDI

The paper introducing Coo-BDI [3] ended with the following statement:

> *We are currently working with the authors of [27] to realize this extension..*

The planned extension has consisted in the design and implementation of a unified architecture for highly cooperative BDI agents meeting the following requirements:

- messages adhere to the form proposed in [27], including a ⟨`tellHow, SenderId, Plan`⟩ performative allowing the receiver to add `Plan` to its plan library if `SenderId` is trusted, and
- plans are associated with access specifiers as in Coo-BDI so that agents can decide when a plan should be shared with others by means of a `tellHow` message.

Together with J. F. Hübner and R. H. Bordini we worked one year to finish the design and implementation of our planned extension, and finally the Coo-BDI approach was successfully and smoothly integrated with AgentSpeak [9, 29] in the context of Jason [10]. Jason implemented the operational semantics

* There are only 10 types of people in the world: those who understand binary, and those who don't.

C. Sakama et al. (Eds.): DALT 2011, LNAI 7169, pp. 95–101, 2012.

given in [9] as well as the extensions in [27], giving the necessary formal and practical basis for plan exchange among BDI agent in the way required by Coo-BDI. The obtained language was named Coo-AgentSpeak and was presented at AAMAS 2004 [4]. The extensions purposely made to Jason for supporting Coo-AgentSpeak features are part of the standard Jason release.

Encouraged by the promising results, we explored the applicability of the Coo-BDI principles to other concrete scenarios. In particular, we were interested in investigating if and how Web Services (WSs) technologies could support a component, described in terms of beliefs, desires and intentions, that dynamically adapts its behavior to new environments (namely, a Coo-BDI agent). A positive answer came from CooWS [11] which implements the ideas behind the Coo-BDI by means of WS technologies. In CooWS plan bodies are expressed in BPEL [1], a high-level scripting language for Web Services built on top of WSDL [12]. Agents able to execute a BPEL specification can execute the body of any plan, making the exchange of plans among agents a fruitful extension of the basic BDI architecture.

In parallel with this practical research activity, theoretical work was carried out for finding a BDI logic suitable for modeling the behavior of Coo-BDI agents. BDI^{ATL} [26] was the result of that effort. By replacing ATL* (Alternating-Time Temporal Logic [2]) with CTL* (an extension of Computation Tree Logic and Linear Temporal Logic [20]) in Rao and Georgeff's BDI logic [32, 30, 31], BDI^{ATL} allows us to express new commitment strategies that could not be defined there. In particular, we can express three variants of Rao and Georgeff's "open minded" commitment: "independent open minded", "optimistic open minded", and "pessimistic open minded". In these commitment strategies the new features that ATL* adds to CTL*, namely *cooperation modalities*, are exploited for expressing the way of thinking of rational Coo-BDI agents.

After the intense activity of the beginning, research on Coo-BDI slackened for a few years during which we pursued other scientific goals, including that of deepening our knowledge on semantic web issues. When the competencies acquired on these themes in general, and on ontology matching [21] in particular, were mature enough, an inspired intuition of A. Ricci gave us the chance to resume Coo-BDI and apply to it the techniques we were experimenting in other domains. The result was CooL-AgentSpeak [24], the "Cooperative Description-Logic AgentSpeak" language integrating Coo-BDI and AgentSpeak-DL [28] and enhancing them with *ontology matching capabilities*. In CooL-AgentSpeak, search for a plan takes place as in Coo-BDI. However, handling an event is more flexible as it is not based solely on unification and on the subsumption relation between concepts as in AgentSpeak-DL, but also on ontology matching. Belief querying and updating take advantage of ontological matching as well. The syntax of the language and motivating scenarios for its adoption are given. A sketch of the operational semantics and of how CooL-AgentSpeak can be implemented on top of JASDL [23] are also provided.

2 The Lives of the Others

Many research activities carried out under the agents and MASs umbrella share with Coo-BDI the idea of exchanging knowledge among peers that, otherwise, could not properly cope with some situations.

M. Baldoni, C. Baroglio, A. Martelli, V. Patti and C. Schifanella [5–8] face the issue of allowing an entity to play a role in an interaction ruled by a choreography, even when it owns no policy conforming to that role. The scenario of interest is Service-oriented Computing. As the authors recognize, in an agent framework the solution might easily come from a Coo-BDI-like approach: one might think of dynamically enriching the set of behaviors of the agent, which failed the conformance test, by asking other agents to supply a correct interaction policy. In Service-oriented Computing, however, a Coo-BDI-like approach can not be applied since in that scenario it is fundamental that knowledge is available before the interaction among the peers takes place.

The work by S. Costantini, P. Dell'Acqua and L. M. Pereira [15] discusses issues related to learning rules from other agents. The origins of that work date back to 2005, with the prototype implementation presented in [19], developed in DALI [18]. In 2008 that implementation has been enriched with temporal-logic-like operators [14, 17], and experiments in Ambient Intelligent applications have been carried out [16]. In the more recent paper [15], the authors further enrich the approach with a meta-evaluation component that prevents agents to blindly accept and incorporate new knowledge by allowing them to evaluate (and thus possibly discard) it according to its usefulness. The proposal adds to Coo-BDI the very relevant aspect of meta-reasoning for evaluating, activating and de-activating the new knowledge, where evaluation may in principle affect the level of trust of source agents.

The work by Meneguzzi and Luck [25] describes how a procedural agent model can be modified to allow an agent to build new plans at runtime by chaining existing fine-grained plans from a plan library into high-level plans. The applicability of the approach is demonstrated through a modification to the AgentSpeak architecture, where declarative and procedural aspects are combined together. Meneguzzi and Luck propose an integration with the Coo-BDI approach as a possible future extension to their architecture to partially overcome efficiency issues, since getting plans from other planning-capable agents may significantly reduce the amount of time spent to create plans from scratch.

The Coo-BDI approach to plan failure has been easily incorporated into the AgentSpeak meta-interpreter designed and implemented by M. Winikoff [34] and into the guidelines on how to create multi-agent systems using Erlang provided by C. Varela, C. Abalde, L. M. Castro and J. Gulías [33].

Finally, the framework Agent Coordination and Cooperation Cognitive Model, AC^3M [13], exhibits connections with Coo-BDI as well: the relationships between coordination, cooperation, BDI and OODA (Observe-Orient-Decide-Act cycle) are analyzed, with a particular focus on uncertain environments.

3 The Future

Research on Coo-BDI has not been financed within a specific project, but has been mainly driven by the willingness of several researchers to collaborate together, by exploiting cross-fertilization fostered by their rather different research backgrounds. Nevertheless, in these eight years the main ideas coming out from this collaboration have proved to have a certain influence on the research community of multi-agent systems, and we believe that there are still many interesting opportunities for improving and extending them in the near future.

Cooperative multi-agent systems find their natural applications in mobile code, context-aware and self-adaptive systems, but also semantic web applications. The most recent and interesting extensions to AgentSpeak discussed in [24] open new interesting scenarios in the intersection of multi-agent systems and advanced semantic web applications, including the Linked Open Data and the Federated Social Web. However, as we highlighted in the IAT 2011 paper, "cross-ontological" knowledge and reasoning may lead to unwanted behavior. Precision and recall of the best performing ontology matching algorithms seldom reach 100% on real ontologies (see `http://oaei.ontologymatching.org/2010/results/benchmarks/index.html`), and this means that using real ontologies and real ontology matchers, wrong matches might be returned, with possibly destructive consequences.

In order to cope with the intrinsic limitations of ontology matching techniques available today, we would greatly benefit from meta-reasoning capabilities similar to those discussed in [15]. Such capabilities might in fact allow agents to reason on the consequences of adopting new plans involving cross-ontological knowledge for ensuring a better control on which plans might be safely incorporated into the plan base, thus limiting risks.

More in general, safety and security are properties of paramount importance for cooperative multi-agent systems, especially when exploited in the context of mobile code, and much work still have to be done to make Coo-BDI usable in practice in contexts where safety and security are serious concerns. Interesting research directions include static and dynamic typechecking and verification of Coo-BDI agents, exploiting for instance session types [22].

The investigation of safety issues and the implementation of CooL-AgentSpeak in Jason is another short term research goal. The far future is too far to be predicted (especially when projects are not funded!), but we are confident that we will be able to talk about Coo-BDI in the next 10000 years[1]!

References

1. Alves, A., et al.: Web Services Business Process Execution Language version 2.0, public review draft, August 23 (2006), `http://docs.oasis-open.org/wsbpel/2.0/wsbpel-specification-draft.html` (accessed on August 30, 2011)

[1] Check the footnote in the first page...

2. Alur, R., Henzinger, T.A., Kupferman, O.: Alternating-time temporal logic. Journal of the ACM 49(5), 672–713 (2002)
3. Ancona, D., Mascardi, V.: Coo-BDI: Extending the BDI Model with Cooperativity. In: Leite, J., Omicini, A., Sterling, L., Torroni, P. (eds.) DALT 2003. LNCS (LNAI), vol. 2990, pp. 109–134. Springer, Heidelberg (2004)
4. Ancona, D., Mascardi, V., Hübner, J.F., Bordini, R.H.: Coo-AgentSpeak: Cooperation in AgentSpeak through plan exchange. In: Proceedings of the 3rd International Joint Conference on Autonomous Agents and Multiagent Systems, AAMAS 2004, pp. 696–705. IEEE Computer Society (2004)
5. Baldoni, M., Baroglio, C., Martelli, A., Patti, V., Schifanella, C.: Interaction Protocols and Capabilities: A Preliminary Report. In: Alferes, J.J., Bailey, J., May, W., Schwertel, U. (eds.) PPSWR 2006. LNCS, vol. 4187, pp. 63–77. Springer, Heidelberg (2006)
6. Baldoni, M., Baroglio, C., Martelli, A., Patti, V., Schifanella, C.: The need of capability requirements inside choreographies and interaction protocols. In: Yan, Y., Zhang, L. (eds.) Proceedings of the International Workshop on Service Oriented Techniques, SOT 2006, pp. 17–24 (2006)
7. Baldoni, M., Baroglio, C., Martelli, A., Patti, V., Schifanella, C.: Preserving players goals: a choreography-driven matchmaking approach. In: Baldoni, M., Boccalatte, A., De Paoli, F., Martelli, M., Mascardi, V. (eds.) Proceedings of the 8th AI*IA/TABOO Joint Workshop "From Objects to Agents", WOA 2007, pp. 132–139. Seneca Edizioni Torino (2007)
8. Baldoni, M., Baroglio, C., Martelli, A., Patti, V., Schifanella, C.: Reasoning on choreographies and capability requirements. International Journal of Business Process Integration and Management 2(4), 247–261 (2007)
9. Bordini, R.H., Moreira, Á.F.: Proving BDI properties of agent-oriented programming languages. Annals of Mathematics and Artificial Intelligence 42, 197–226 (2004)
10. Bordini, R.H., Wooldridge, M., Hübner, J.F.: Programming Multi-Agent Systems in AgentSpeak using Jason. John Wiley & Sons (2007)
11. Bozzo, L., Mascardi, V., Ancona, D., Busetta, P.: COOWS: Adaptive BDI agents meet service-oriented computing. In: Gleizes, M.P., Kaminka, G.A., Nowé, A., Ossowski, S., Tuyls, K., Verbeeck, K. (eds.) Proceedings of the 3rd European Workshop on Multi-Agent Systems, EUMAS 2005, p. 473. Koninklijke Vlaamse Academie van Belie voor Wetenschappen en Kunsten (2005); longer version of this paper also appeared in the Proceedings of the WWW/Internet 2005 Conference, edited by P. Isaìas and M. B. Nunes, vol. II, pp. 205–209 (2005)
12. Christensen, E., Curbera, F., Meredith, G., Weerawarana, S.: Web Services Description Language (WSDL) 1.1, W3C note, March 15 (2001), `http://www.w3.org/TR/wsdl` (accessed on August 30, 2011)
13. Consoli, A., Tweedale, J., Jain, L.C.: An Architecture for Agent Coordination and Cooperation. In: Apolloni, B., Howlett, R.J., Jain, L.C. (eds.) KES 2007, Part III. LNCS (LNAI), vol. 4694, pp. 934–940. Springer, Heidelberg (2007)
14. Costantini, S., Dell'Acqua, P., Pereira, L.M.: A multi-layer framework for evolving and learning agents. In: Proceedings of the AAAI 2008 Workshop on Metareasoning: Thinking about Thinking. Stanford University, AAAI Press (2008)
15. Costantini, S., Dell'Acqua, P., Pereira, L.M.: Conditional Learning of Rules and Plans by Knowledge Exchange in Logical Agents. In: Pasche, A. (ed.) RuleML 2011 - Europe. LNCS, vol. 6826, pp. 250–265. Springer, Heidelberg (2011)

16. Costantini, S., Dell'Acqua, P., Pereira, L.M., Toni, F.: Learning and evolving agents in user monitoring and training. In: Proceedings of the 48th National Conference of the Italian Association for Computer Science and Automatic Computation, AICA Conference 2010 (2010)
17. Costantini, S., Dell'Acqua, P., Pereira, L.M., Tsintza, P.: Runtime verification of agent properties. In: Proceedings of the International Conference on Applications of Declarative Programming and Knowledge Management, INAP 2009 (2009)
18. Costantini, S., Tocchio, A.: The DALI Logic Programming Agent-Oriented Language. In: Alferes, J.J., Leite, J. (eds.) JELIA 2004. LNCS (LNAI), vol. 3229, pp. 685–688. Springer, Heidelberg (2004)
19. Costantini, S., Tocchio, A.: Learning by knowledge exchange in logical agents. In: Corradini, F., De Paoli, F., Merelli, E., Omicini, A. (eds.) Proceedings of the 6th AI*IA/TABOO Joint Workshop "From Objects to Agents", WOA 2005, pp. 1–8. Pitagora Editrice Bologna (2005)
20. Emerson, E.A., Halpern, J.Y.: "Sometimes" and "not never" revisited: on branching versus linear time temporal logic. Journal of the ACM 33(1), 151–178 (1986)
21. Euzenat, J., Shvaiko, P.: Ontology Matching. Springer, Heidelberg (2007)
22. Honda, K.: Types for Dynamic Interaction. In: Best, E. (ed.) CONCUR 1993. LNCS, vol. 715, pp. 509–523. Springer, Heidelberg (1993)
23. Klapiscak, T., Bordini, R.H.: JASDL: A Practical Programming Approach Combining Agent and Semantic Web Technologies. In: Baldoni, M., Son, T.C., van Riemsdijk, M.B., Winikoff, M. (eds.) DALT 2008. LNCS (LNAI), vol. 5397, pp. 91–110. Springer, Heidelberg (2009)
24. Mascardi, V., Ancona, D., Bordini, R.H., Ricci, A.: CooL-AgentSpeak: Enhancing AgentSpeak-DL agents with plan exchange and ontology services. In: Boissier, O., Bradshaw, J., Cao, L., Fischer, K., Hacid, M.-S. (eds.) Proceedings of the IEEE/WIC/ACM International Conference on Intelligent Agent Technology, IAT 2011, pp. 109–116. IEEE Computer Society (2011)
25. Meneguzzi, F., Luck, M.: Composing High-Level Plans for Declarative Agent Programming. In: Baldoni, M., Son, T.C., van Riemsdijk, M.B., Winikoff, M. (eds.) DALT 2007. LNCS (LNAI), vol. 4897, pp. 69–85. Springer, Heidelberg (2008)
26. Montagna, R., Delzanno, G., Martelli, M., Mascardi, V.: BDI^{ATL}: An alternating-time BDI logic for multiagent systems. In: Gleizes, M.P., Kaminka, G.A., Nowé, A., Ossowski, S., Tuyls, K., Verbeeck, K. (eds.) Proceedings of the 3rd European Workshop on Multi-Agent Systems, EUMAS 2005, pp. 214–223. Koninklijke Vlaamse Academie van Belie voor Wetenschappen en Kunsten (2005)
27. Moreira, Á.F., Vieira, R., Bordini, R.H.: Extending the Operational Semantics of a BDI Agent-Oriented Programming Language for Introducing Speech-Act Based Communication. In: Leite, J., Omicini, A., Sterling, L., Torroni, P. (eds.) DALT 2003. LNCS (LNAI), vol. 2990, pp. 135–154. Springer, Heidelberg (2004)
28. Moreira, Á.F., Vieira, R., Bordini, R.H., Hübner, J.F.: Agent-Oriented Programming with Underlying Ontological Reasoning. In: Baldoni, M., Endriss, U., Omicini, A., Torroni, P. (eds.) DALT 2005. LNCS (LNAI), vol. 3904, pp. 155–170. Springer, Heidelberg (2006)
29. Rao, A.S.: AgentSpeak(L): BDI Agents Speak Out in a Logical Computable Language. In: Perram, J.W., Van de Velde, W. (eds.) MAAMAW 1996. LNCS, vol. 1038, pp. 42–55. Springer, Heidelberg (1996)
30. Rao, A.S., Georgeff, M.P.: Asymmetry thesis and side-effect problems in linear-time and branching-time intention logics. In: Mylopoulos, J., Reiter, R. (eds.) Proceedings of the 12th International Joint Conference on Artificial Intelligence, IJCAI 1991, pp. 498–505. Morgan Kaufmann (1991)

31. Rao, A.S., Georgeff, M.P.: Deliberation and intentions. In: D'Ambrosio, B., Smets, P. (eds.) Proceedings of the 7th Conference on Uncertainty in Artificial Intelligence, UAI 1991. Morgan Kaufmann (1991)
32. Rao, A.S., Georgeff, M.P.: Modelling rational agents within a BDI-architecture. In: Proceedings of the 2nd International Conference of Principles of Knowledge Representation and Reasoning, KR 1991. Morgan Kaufmann Publishers (1991)
33. Varela, C., Abalde, C., Castro, L.M., Gulías, J.: On modelling agent systems with Erlang. In: Cesarini, F., Wadler, P. (eds.) 3rd ACM SIGPLAN Workshop on Erlang, Proceedings, pp. 65–70. ACM (2004)
34. Winikoff, M.: An AgentSpeak Meta-interpreter and Its Applications. In: Bordini, R.H., Dastani, M.M., Dix, J., El Fallah Seghrouchni, A. (eds.) PROMAS 2005. LNCS (LNAI), vol. 3862, pp. 123–138. Springer, Heidelberg (2006)

A Distributed Architecture for Norm-Aware Agent Societies: A Retrospective

Andrés García-Camino[1], Juan-Antonio Rodríguez-Aguilar[2], Carles Sierra[2], and Wamberto W. Vasconcelos[3]

[1] Independent Researcher
andres@garcia-camino.es
[2] IIIA-CSIC, Campus UAB 08193 Bellaterra, Catalunya, Spain
{jar,sierra}@iiia.csic.es
[3] Dept. of Computing Science, Univ. of Aberdeen, Aberdeen AB24 3UE, UK
wvasconcelos@acm.org

Abstract. We provide a retrospective on the research leading to and following our paper "A Distributed Architecture for Norm-Aware Agent Societies" [1], presented at DALT 2005. We do so by giving the context and motivation for that research, listing its contributions, and discussing the main developments of the research and its impact.

1 Introduction

We provide a retrospective on the research reported in the paper "A Distributed Architecture for Norm-Aware Agent Societies" [1], presented at DALT 2005. That paper described a distributed architecture to endow multi-agent systems with a social layer in which normative positions are explicitly represented and managed via *institutional rules*. These rules operate on a representation of the execution states of a multi-agent system. The paper presented the syntax and semantics of institutional rules and an interpreter for them. The approach achieved greater precision and expressiveness by having constraints as part of the rules. Finally, the paper proposed means to connect rules and states in a distributed architecture, whereby a team of administrative agents employ a tuple space to guide the execution of a multi-agent system.

This retrospective is organised as follows. In Section 2 we give the context and motivation for the research. Section 3 reviews the representation of norms and institutional rules, and mechanisms for processing them. We revisit the computational infrastructure based on a shared tuple space in Section 4 and in Section 5 we report on how the research was further developed and its impact in the state-of-the-art. Finally, we draw conclusions in Section 6.

2 Context and Motivation of Research

The work reported in [1] was carried out within García-Camino's PhD research [2]. The work was influenced by research on *electronic institutions* (EIs, for short), especially Esteva's PhD thesis [3], the AMELI middleware [4] and the Electronic

C. Sakama et al. (Eds.): DALT 2011, LNAI 7169, pp. 102–110, 2012.

Institutions Development Environment (EIDE) [5]. Another influence was the Sustainable Lifecycles in Information Ecosystems (SLIE) European project [6]. These efforts helped define a software engineering perspective on electronic institutions, expanding and grounding earlier theoretical work (*e.g.*, [7,8]).

The research reported in [1] was also motivated by a gap between theoretical work on norms for multi-agent systems [9,10] and implementation/engineering concerns. More specifically, we provided clear connections between a declarative formal specification of norms with agents' behaviours, also providing a computational infrastructure to support the implementation of multi-agent systems.

3 Representation and Processing of Norms

Norms are represented in [1] as atomic formulae $obl(S, W, \bar{I})$, $per(S, W, \bar{I})$ and $prh(S, W, \bar{I})$, standing for, respectively, an obligation, a permission and a prohibition to send a message $\bar{I}$ in a state W of a scene S[1]. The normative position of an agent is its "social burden", that is, the obligations, permissions and prohibitions associated with the agent. We show in Fig. 1 the architecture proposed in [1] and how its components fit together. The architecture provides a *social layer* for multi-agent systems specified via electronic institutions [3]. EIs specify the kinds and order of interactions among software agents with a view to achieving global and individual goals. The diagram shows a tuple space in which *institutional states* $\Delta_0, \Delta_1, \ldots$ are stored; these states contain all norms and other information that hold in specific points of time during the EI enactment.

The normative positions of agents are updated via *institutional rules.* These are constructs of the form LHS $\rightsquigarrow$ RHS where LHS describes a condition of the current institutional state and RHS depicts how it should be updated, giving rise to the next institutional state. The architecture is built around a shared tuple space [11] – a kind of blackboard system that can be accessed asynchronously by different administrative agents. In our diagram our administrative agents are shown in grey: the institutional agent updates the institutional state using the institutional rules; the governor agents work as "escorts" or "chaperons" to the external, heterogeneous software agents, writing onto the tuple space the messages to be exchanged.

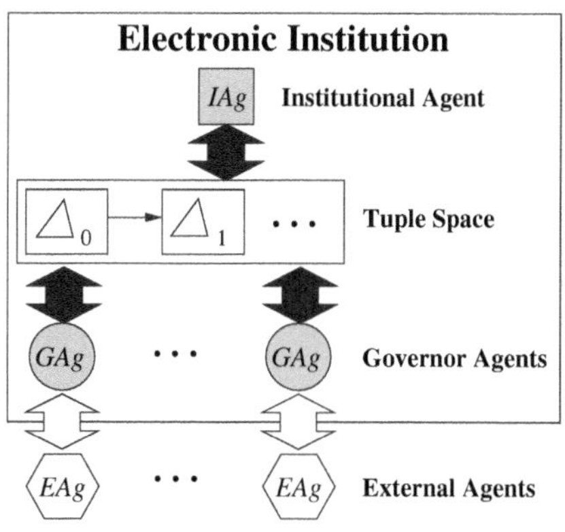

Fig. 1. Architecture Proposed in [1]

[1] States and scenes are means to break down complex EIs [3,8]. For instance, a virtual auction institution has scenes addressing agents' registration, the actual auction room, payment/delivery scenes and departure scenes. Each scene is decomposed into states, connected by expected illocutions (messages) from/to the various concerned parties.

An important contribution of [1] to research on normative systems has been the use of rules to update normative positions, adding and removing norms to/from institutional states. Constraints [12] play a special role in our approach, allowing a fine-grained and precise representation of the context in which rules should apply, and how these match with institutional states. A constraint C is of the form $\mathsf{T} \lhd \mathsf{T}'$, where T, T' are first-order terms, and $\lhd \in \{=, \neq, >, \geq, <, \leq\}$; $\Gamma = \{\mathsf{C}_1, \ldots, \mathsf{C}_n\}$ denotes a set of constraints. $\Gamma_1 \sqsubseteq \Gamma_2$ holds iff $\mathit{satisfy}(\Gamma_1, \Gamma_1')$ and $\mathit{satisfy}(\Gamma_2, \Gamma_2')$ hold and for every constraint $(\bot_1 \lhd X \lhd \top_1)$ in Γ_1', there is a constraint $(\bot_2 \lhd X \lhd \top_2)$ in Γ_2', such that $\mathit{max}(\bot_1, \bot_2) \geq \bot_1$ and $\mathit{min}(\bot_1, \bot_2) \leq \bot_1$, where $\bot_i, \top_i, i = 1, 2$ are arbitrary values. Relation $\mathit{satisfy}(\Gamma, \Gamma')$ holds, for two sets of constraints Γ, Γ' iff Γ can be satisfied and Γ' is the smallest set obtained from Γ such that:

- if both $(\mathsf{T} \lhd X), (X \lhd' \mathsf{T}') \in \Gamma$ then $(\mathsf{T} \lhd X \lhd' \mathsf{T}') \in \Gamma'$.
- if $(X \lhd \mathsf{T}) \in \Gamma$ then $(-\infty < X \lhd \mathsf{T}) \in \Gamma'$.
- if $(\mathsf{T} \lhd X) \in \Gamma$ then $(\mathsf{T} \lhd X < \infty) \in \Gamma'$.

Γ' contains a syntactic variation of the elements in Γ in which the constraints of each variable are *expanded* to be within an interval – two limits, $-\infty, \infty$, represent the lowest and highest value any variable may have.

We extended a conventional rule interpreter [13] to handle constraints in rules, shown in Fig. 2 as a logic program, interspersed with built-in Prolog predicates (each clause is shown with a number on its left). Clause 1 contains the top most

1. $\mathsf{s}^*(\Delta, \mathsf{Rs}, \Delta') \leftarrow$
   $\mathtt{findall}(\langle \mathsf{RHS}, \Sigma \rangle, (\mathtt{member}((\mathsf{LHS} \rightsquigarrow \mathsf{RHS}), \mathsf{Rs}), \mathsf{s}_l^*(\Delta, \mathsf{LHS}, \Sigma)), \mathsf{RHSs}),$
   $\mathsf{s}_r'(\Delta, \mathsf{RHSs}, \Delta')$

2. $\mathsf{s}_l^*(\Delta, \mathsf{LHS}, \Sigma) \leftarrow \mathtt{findall}(\sigma, \mathsf{s}_l(\Delta, \mathsf{LHS}, \sigma), \Sigma)$
3. $\mathsf{s}_l(\Delta, (\mathsf{A} \wedge \mathsf{LHS}), \sigma_1 \cup \sigma_2) \leftarrow \mathsf{s}_l(\Delta, \mathsf{A}, \sigma_1), \mathsf{s}_l(\Delta, \mathsf{LHS}, \sigma_2)$
4. $\mathsf{s}_l(\Delta, \neg\mathsf{LHS}, \sigma) \leftarrow \neg\mathsf{s}_l(\Delta, \mathsf{LHS}, \sigma)$
5. $\mathsf{s}_l(\Delta, \mathsf{B}, \sigma) \leftarrow \mathtt{member}(\mathsf{B} \cdot \sigma, \Delta), \mathit{constrs}(\Delta, \Gamma), \mathit{satisfy}(\Gamma \cdot \sigma, \Gamma')$
6. $\mathsf{s}_l(\Delta, \mathsf{C}, \sigma) \leftarrow \mathit{constrs}(\Delta, \Gamma), \{\mathsf{C} \cdot \sigma\} \sqsubseteq \Gamma$

7. $\mathsf{s}_r'(\Delta, \mathsf{RHSs}, \Delta') \leftarrow$
   $\mathtt{findall}(\Delta'', (\mathtt{member}(\langle \mathsf{RHS}, \Sigma \rangle, \mathsf{RHSs}), \mathtt{member}(\sigma, \Sigma), \mathsf{s}_r(\Delta, \mathsf{RHS} \cdot \sigma, \Delta'')), \mathit{All\Delta}),$
   $\mathit{merge}(\mathit{All\Delta}, \Delta')$
8. $\mathsf{s}_r(\Delta, (\mathsf{U} \wedge \mathsf{RHS}), \Delta_1 \cup \Delta_2) \leftarrow \mathsf{s}_r(\Delta, \mathsf{U}, \Delta_1), \mathsf{s}_r(\Delta, \mathsf{RHS}, \Delta_2)$
9. $\mathsf{s}_r(\Delta, \oplus\mathsf{B}, \Delta \cup \{\mathsf{B}\})) \leftarrow$
10. $\mathsf{s}_r(\Delta, \ominus\mathsf{B}, \Delta \setminus \{\mathsf{B}\})) \leftarrow$
11. $\mathsf{s}_r(\Delta, \oplus\mathsf{C}, \Delta \cup \{\mathsf{C}\}) \leftarrow \mathit{constrs}(\Delta, C), \mathit{satisfy}([\mathsf{Constr}|C], C')$

Fig. 2. Interpreter for Institutional Rules (reproduced from [1])

definition: given a Δ and a set of rules Rs, it shows how we can obtain the next state Δ' by finding (via the built-in `findall` predicate[2]) all those rules in Rs

[2] ISO Prolog built-in `findall/3` obtains all answers to a query (2nd argument), recording the values of the 1st argument as a list stored in the 3rd argument.

(picked by the `member` built-in) whose LHS holds in Δ (checked via the auxiliary definition $\mathbf{s}_l^*$). This clause then uses the RHS of those rules with their respective sets of substitutions Σ as the arguments of $\mathbf{s}_r'$ to finally obtain Δ'.

Clause 2 implements $\mathbf{s}_l^*$: it finds all the different ways (represented as individual substitutions σ) that the left-hand side LHS of a rule can be matched in an institutional state Δ – the individual σ's are stored in sets Σ of substitutions, as a result of the `findall/3` execution. In clause 6, $constrs(\Delta, \Gamma), \Gamma \subseteq \Delta$, holds iff for every $\mathsf{C} \in \Delta$ then $\mathsf{C} \in \Gamma$.

Clause 7 shows how $\mathbf{s}_r'$ computes the new state from a list RHSs of pairs $\langle \mathsf{RHS}, \Sigma \rangle$ (obtained in the second body goal of clause 1): it picks out (via predicate `member/2`) each individual substitution $\sigma \in \Sigma$ and uses it in RHS to compute via $\mathbf{s}_r$ a partial new institutional state Δ'' which is stored in $All\Delta$. $All\Delta$ contains a set of partial new institutional states and these are combined together via the *merge*/2 predicate – it joins all the partial states, removing any replicated components. A garbage collection mechanism can be also added to the functionalities of *merge*/2 whereby constraints whose variables are not referred in Δ are discarded.

4 Computational Infrastructure

We refer back to Fig. 1: in its centre we show a tuple space [11] – this is a blackboard system with accompanying operations to manage its entries. Our agents, depicted as a rectangle (labelled *IAg*), circles (labelled *GAg*) and hexagons (labelled *EAg*) interact (directly or indirectly) with the tuple space, reading and deleting entries from it as well as writing entries onto it. We proposed means to represent institutional states with a view to maximising asynchronous aspects (*i.e.*, agents should be allowed to access the tuple space asynchronously) and minimising housekeeping (*i.e.*, not having to move information around).

The top most rectangle in Fig. 1 depicts our *institutional agent IAg*, responsible for updating the institutional state, applying $\mathbf{s}^*$. The circles below the tuple space represent the *governor agents GAgs*, responsible for following the EI "chaperoning" the *external agents EAgs*. The external agents are arbitrary heterogeneous software or human agents that actually enact an EI to ensure that they conform to the required behaviour, each external agent is provided with a governor agent with which it communicates to take part in the EI. Governor agents ensure that external agents fulfil all their social duties during the enactment of an EI. In our diagram, we show the access to the tuple space as black block arrows; communication among agents are the white block arrows.

```
main:-
  out(current_state(0)),
  time_step(T),
  loop(T).

loop(T):-
  sleep(T),
  no_one_updating,
  in(current_state(N)),
  get_state(N,Delta),
  inst_rules(Rules),
  s*(Delta,Rules,NewDelta),
  write_onto_space(NewDelta),
  NewN is N + 1,
  out(current_state(N)),
  loop(T).
```

Fig. 3. Institutional Agent

We show in Fig. 3 a Prolog implementation for the institutional agent *IAg*. It bootstraps the architecture by creating an initial value 0 for the current state (lines 2-3); the initial institutional state is empty. In line 3 the institutional agent obtains via `time_step`/1 a value `T`, an attribute of the EI enactment setting up the frequency new institutional states should be computed.

The *IAg* agent then enters a loop (lines 5-14) where it initially (line 6) sleeps for `T` milliseconds – this guarantees that the frequency of the updates will be respected. *IAg* then checks via `no_one_updating`/0 (line 7) that there are no governor agents currently updating the institutional state with their utterances – `no_one_updating`/0 succeeds if there are no `updating`/2 tuples in the space. Such tuples are written by the governor agents to inform the institutional agent it has to wait until their utterances are written onto the space.

When the agent *IAg* is sure there are no more governor agents updating the tuple space then it removes the `current_state`/1 tuple (line 8) thus preventing any governor agent from trying to update the tuple space (the governor agent checks in line 7 of Fig. 4 if such entry exists – if it does not, then the flow of execution is blocked on that line). The agent *IAg* then obtains via predicate `get_state`/2 all those tuples pertaining to the current institutional state `N` and stores them in `Delta`; the institutional rules are obtained in line 10 – they are also stored in the tuple space so that any of the agents can examine them. In line 11 `Delta` and `Rules` are used to obtain the next institutional state `NewDelta` via predicate `s*`/2 and its implementation in Fig 2). In line 12 the new institutional state `NewDelta` is written onto the tuple space, then the tuple recording the identification of the current state is written onto the space (line 14) for the next update. Finally, in line 15 the agent loops[3].

```
1 main:-
2   connect_ext_ag(Ag),
3   root_scene(Sc),
4   initial_state(Sc,St),
5   loop([Ag,Sc,St,Role]).

6 loop(Ctl):-
7   rd(current_state(N)),
8   Ctl = [Ag|_],
9   out(updating(Ag,N)),
10  get_state(N,Delta),
11  findall([A,NC],(p(Ctl):-A,p(NC)),ANCs),
12  social_analysis(ANCs,Delta,Act,NewCtl),
13  perform(Act),
14  in(updating(Id,N)),
15  loop(NewCtl).
```

Fig. 4. Governor Agent

Distinct threads will execute the code for the governor agents *GAg* shown in Fig. 4. Each of them will connect to an external agent via predicate `connect_ext_ag`/1 and obtain its identification `Ag`, then find out (line 3) about the EI's root scene (where all agents must initially report to [3]) and that scene's initial state (line 4). In line 5 the governor agent makes the initial call to `loop`/1: the `Role` variable is not yet instantiated at that point, as a role is assigned to the agent when it joins the EI. The governor agents then will loop through lines 6-15, initially checking in line 7 if they are allowed to update the current institutional state, adding their utterances. Only if the `current_state`/1 tuple is on the space

[3] For simplicity we did not show the termination conditions for the loops of the institutional and governor agents. These conditions are prescribed by the EI specification and should appear as a clause preceding the loop clauses of Figs. 3 and 4.

then does the flow of execution of the governor agent move to line 8, where it obtains the identifier Ag from the control list Ctl; in line 9 a tuple updating/2 is written out onto the space. This tuple informs the institutional agent that there are governors updating the space and hence it should wait to update the institutional state. In line 10 the governor agent reads all those tuples pertaining to the current institutional state. In line 11 the governor agent collects all those actions send/1 and receive/1 in the EI specification which are associated with its current control [Ag,Sc,St,Role]. In line 12, the governor agent interacts with the external agent and, taking into account all constraints associated with Ag, obtains an action Act that is performed in line 14 (*i.e.*, a message is sent or received). In line 14 the agent removes the updating/2 tuple and in line 15 the agent starts another loop.

We were able to claim that the resulting society of agents is endowed with norm-awareness because their behaviour is regulated by the governor agents depicted above. The social awareness of the governor agent, in its turn, stems from two features: *i)* its access to the institutional state where obligations, prohibitions and permissions are recorded (as well as constraints on the values of their variables); *ii)* its access to the set of possible actions prescribed in the protocol. With this information, we can define various alternative ways in which governor agents, in collaboration with their respective external agents, can decide on which action to carry out.

We show in Fig. 5 a definition for predicate social_analysis/4. Its first subgoal removes from the list ANCs all those utterances that are prohibited from being sent, obtaining the list ANCsWOPrhs. The second subgoal ensures that obligations are given adequate priority: the list ANCsWOPrhs is further refined to get the obligations among the actions and store them in the list ANCsObls – if there are no obligations, then ANCsWOPrhs is the same as ANCsObls. Finally, in the third subgoal, an action is chosen from ANCsObls and customised in collaboration with the external agent.

```
social_analysis(ANCs,Delta,Act,NewCtr):-
  remove_prhs(ANCs,Delta,ANCsWOPrhs),
  select_obls(ANCsWOPrhs,Delta,ANCsObls),
  choose_customise(ANCsObls,Delta,Act,NewCtr).
```

Fig. 5. Definition of Social Analysis

5 Developments and Impact

The research reported in [1] was further developed in many ways. We refined, extended and related the rule-based approach to normative-oriented programming desiderata in [14], also exploring the approach in an auction scenario. In [15] we consolidated our approach, offering the pragmatics of our rule-based language, and how to represent and enact protocols; in that paper we also carry out an expressiveness analysis of the language, comparing it with other similar approaches. A shorter version of [1] appears as [16].

Our rule-based approach to norm-oriented programming and the tuple-space centered architecture allowed us to extend AMELI [4]: in [17] we presented

AMELI$^+$, a layered and distributed architecture with a team of administrative agents responsible for the "housekeeping" of rules and propagation of norms among various concurrent scenes. In [18] we developed an algorithm to deal with normative conflicts in a distributed setting.The use of constraints to increase precision and expressiveness of a formalism influenced the work reported in [19,20]. However, in this research constraints were used in the norm themselves (and not in rules adding/removing norms). The approach to use rules in order to give norms an operational semantics was also adopted in [21] and, subsequently, in [22].

The seminal ideas of [1] provided us with a vantage point from which various issues could be conveniently explored. The impact of this research was very noticeable, leading to distributed and highly scaleable architectures for multi-agent systems, also providing an explicit account of normative aspects and mechanisms for their management. Alternative formulations of our distributed architecture were proposed in [23] and in [24]; the concept of administrative agents stemmed from early work on EIs [3,7], but in [1] these were presented in a compact and self-contained fashion, being explicitly related with the information model and representation of norms.

6 Conclusions

This is a retrospective on the work reported [1], listing its context, the main ideas and contributions, and assessing its developments, influence and impact. The proposal of a formalism for norm representation which was expressive yet of practical use, and coupled with conceptual/architectural concerns, paved the way to the development of alternative formalisms and associated mechanisms and architecures.

References

1. García-Camino, A., Rodríguez-Aguilar, J.A., Sierra, C., Vasconcelos, W.W.: A Distributed Architecture for Norm-Aware Agent Societies. In: Baldoni, M., Endriss, U., Omicini, A., Torroni, P. (eds.) DALT 2005. LNCS (LNAI), vol. 3904, pp. 89–105. Springer, Heidelberg (2006)
2. García-Camino, A.: Normative Regulation of Open Multi-Agent Systems. PhD thesis, Universitat Autònoma de Barcelona, Spain (2009); IIIA monography, Vol. 35
3. Esteva, M.: Electronic Institutions: From Specification to Development. PhD thesis, Universitat Politècnica de Catalunya, Spain (2003); IIIA monography, Vol. 19
4. Esteva, M., Rosell, B., Rodríguez-Aguilar, J.A., Arcos, J.L.: AMELI: An agent-based middleware for electronic institutions. In: Jennings, N., et al. (eds.) Procs. 3rd Int'l Joint Conf. on Autonomous Agents & Multiagent Systems (AAMAS 2004), pp. 236–243. ACM (2004)
5. Esteva, M., Rodriguez-Aguilar, J.A., Arcos, J.L., Sierra, C., Noriega, P., Rosell, B., de la Cruz, D.: Electronic institutions development environment. In: Procs. 7th Int'l Joint Conf. on Autonomous Agents & Multiagent Systems (AAMAS 2008), pp. 1657–1658. IFAAMAS, Richland (2008)

6. Vasconcelos, W.W., Robertson, D., Agustí, J., Sierra, C., Wooldridge, M.J., Parsons, S., Walton, C.D., Sabater, J.: A Lifecycle for Models of Large Multi-agent Systems. In: Wooldridge, M.J., Weiß, G., Ciancarini, P. (eds.) AOSE 2001. LNCS, vol. 2222, pp. 297–318. Springer, Heidelberg (2002)
7. Esteva, M., Rodríguez-Aguilar, J.-A., Sierra, C., Garcia, P., Arcos, J.-L.: On the Formal Specification of Electronic Institutions. In: Sierra, C., Dignum, F.P.M. (eds.) AgentLink 2000. LNCS (LNAI), vol. 1991, pp. 126–147. Springer, Heidelberg (2001)
8. Vasconcelos, W.: Logic-Based Electronic Institutions. In: Leite, J., Omicini, A., Sterling, L., Torroni, P. (eds.) DALT 2003. LNCS (LNAI), vol. 2990, pp. 221–242. Springer, Heidelberg (2004)
9. Dignum, F.: Autonomous agents with norms. Art. Intell. & Law 7, 69–79 (1999)
10. Verhagen, H.: Norm Autonomous Agents. PhD thesis, Stockholm University (2000)
11. Carriero, N., Gelernter, D.: Linda in context. Comm. of the ACM 32 (1989)
12. Jaffar, J., Maher, M.J., Marriott, K., Stuckey, P.J.: The semantics of constraint logic programs. Journal of Logic Programming 37, 1–46 (1998)
13. Vianu, V.: Rule-based languages. Annals of Mathematics and Artificial Intelligence 19, 215–259 (1997)
14. García-Camino, A., Rodríguez-Aguilar, J.A., Sierra, C., Vasconcelos, W.: A rule-based approach to norm-oriented programming of electronic institutions. ACM SIGecom Exchanges 5, 33–40 (2006)
15. García-Camino, A., Rodríguez-Aguilar, J.A., Sierra, C., Vasconcelos, W.: Constraint rule-based programming of norms for electronic institutions. Autonomus Agents and Multi-Agent Systems 18, 186–217 (2009)
16. García-Camino, A., Rodríguez-Aguilar, J.A., Sierra, C., Vasconcelos, W.: Norm-oriented programming of electronic institutions. In: 5th Int'l Joint Conf. on Autonomous Agents and Multiagent Systems, AAMAS 2006 (2006)
17. García-Camino, A., Rodríguez-Aguilar, J.-A., Vasconcelos, W.W.: A Distributed Architecture for Norm Management in Multi-Agent Systems. In: Sichman, J.S., Padget, J., Ossowski, S., Noriega, P. (eds.) COIN 2007. LNCS (LNAI), vol. 4870, pp. 275–286. Springer, Heidelberg (2008)
18. Gaertner, D., García-Camino, A., Noriega, P., Rodríguez-Aguilar, J.A., Vasconcelos, W.: Distributed norm management in regulated multi-agent systems. In: 6th Int'l Joint Conf. on Autonomous Agents and Multiagent Systems, AAMAS 2007 (2007)
19. Kollingbaum, M.J., Vasconcelos, W.W., García-Camino, A., Norman, T.J.: Conflict Resolution in Norm-Regulated Environments Via Unification and Constraints. In: Baldoni, M., Son, T.C., van Riemsdijk, M.B., Winikoff, M. (eds.) DALT 2007. LNCS (LNAI), vol. 4897, pp. 158–174. Springer, Heidelberg (2008)
20. Kollingbaum, M.J., Vasconcelos, W.W., García-Camino, A., Norman, T.J.: Managing Conflict Resolution in Norm-Regulated Environments. In: Artikis, A., O'Hare, G.M.P., Stathis, K., Vouros, G.A. (eds.) ESAW 2007. LNCS (LNAI), vol. 4995, pp. 55–71. Springer, Heidelberg (2008)
21. Aldewereld, H., Dignum, F., García-Camino, A., Noriega, P., Rodríguez-Aguilar, J.A., Sierra, C.: Operationalisation of norms for usage in electronic institutions. In: Procs. 5th Int'l Conf. on Autonomous Agents and Multiagent Systems (AAMAS 2006), pp. 223–225. ACM, New York (2006)

22. Aldewereld, H., Álvarez Napagao, S., Dignum, F., Vázquez-Salceda, J.: Making norms concrete. In: Procs. 9th Int'l Conf. on Autonomous Agents and Multiagent Systems (AAMAS 2010), pp. 807–814. IFAAMAS, Richland (2010)
23. Okuyama, F., Bordini, R., da Rocha Costa, A.: A Distributed Normative Infrastructure for Situated Multi-agent Organisations. In: Baldoni, M., Son, T.C., van Riemsdijk, M.B., Winikoff, M. (eds.) DALT 2008. LNCS (LNAI), vol. 5397, pp. 29–46. Springer, Heidelberg (2009)
24. Felicíssimo, C.H., de Lucena, C.J.P., Briot, J.P.: A norm-based approach for the modeling of open multiagent systems. In: Procs. Int'l Conf. on Agents & Artificial Intelligence (ICAART 2009), pp. 540–546 (2009)

Speech-Act Based Communication: Progress in the Formal Semantics and in the Implementation of Multi-agent Oriented Programming Languages

Álvaro F. Moreira[1], Renata Vieira[2], and Rafael H. Bordini[1]

[1] Institute of Informatics
Federal University of Rio Grande do Sul
CP 15064, CEP 91501-970, Porto Alegre – RS, Brazil
{alvaro.moreira,r.bodini}@inf.ufrgs.br
[2] Faculdade de Informática
Pontifícia Universidade Católica do Rio Grande do Sul
CP 275, CEP 93022-000, Porto Alegre – RS, Brazil
renata@pucrs.br

Abstract. In this paper we revisit the motivations and the initial developments that led to our DALT 2003 paper *Extending the Operational Semantics of a BDI Agent-Oriented Programming Language for Introducing Speech-Act Based Communication.* We then discuss our own follow-up work which consisted in formally defining a larger set of speech-act based performatives and deploying them in *Jason*, a fully-fledged implementation of AgentSpeak. Subsequent research referring to the computationally grounded semantics of speech-act based agent communication that we introduced in that paper is also discussed.

1 Introduction

In [13], we introduced an operational semantics of speech-act based communication for AgentSpeak(L) [16], defining semantic rules for handling some of the performatives defined by Searle [19]. We were motivated mainly by two facts: first we realised that, at that time, the semantics for agent-oriented programming languages was given only at a very abstract level and important social and pragmatical aspects, such as inter-agent communication, were completely neglected. Second, previous attempts at giving semantics for agent communication were based on the approach in [11], asserting pre and post conditions on mental states of agents expressed in the modal logic introduced in [7]. Although that was a well-established way of defining the meaning of speech-act based communication, it lacked a computational interpretation and could not, therefore, be used for guiding the implementation of programming languages.

Given that state of affairs, and also our interest in developing AgentSpeak(L) into a core language for investigating agent-oriented languages (both on their formal and practical aspects), we endeavoured to define a computationally grounded

C. Sakama et al. (Eds.): DALT 2011, LNAI 7169, pp. 111–116, 2012.

semantics for speech-act communication in a way that could be used as a direct guide for the implementation of multi-agent programming languages.

The operational semantics given in our DALT-2003 paper was an extension of the formal semantics of AgentSpeak(L) which was first presented in [14] and further developed in [3]. We started by considering the performatives *Tell*, *Untell*, *Achieve*, *Unachieve*, *TellHow*, *UntellHow* and by formalising only the effects of receiving these illocutionary forces on the computational interpretation — formalised in [3] — of beliefs, desires, and intentions of AgentSpeak agents.

When working in that direction, we realised it was important to keep track of the source of the messages being exchanged along an agent's execution. For that purpose, all the atomic predicates in the belief base were annotated with their *source of information*. Those annotations can be of 3 different types: *self* when it comes from the internal plan execution of the agent, *percept* when it derives from the agent perception of its environment, and it can also be an agent's ID when the message has been sent by another agent.

In our semantics, the performatives *Tell* and *Untell* affect the belief base of the agent by respectively adding and removing beliefs from it. The performatives *Achieve* and *Unachieve* add new events in the agent's set of events. These events, later when handled in an agent reasoning cycle, might have effects on the intentions of the receiving agent (i.e., pursuing a new intention with *Achieve* and dropping an intention with *Unachieve*). Plans can also be communicated with *TellHow* and *UntellHow*, for respectively adding and removing a plan from the agent's plans library.

At around the same time, some of us were working on a fully-fledged implementation of an extension of AgentSpeak (that eventually culminated in platform called *Jason* [4]). It became clear that the work on the semantics of communication was crucial and had to be pursued further.

2 Improvements to the Original Proposal

Following the DALT paper, in [22] we extended the formal treatment to a larger set of performatives. Besides those already considered, we also defined the operational semantics for sending and receiving *AskIf*, *AskAll*, and *AskHow* messages.

The sender of a message with performative *AskIf* gets blocked (i.e., the intention that originated the message sending has its execution suspended) until it gets a reply saying whether the content of the message is true for the receiving agent. Similarly, the intention that originated an *AskAll* gets suspended until it gets the set of answers that make the content of the message true for the receiver. The intention that gave rise to an *AskHow* message is suspended until it obtains a set of plans that match, for the receiver, the triggering event in the message's content.

We also generalised the content of the messages allowing agents to send and receive sets of predicates and sets of plans instead of only a single predicate and a single plan (as it was the case in the DALT original paper). As before, our main concern was to give an account of the effects that communication based on speech-acts have on a computational interpretation of the agent's mental states. Hence, questions such as the mechanism for actual message exchange and for synchronisation were not taken into account in detail, although more of that aspect was formalised in the extended paper than in the original DALT paper.

3 Some Subsequent Related Research

In this section we discuss subsequent related research in agent programming that cited our work published in post-proceedings of DALT–2003. Since communication is intrinsically related to collaborative action, task distribution, and planning, much of the work which took ours as basis go in that direction. One of the first papers that referred to the operational semantics we presented back then was [1]. That paper presents an approach for plan exchange among BDI agent, based on the operational semantics of speech-act based communication for AgentSpeak, including special illocutionary forces for the communication of plans.

The importance of communication for achieving goals in multi-agent systems, and how an agent can delegate tasks to other agents, is stressed in [5]. The authors of that paper emphasise the importance of having precise semantics for goal delegation, as well as issues related to commitment, trust, and organisational structures, as indeed we conjectured when presenting the semantics proposed in our DALT–2003 paper.

AgentSpeak was extended in two ways in [6]. First, that work puts forward the use of "execution monitoring" to enable agents to reflect on their past endeavours. Second, they extend the semantics and syntax of the language to allow for user-defined monitoring strategies. This allows agent designers to use execution monitoring so as to balance the focus of an agent's behaviour in a way that is appropriate for particular application domains.

The notation we first proposed in our DALT 2003 paper was adapted by [9] in their operational semantics for learning intentionally. Intentional learning intends to keep reasons for action updated while keeping MAS-consistency in order to facilitate coordination. Such "reasons to act" in some particular way rather than another are usually expressed in the context part of plans. When an agent detects a failed execution of some intention, it desires to update its "practical reasons".

The work in [2] developed a semantics based on commitments and arguments for conversational agents. Their formal framework uses three basic elements: social commitments, actions that agents apply to these commitments, and arguments that agents use to support their actions. Their logical model gathers these elements and the existing relations between them within the same framework. The semantics reflects the dynamics of agent communication. It also establishes an important link between commitments as a deontic concept and arguments. They offer a way to express the temporal aspects related to the handling of commitments and arguments. On the other hand, they also capture the actions that agents are committed to achieve.

Unlike mental semantics, the semantics in the work mentioned above can be verified even for agents that are not programmed using a programming language based on mentalistic notions and with formal semantics. The reason is that it is expressed in terms of public commitments and arguments and not in terms of private mental states, as originally proposed by Singh [20]. The compliance of agents with this semantics can be checked by verifying whether the agents behave in accordance with their commitments and arguments. It is thus a prescriptive theory serving to establish rules regulating the behaviour of agents when communicating. The authors claim that it can be used for specifying agent communication protocols implementing such rules. They claim that equipping these protocols with an operational semantics like the one proposed in our DALT paper will be of great importance as a framework for designing and implementing normative agent communication.

In [12], a technique that enables new plans to be added to a plan library, extending their previous work to include the chaining of subplans, is presented. The mechanism makes use of plan patterns. In this way, they allow an agent to discover new ways of achieving goals through local planning and the delegation of tasks. As cooperation between agents requires communication, they refer to our DALT paper and they closely followed three of our proposed performatives: *Ask*, *Tell*, and *Achieve*.

The work in [17] points out that an aspect of agent architecture which is not always provided in existing agent programming frameworks is a mechanism for goal adoption. In their approach, the agent is endowed with a set of (suspended) goals at start-up. They refer to our DALT paper as an example of a framework that does allow goal adoption through communication.

In [21], richer state and action representations are given and are compared to the usual definition of a belief base and its update in AgentSpeak. That paper also refers to our proposed language extension regarding communication (as presented in our DALT paper), saying that such features can be realised in the underlying background theory they provide by specifying how beliefs and goals are affected by speech acts.

Recent work is still alerting to the fact that communication is essential for complex sophisticated collaborative planning, and goals failure handling (e.g., [18]. Also such research efforts recognise the role of communication in rational agents, particularly in the process of goal adoption. In fact, agent communication is presented as a common source of motivation for agent action. In those recent discussions, our work is still remembered.

4 Future Developments

We believe that the next steps in the development of multi-agent programming languages will still be focused on communication. This is an aspect where agent-oriented languages can impact in the software engineering of complex and intelligent systems when compared with other general purpose programming languages. Our work on proposing an operational semantics for modelling the effects of illocutionary forces over a computational interpretation of the mental states of agents was just a first step in a much larger research programme.

Recently, our research has focused on another important aspect of agent communication which is a common understanding of the information exchanged between agents. In [15,8] we proposed AgentSpeak-DL, a variant of AgentSpeak(L) having a description logic, instead of predicate logic, as the underlying logic, and in [10] an extension of *Jason* with underlying ontological reasoning was presented.

Besides allowing more structured belief bases, which are essentially ontologies defined in a description logic, we believe that the combination of speech-act based communication with ontological reasoning can open up a richer set of possibilities for agent deliberation. This is because with such an approach agents can not only count on reasoning over their internal beliefs but they can also count on deliberation based on the information that can be derived from the content of messages from other agents, as well as ontological reasoning based on ontologies available on the Web.

References

1. Ancona, D., Mascardi, V., Hubner, J.F., Bordini, R.H.: Coo-agentspeak: Cooperation in AgentSpeak through plan exchange. In: Proceedings of the Third International Joint Conference on Autonomous Agents and Multiagent Systems, AAMAS 2004, vol. 2, pp. 696–705. IEEE Computer Society (2004)
2. Bentahar, J., Moulin, B., Meyer, J.-J.C., Lespérance, Y.: A New Logical Semantics for Agent Communication. In: Inoue, K., Satoh, K., Toni, F. (eds.) CLIMA 2006. LNCS (LNAI), vol. 4371, pp. 151–170. Springer, Heidelberg (2007)
3. Bordini, R.H., Moreira, Á.F.: Proving BDI properties of agent-oriented programming languages: The Asymmetry Thesis principles in AgentSpeak(L). Annals of Mathematics and Artificial Intelligence 42(1-3), 197–226 (2004)
4. Bordini, R.H., Hübner, J.F., Wooldridge, M.: Programming multi-agent systems in AgentSpeak using Jason. Wiley, Chichester (2007)
5. Braubach, L., Pokahr, A., Moldt, D., Lamersdorf, W.: Goal Representation for BDI Agent Systems. In: Bordini, R.H., Dastani, M.M., Dix, J., El Fallah Seghrouchni, A. (eds.) PROMAS 2004. LNCS (LNAI), vol. 3346, pp. 44–65. Springer, Heidelberg (2005)
6. Cleaver, T.W., Sattar, A., Ferdous, R.: User defined monitoring strategies for bdi agent programs. In: Proceedings of the Fifth International Joint Conference on Autonomous Agents and Multiagent Systems, pp. 1055–1057. ACM (2006)
7. Cohen, P.R., Levesque, H.J.: Intention is choice with commitment. Artificial Intelligence 42(3), 213–261 (1990)
8. Fuzitaki, C., Moreira, Á., Vieira, R.: Ontology Reasoning in Agent-Oriented Programming. In: da Rocha Costa, A.C., Vicari, R.M., Tonidandel, F. (eds.) SBIA 2010. LNCS (LNAI), vol. 6404, pp. 21–30. Springer, Heidelberg (2010)
9. Guerra-Hernández, A., Castro-Manzano, J.M., El-Fallah-Seghrouchni, A.: Toward an AgentSpeak(L) Theory of Commitment and Intentional Learning. In: Gelbukh, A., Morales, E.F. (eds.) MICAI 2008. LNCS (LNAI), vol. 5317, pp. 848–858. Springer, Heidelberg (2008)

10. Klapiscak, T., Bordini, R.H.: JASDL: A Practical Programming Approach Combining Agent and Semantic Web Technologies. In: Baldoni, M., Son, T.C., van Riemsdijk, M.B., Winikoff, M. (eds.) DALT 2008. LNCS (LNAI), vol. 5397, pp. 91–110. Springer, Heidelberg (2009)
11. Labrou, Y., Finin, T.: A semantics approach for KQML—a general purpose communication language for software agents. In: Proceedings of the Third International Conference on Information and Knowledge Management (CIKM 1994), pp. 447–455. ACM Press (1994)
12. Meneguzzi, F., Luck, M.: A new logical semantics for agent communication. In: From Agent Theory to Agent Implementatio, 6th Internatinal Workshop. Helds in Conjunction with AAMAS 2008 (2008)
13. Moreira, Á.F., Vieira, R., Bordini, R.H.: Extending the Operational Semantics of a BDI Agent-Oriented Programming Language for Introducing Speech-Act Based Communication. In: Leite, J., Omicini, A., Sterling, L., Torroni, P. (eds.) DALT 2003. LNCS (LNAI), vol. 2990, pp. 135–154. Springer, Heidelberg (2004)
14. Moreira, Á.F., Bordini, R.H.: An operational semantics for a BDI agent-oriented programming language. In: Proceedings of the Workshop on Logics for Agent-Based Systems (LABS 2002), Held in Conjunction with the Eighth International Conference on Principles of Knowledge Representation and Reasoning (KR 2002), Toulouse, France, April 22-25, pp. 45–59 (2002)
15. Moreira, Á.F., Vieira, R., Bordini, R.H., Hübner, J.F.: Agent-Oriented Programming with Underlying Ontological Reasoning. In: Baldoni, M., Endriss, U., Omicini, A., Torroni, P. (eds.) DALT 2005. LNCS (LNAI), vol. 3904, pp. 155–170. Springer, Heidelberg (2006)
16. Rao, A.S.: AgentSpeak(L): BDI Agents Speak Out in a Logical Computable Language. In: Perram, J., Van de Velde, W. (eds.) MAAMAW 1996. LNCS (LNAI), vol. 1038, pp. 42–55. Springer, Heidelberg (1996)
17. van Riemsdijk, M.B., Dastani, M., Winikoff, M.: Goals in agent systems: a unifying framework. In: 7th International Joint Conference on Autonomous Agents and Multiagent Systems (AAMAS 2008), Estoril, Portugal, May 12-16, vol. 2, pp. 713–720. IFAAMAS (2008)
18. Sardiña, S., Padgham, L.: A BDI agent programming language with failure handling, declarative goals, and planning. Autonomous Agents and Multi-Agent Systems 23(1), 18–70 (2011)
19. Searle, J.R.: Speech Acts: An Essay in the Philosophy of Language. Cambridge University Press, Cambridge (1969)
20. Singh, M.P.: Agent communication languages: Rethinking the principles. IEEE Computer 31(12), 40–47 (1998)
21. Thielscher, M.: Integrating Action Calculi and AgentSpeak: Closing the gap. In: Principles of Knowledge Representation and Reasoning: Proceedings of the Twelfth International Conference, KR 2010, Toronto, Ontario, Canada, May 9-13, pp. 79–89. AAAI Press (2010)
22. Vieira, R., Moreira, Á.F., Wooldridge, M., Bordini, R.H.: On the formal semantics of speech-act based communication in an agent-oriented programming language. Journal of Artificial Intelligence and Research (JAIR) 29, 221–267 (2007)

Specifying and Enforcing Norms in Artificial Institutions: A Retrospective Review*

Nicoletta Fornara[1] and Marco Colombetti[1,2]

[1] Università della Svizzera italiana, via G. Buffi 13, 6900 Lugano, Switzerland
{nicoletta.fornara,marco.colombetti}@usi.ch
[2] Politecnico di Milano, piazza Leonardo Da Vinci 32, Milano, Italy
marco.colombetti@polimi.it

In this short contribution we explain how our research has evolved from the publication of the following paper [2] with respect to its relevant aspects. This paper proposes a model of norms whose content is related to time, which are specified at design time and therefore are expressed in terms of *roles* played by the agents. Those norms have an *activation event* that is used to express the template of the events that when happen, provided that certain conditions hold, transform the norm in a *social commitment*. This dynamic evolution of norms is formalized by means of *ECA-rules*. Another relevant contribution is that the model of norms presented in this paper makes it possible to specify two types of sanctions for norms enforcement: *active sanctions* and *passive sanctions*.

A significant evolution of this model has been the adoption of a different formal language for the specification of static and dynamic aspects of norms, a choice that brought us to extend and partially change our model of norms. Indeed starting from 2009 we adopted standard Semantic Web Technologies [5] for modeling, describing the evolution in time, and monitoring norms [4,1]. In particular, we decided to represent as much knowledge as possible in OWL 2 DL.

The main advantage of this choice is that when knowledge is represented in OWL 2 DL the reasoning process is decidable and fairly efficient, and reasoners are freely available and widely used. Moreover, Semantic Web Technologies are increasingly becoming a standard for Internet applications, and thus it is easier to find available ontologies to be re-used for certain application domains (like for instance the Friend of a Friend (FOAF) ontology), and suitable tools for editing and implementing them. The fact that Semantic Web Technologies are standard is crucial for the realization of very important for open interoperable systems, which we regard as an important aspect for future applications running on the Internet.

Semantic Web languages are very powerful for representing concepts, domain knowledge, and for sharing them. Unfortunately, the adoption of these languages for the specification of the dynamic aspects of norms is not straightforward, and we had to tackle an open research question: how can a language like OWL be used for temporal and deontic reasoning?

* The first author is supported by the project number 11115-KG funded by the Hasler Foundation.

C. Sakama et al. (Eds.): DALT 2011, LNAI 7169, pp. 117–119, 2012.

In our first proposal [4] we started to model temporal propositions, social commitments, and norms using OWL 2 DL[1], and with the additional use of SWRL (Semantic Web Rule Language)[2] rules we succeeded in describing their temporal evolution. We used an OWL 2 DL reasoner (firstly Pellet[3] and subsequently HermiT [4]) for reasoning on the ontology containing individuals used to represent concrete instances of norms. To perform run-time monitoring of the evolution in time of the commitments representing specific obligations and prohibitions created when norms are activated, we used a Java program together with OWL-API for accessing the ontology, in order to simulate the elapsing of time.

The first problem that we tackled in this phase was related to the representation of time: we decided to include in our ontology the OWL Time Ontology[5], with some additional SWRL rules used to increase its deductive power; however, given that the OWL Time ontology has a weak axiomatization of temporal entities we did not succeed in performing full temporal reasoning. Secondly we had a problem with the fact that in standard OWL 2 DL, reasoning is carried out under the *open world assumption.* But, to deduce that an obligation is violated if there is no evidence that the relevant action has been performed before its deadline, we need to perform *closed world reasoning* on certain classes of action. To solve this problem we extended the Java program in charge of representing the elapsing of time with the functionalities necessary to perform close world reasoning on certain classes. In particular we assumed that when the system is unable to infer that an action has been performed in the past, this is sufficient evidence that the action has not been performed.

In our subsequent work [1] we continued this line of research. In particular we realized that for efficiently modeling and simulating the temporal evolution of the obligations, prohibitions, and social commitments used to represent the semantics of certain communicative acts, it is better to model them with different constructs. Therefore we started to propose a new ontology of obligations in OWL 2 DL and SWRL rules, with the following characteristics: (i) obligations have a content that is related to time in order to represent deadlines, an activation condition, and an end condition used for deducing if an obligation is canceled; (ii) the content of an obligation is represented as an OWL class of possible actions: an instance of such a class has to be performed within a given deadline in order to fulfill the obligation; (iii) also the activation and end conditions are represented as OWL classes of events (a superclass of actions). The main advantage of using OWL classes to specify contents, activation conditions, and end conditions, is that at design time it is possible to describe the general templates of the required events, while at run time any concrete event

1 http://www.w3.org/2007/OWL/wiki/OWL_Working_Group
2 http://www.w3.org/Submission/SWRL/
3 http://clarkparsia.com/pellet/
4 http://owlapi.sourceforge.net/download.html
5 http://www.w3.org/TR/owl-time/, http://www.w3.org/2006/time.rdf

satisfying the template will constitute a relevant realization of it, and this can be established by standard OWL reasoning.

The temporal evolution of the state of the system is simulated using as input a set of events/actions together with the instant of time at which those events happen. As in our first proposal [4], we simulate the elapsing of time with a Java program that asserts that the current instant of time has elapsed. As we have already pointed out, the Java program is also used to implement the closed-world reasoning necessary to deduce the state of obligations.

Currently we are continuing this line of research by extending the ontology of obligations that we use to model the activation of norms, and that we plan to use to express the semantics of commissive communicative acts (like promises), with a model of prohibitions and social commitments, that we plan to use to express more complex norms and the semantics of assertives communicative acts. All these concepts are part of a larger model of artificial institutions, called OCeAN, that in 2009 we have formalized using Discrete Event Calculus[3] and are now specifying using Semantic Web Technologies, with the goal of using it in the implementation of an e-marketplace. An important aspect of this work is the study of an efficient software architecture for an open interaction system designed using these concepts and functionalities. In particular, we plan to study the mechanism by which agents start to play certain roles, efficient mechanisms for the enforcement of norms, and how to treat the interconnections among multiple artificial institutions.

References

1. Fornara, N.: Specifying and Monitoring Obligations in Open Multiagent Systems using Semantic Web Technology. In: Semantic Agent Systems: Foundations and Applications. SCI, ch. 2, pp. 25–46. Springer, Heidelberg (2011)
2. Fornara, N., Colombetti, M.: Specifying and Enforcing Norms in Artificial Institutions. In: Baldoni, M., Son, T.C., van Riemsdijk, M.B., Winikoff, M. (eds.) DALT 2008. LNCS (LNAI), vol. 5397, pp. 1–17. Springer, Heidelberg (2009)
3. Fornara, N., Colombetti, M.: Specifying Artificial Institutions in the Event Calculus. In: Dignum, V. (ed.) Handbook of Research on Multi-Agent Systems: Semantics and Dynamics of Organizational Models. Information science reference, ch. XIV, pp. 335–366. IGI Global (2009)
4. Fornara, N., Colombetti, M.: Representation and monitoring of commitments and norms using OWL. AI Commun. 23(4), 341–356 (2010)
5. Hitzler, P., Krötzsch, M., Rudolph, S.: Foundations of Semantic Web Technologies. Chapman & Hall/CRC (2009)

A Retrospective on the Reactive Event Calculus and Commitment Modeling Language

Paolo Torroni[1], Federico Chesani[1], Paola Mello[1], and Marco Montali[2]

[1] DISI, University of Bologna, Italy
{paolo.torroni,federico.chesani,paola.mello}@unibo.it
[2] KRDB, Free University of Bozen-Bolzano, Italy
montali@inf.unibz.it

Abstract. *Social commitments in time: Satisfied or compensated* was the title of a presentation given at the 7th DALT workshop edition [34] in which we proposed a layered architecture for modeling and reasoning about social commitments. We gave emphasis to modularity and to the need of accommodating certain temporal aspects in order for a commitment modeling framework to be flexible enough to adapt to diverse commitment theories, and expressive enough to model realistic scenarios. We grounded the framework on two formalisms: the Reactive Event Calculus ($\mathcal{REC}$) and the Commitment Modeling Language ($\mathcal{CML}$). In this retrospective, we review recent developments of this line of work, and discuss our contribution in a broader context of related research.

1 A Short Introduction to $\mathcal{REC}$ and $\mathcal{CML}$

Social commitments are a well-known concept in Multi-Agent Systems (MAS) research [8, 31]. They are commitments made from an agent to another agent to bring about a certain property. In broad terms, a social commitment represents the commitment that an agent, called *debtor*, has towards another agent, called *creditor*, to bring about some property or state of affairs, which is the *subject* of the commitment. In some instantiations of this idea, such as [18, 37], the subject of a commitment is a temporal logic formula.

Representing the commitments that the agents have to one another and specifying constraints on their interactions in terms of commitments provides a principled basis for agent interactions [35]. From a MAS modelling perspective, a role can be modelled by a set of commitments. For example, a seller in an online market may be understood as committing to its price quotes and a buyer may be understood as committing to paying for goods received. Commitments also serve as a natural tool to resolve design ambiguities. The formal semantics enables verification of conformance and reasoning about the MAS specifications [17] to define core interaction patterns and build on them by reuse, refinement, and composition.

Central to the whole approach is the idea of manipulation of commitments: their creation, discharge, delegation, assignment, cancellation, and release, since commitments are stateful objects that change in time as events occur. Time

C. Sakama et al. (Eds.): DALT 2011, LNAI 7169, pp. 120–127, 2012.

and events are, therefore, essential elements. Literature distinguishes between *base-level* commitments, written $\mathsf{C}(x, y, p)$, and *conditional* commitments, written $\mathsf{CC}(x, y, p, q)$ (x is the debtor, y is the creditor, and p/q are properties). $\mathsf{CC}(x, y, p, q)$ signifies that if p is brought out, x will be committed towards y to bring about q.

In our DALT 2009 paper *Social commitments in time: Satisfied or compensated* [34], we drew inspiration from work by Mallya *et al.* [24] and gave emphasis to temporal aspects of commitments. We wanted to propose an expressive enough notation, to be able to model commitment properties that have to be satisfied at specific time points or along specific intervals, and introduce a notion of compensation, with a mind on some scenarios in which social commitments may realistically be used. To this end, we identified a number of desiderata for social commitment frameworks. We then defined a new notation for commitments and commitment specification programs: the Commitment Modeling Language ($\mathcal{CML}$). Finally, we proposed an abstract commitment framework architecture and a concrete instance of it that supports $\mathcal{CML}$. In such an instance, temporal reasoning with commitments is operationalized using the Reactive Event Calculus ($\mathcal{REC}$), and various verification tasks can be accomplished thanks to an underlying declarative, computational logic-based framework.

The architecture proposed in [34] consists of four layers: a *user application* layer, a *commitment modeling* layer, a *temporal representation and reasoning* layer, and a *reasoning and verification* layer.

On the top layer, the user can define contracts or social interaction rules using commitments. Such definitions are based on a language provided by the layer below. The commitment modeling language is implemented using a temporal representation and reasoning framework, which is in turn built on top of a more general reasoning and verification framework, which lies at the bottom layer. It is important to rely on a formal framework that accommodates various forms of verification, because in this way commitments can be operationalized and the user can formally analyze commitment-based contracts, reason on the state of commitments, plan for actions needed to reach states of fulfillment, and track the evolution of commitments at run-time. Indeed, the underlying reasoning and verification layer must be powerful enough to accommodate temporal representation and reasoning.

Our proposal also included a concrete instance of such an architecture. We report it here (see Fig. 1). At the bottom of the stack lay a number of Prolog+CLP modules, which implement the SCIFF family of proof-procedures and provide the SCIFF language to the layer above [1]. The SCIFF framework is based on abductive logic programming and it consists of a declarative specification language and a family of proof-procedures for reasoning from SCIFF specifications. Some kinds of reasoning are: deduction, hypothetical reasoning, static verification of properties, compliance checking and run-time monitoring. In general, SCIFF comes in handy for a number of useful tasks in the context of agent interaction. Its main metaphor is that of *expectation* about events. A simple introduction to SCIFF and its usage is given in [35], where expectations are

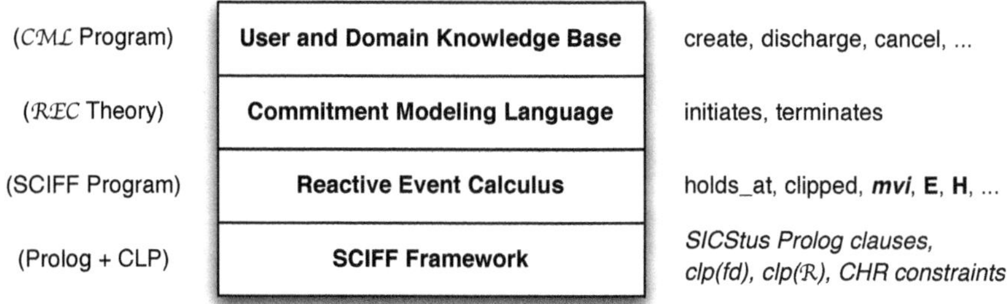

Fig. 1. Social commitment framework architecture

discussed in relation with commitments. The CLP solvers integrated in SCIFF can work with discrete and dense domains, depending on the application needs, and they are particularly useful for reasoning along the temporal dimension.

On top of the SCIFF layer we find the $\mathcal{REC}$: a SCIFF implementation of the $\mathcal{EC}$, which enables runtime verification [9]. In the third layer, the constructs that define $\mathcal{CML}$ are written by way of $\mathcal{REC}$ theories. Thus this layer provides the top layer with the language to write a $\mathcal{CML}$ program. The top layer consists of user and domain-dependent knowledge encoded into a $\mathcal{CML}$ program.

A sample $\mathcal{CML}$ program taken from [34] is the following one, which models a car rental contract inspired from a scenario due to [24]:

$$create(rent\_a\_car(T_c, T_e), \mathsf{C}(r, c, [T_c, T_c + 2days]great\_car)). \tag{1}$$

$$\begin{aligned} create(car\_broken(T_b), \mathsf{C}(r, c, [T_r]replace\_car)) \leftarrow \\ T_r \leq T_b + 24hours, holds([T_b]viol(\mathsf{C}(r, c, [T_s, T_e]great\_car), T_b)). \end{aligned} \tag{2}$$

Renting a car at time T_c until T_e creates a commitment that for 2 days as of T_c the car does not break down. The car breaking down at a time T_b creates a commitment that the car must be replaced within 24 hours of the incident, if the breakdown has caused a breach of commitment.

2 Recent Developments

Our implementation of $\mathcal{REC}$ on top of the SCIFF framework addressed an issue which had initially been introduced in [35], namely the reconciliation of commitments and expectations. Since the publication of [9], the $\mathcal{REC}$ framework has been fully implemented and is now distributed within the j-$\mathcal{REC}$ tool for run-time monitoring [10]. j-$\mathcal{REC}$, which embeds a tuProlog reasoner,[1] can be downloaded from `http://www.inf.unibz.it/~montali/tools.html#jREC`.

A significant and recent research direction, which is still subject of ongoing work, is monitoring and diagnosis of business contract exceptions. In [20–22],

[1] `http://sourceforge.net/projects/tuprolog`

Kafalı *et al.* study misalignment of commitments with temporal constraints. Misalignment is an undesirable situation in contract-regulated interactions, because it may bring about exceptions. To detect and therefore address occurrences of misalignment in an intrinsically distributed environment such as a multi-agent system or e-commerce setting, in [20] the authors present a diagnosis algorithm where agents reason based on the current states of their commitments. They also provide a method for automatic realignment, which can be applied by an agent when the diagnosis algorithm identifies a misalignment. $\mathcal{REC}$ is used to formalize the agent interactions in a delivery process scenario inspired from e-commerce.

As misalignments are typically due to mistakes in the delegation process, [21] and its extended version [22] focus on the notion of delegation. The authors propose a systematic classification of commitment delegation types, and identify *similarity* relations, to formalize connections among commitments. Understanding similarities enables handling exceptions in contract-regulated systems. In particular, it helps identifying possible reasons of exceptions by considering time-related commitments and "improper" ways of delegating such commitments, which may bring about inconsistent states. Again, the exception diagnosis framework is implemented in $\mathcal{REC}$.

The theoretical foundations of $\mathcal{REC}$, which we started to investigate in [9], were further explored in [11]. There we evaluate $\mathcal{REC}$ theoretically, discussing its formal properties and the use of negation, as well as from a practical perspective, by means of a examples dealing with quantitative temporal aspects, violations and compensations. On the application side, a recent survey [7] shows how $\mathcal{REC}$ has been applied to a variety of application domains, namely business process modeling, service-oriented computing, clinical guidelines and multi-agent systems. With respect to these different global computing domains, the survey identifies some challenges posed by concrete monitoring applications, showing how $\mathcal{REC}$ addresses them.

With respect to the multi-agent systems domain, we found that $\mathcal{REC}$ is successful not only in modeling and reasoning about e-commerce style contracts, but also in representing and reasoning upon the dynamic relations between agents and roles in multi-agent organizations [12] and in the context of agent-based simulation [13], for example to dynamically evaluate whether a running simulation is compliant with a given commitment-based contract, or to provide useful information to the interacting agents, helping them exhibit a compliant behaviour.

3 Related Work

We complete this retrospective with a brief survey on recent work by other authors, which is closely related to [9]. Two very relevant stuies by Yolum *et al.* were presented at DALT 2011 [19, 23]. The first one studies commitments in relation to each other. Following and extending our formalization of commitments based on $\mathcal{REC}/\mathcal{CML}$ [34, 9] Günay and Yolum identify key *conflict* relations among commitments. Conflict detection enables detecting a commitment violation before the actual violation occurs during agent interaction, and this knowledge can be used to guide an agent to avoid the violation. It can also be used during creation of multi-agent contracts to identify conflicts in the contracts. The authors implement their method in $\mathcal{REC}$. The second article, by Kafalı and Yolum, proposes a method to check if an agent's state complies with its projections, i.e., what they expect the outcome of a commitment-based contract to be, based on its content as well as their past experiences and the current world state. These projected states represent an agent's expectations from the future. The authors also propose a satisfiability relation, to check if an agent's state complies with its projections, and relate satisfiability with the occurrence of exceptions. The examples used in the paper show the importance of an explicit representation of (metric) time, especially in the subject of a commitment.

El Menshawy *et al.* [16, 26] addresses verification of social commitments and time following an approach alternative to our rule-based $\mathcal{REC}/\mathcal{CML}$ languages. The authors focus on the semantics of commitment operations, and propose a logical model based on an original extension of CTL^* with commitments and operations, and a new definition of assignment and delegation operations by considering the relationship between the original and new commitment contents. For the verification task, they rely on off-the-shelf symbolic model checkers such as NuSMV and MCMAS. The reader may be interested in comparing model checking-based and logic programming-based verification, especially in the context of domains that naturally lend themselves to declarative specifications, such as open multi-agent systems whose interactions are specified by social commitments. Montali *et al.* [28] present such a comparison, based on experimental results. Unfortunately, there is not much literature on this topic, also due to lack of benchmarks.

In a number of recent publications [4–6, 3, 25], Marengo *et al.* focus on the distinction between regulative and constitutive rules, and propose a new formalization of commitments where temporal regulations are incorporated as content of the commitments, using LTL as an underlying temporal language. This line of research suggests a possible future development of the $\mathcal{REC}/\mathcal{CML}$ framework, in which a explicit representation of time and the distinction between regulative and constitutive rules are combined in a unified framework. Some preliminary results on the formal relations between LTL and SCIFF are discussed in [27].

Frameworks for reasoning about events in time are rapidly gaining importance. In [2], Artikis *et al.* review representative approaches of logic-based event recognition, which is a key issue for many new applications that require efficient techniques for automated transformation of large data volumes into operational knowledge. A direction for future research is the evaluation of $\mathcal{REC}$'s reasoning efficiency, both theoretically and empirically. Although $\mathcal{REC}$ is implemented and used, such a systematic evaluation is still missing. Efficiency of temporal reasoning frameworks is an issue also for Patkos *et al.* [29, 30], who use the Jess rule-based system[2] to implement their Event Calculus reasoner. Urovi *et al.* [36] study selected versions of the Event Calculus to support efficient temporal reasoning without compromising the expressive power required to specify

[2] `http://www.jessrules.com`

norm-governed systems. Pros and cons of different implementations of the Event Calculus, taking into account reactivity, efficiency, intended application, and amenability to formal analysis, are also discussed by Chesani *et al.* in [11, 7].

Other interesting proposals for temporal representation and reasoning in the context of multi-agent systems are the action languages recently introduced by Pontelli *et al.*, applied to multi-agent planning [15] and commitment specification [32, 33]. In these last two articles, the authors show how the problem of verifying commitments or identifying pending commitments can be posed as queries to a narrative with commitments.

4 Conclusion

The abundance of recent proposals for modeling and representing events in time, especially in the context of commitments, demonstrates that this is a lively area, which has a good potential for further growth while posing at the same time interesting challenges. A reason for that is that there are many new applications requiring efficient and powerful techniques for describing and monitoring events in open domains. One such domain is multi-agent systems, where interactions can be described by way of commitment-based contracts. The $\mathcal{REC}/\mathcal{CML}$ framework we introduced in [34, 9] proposed an approach to these issues that aimed to be effective, both in terms of expressiveness (by accommodating metric time) and practical usability (by relying on procedures that make use of efficient, constraint-based solvers). Our initial work motivated further research, in contexts such as multi-agent contract exception handling, organization modeling and simulation.

In the future, we plan to integrate $\mathcal{REC}/\mathcal{CML}$ in a possible commitment-based middleware for agent development, such as that envisaged by Chopra and Singh [14]. There, instead of low-level communication primitives such as *send* and *receive*, the API would expose commitment-based operations such as *create*, *delegate*, *update*, and so on, and support listeners for commitment-related events. Another challenge we intend to take on is the systematic evaluation of our framework. However, performing an objective analysis of $\mathcal{REC}/\mathcal{CML}$ in relation with other commitment modeling and verification frameworks could be hard, due to a lack of suitable benchmarks. For this reason, in our works we took inspiration from what we considered realistic scenarios, and in [34] we attempted to define a number of desiderata for a commitment modeling framework.

References

1. Alberti, M., Chesani, F., Gavanelli, M., Lamma, E., Mello, P., Torroni, P.: Verifiable agent interaction in abductive logic programming: the SCIFF framework. ACM Transactions on Computational Logic 9(4), 1–43 (2008)
2. Artikis, A., Skarlatidis, A., Portet, F., Paliouras, G.: Logic-based event recognition. Knowledge Engineering Review (to appear)
3. Baldoni, M., Baroglio, C., Marengo, E.: Behavior-oriented commitment-based protocols. In: Proc. 19th ECAI. Frontiers in Artificial Intelligence and Applications, vol. 215, pp. 137–142. IOS Press (2010)

4. Baldoni, M., Baroglio, C., Marengo, E.: Constraints among commitments: Regulative specification of interaction protocols. In: Proc. AC 2010, Toronto, Canada, pp. 2–18 (May 2010), http://users.encs.concordia.ca/~bentahar/AC2010/AC2010.htm
5. Baldoni, M., Baroglio, C., Marengo, E.: Commitment-Based Protocols with Behavioral Rules and Correctness Properties of MAS. In: Omicini, A., Sardina, S., Vasconcelos, W. (eds.) DALT 2010. LNCS, vol. 6619, pp. 60–77. Springer, Heidelberg (2011)
6. Baldoni, M., Baroglio, C., Marengo, E., Patti, V.: Constitutive and regulative specifications of commitment protocols: A decoupled approach. ACM Transactions on on Intelligent Systems and Technology (to appear)
7. Bragaglia, S., Chesani, F., Mello, P., Montali, M., Torroni, P.: Reactive event calculus for monitoring global computing applications. In: Essays in Honour of Marek Sergot: Computational Logic for Normative Systems. Springer, Heidelberg (to appear)
8. Castelfranchi, C.: Commitments: From individual intentions to groups and organizations. In: Proc. 1st ICMAS, pp. 41–48. The MIT Press (1995)
9. Chesani, F., Mello, P., Montali, M., Torroni, P.: Commitment tracking via the reactive event calculus. In: Proc. 21st IJCAI, pp. 91–96. AAAI (2009)
10. Chesani, F., Mello, P., Montali, M., Torroni, P.: A REC-based commitment tracking tool. In: 10th AI*IA/TABOO Italian Joint Workshop "From Objects to Agents", WOA 2009 (2009)
11. Chesani, F., Mello, P., Montali, M., Torroni, P.: A logic-based, reactive calculus of events. Fundamenta Informaticae 105(1-2), 135–161 (2010)
12. Chesani, F., Mello, P., Montali, M., Torroni, P.: Role Monitoring in Open Agent Societies. In: Jędrzejowicz, P., Nguyen, N.T., Howlet, R.J., Jain, L.C. (eds.) KES-AMSTA 2010, Part I. LNCS, vol. 6070, pp. 112–121. Springer, Heidelberg (2010)
13. Chesani, F., Mello, P., Montali, M., Torroni, P.: Monitoring time-aware commitments within agent-based simulation environments. Cybernetics and Systems 42(7), 546–566 (2011)
14. Chopra, A.K., Singh, M.P.: Elements of a Business-Level Architecture for Multiagent Systems. In: Braubach, L., Briot, J.-P., Thangarajah, J. (eds.) ProMAS 2009. LNCS, vol. 5919, pp. 15–30. Springer, Heidelberg (2010)
15. Dovier, A., Formisano, A., Pontelli, E.: An investigation of multi-agent planning in clp. Fundamenta Informaticae 105(1-2), 79–103 (2010)
16. El-Menshawy, M., Bentahar, J., Dssouli, R.: Verifiable Semantic Model for Agent Interactions Using Social Commitments. In: Dastani, M., El Fallah Segrouchni, A., Leite, J., Torroni, P. (eds.) LADS 2009. LNCS, vol. 6039, pp. 128–152. Springer, Heidelberg (2010)
17. Fisher, M., Bordini, R.H., Hirsch, B., Torroni, P.: Computational logics and agents: A road map of current technologies and future trends. Computational Intelligence 23(1), 61–91 (2007)
18. Fornara, N., Colombetti, M.: Operational specification of a commitment-based agent communication language. In: Proc. 1st AAMAS, pp. 536–542. ACM Press (2002)
19. Gunay, A., Yolum, P.: Detecting Conflicts in Commitments. In: Sakama, C., et al. (eds.) DALT 2011. LNCS (LNAI), vol. 7169, pp. 51–66. Springer, Heidelberg (2012)
20. Kafalı, Ö., Chesani, F., Torroni, P.: What Happened to My Commitment? Exception Diagnosis among Misalignment and Misbehavior. In: Dix, J., Leite, J., Governatori, G., Jamroga, W. (eds.) CLIMA XI. LNCS (LNAI), vol. 6245, pp. 82–98. Springer, Heidelberg (2010)
21. Kafali, O., Torroni, P.: Diagnosing commitments: delegation revisited (extended abstract). In: Proc. 10th AAMAS, IFAAMAS, pp. 1175–1176 (2011)

22. Kafalı, Ö., Torroni, P.: Social Commitment Delegation and Monitoring. In: Leite, J., Torroni, P., Ågotnes, T., Boella, G., van der Torre, L. (eds.) CLIMA XII 2011. LNCS, vol. 6814, pp. 171–189. Springer, Heidelberg (2011)
23. Kafali, O., Yolum, P.: A distributed treatment of exceptions in multiagent contracts (preliminary report). In: Proc. 9th DALT, pp. 65–78 (2011)
24. Mallya, A.U., Yolum, p., Singh, M.P.: Resolving Commitments among Autonomous Agents. In: Dignum, F.P.M. (ed.) ACL 2003. LNCS (LNAI), vol. 2922, pp. 166–182. Springer, Heidelberg (2004)
25. Marengo, E., Baldoni, M., Baroglio, C., Chopra, A.K., Patti, V., Singh, M.P.: Commitments with regulations: Reasoning about safety and control in REGULA. In: Proc. 10th AAMAS, IFAAMAS, pp. 843–850 (2011)
26. Menshawy, M.E., Bentahar, J., Qu, H., Dssouli, R.: On the verification of social commitments and time. In: Proc. 10th AAMAS, IFAAMAS, pp. 483–490 (2011)
27. Montali, M.: Specification and Verification of Declarative Open Interaction Models. A Logic-Based Approach. LNBIP, vol. 56, pp. 383–385. Springer, Heidelberg (2010)
28. Montali, M., Torroni, P., Alberti, M., Chesani, F., Gavanelli, M., Lamma, E., Mello, P.: Verification from Declarative Specifications Using Logic Programming. In: Garcia de la Banda, M., Pontelli, E. (eds.) ICLP 2008. LNCS, vol. 5366, pp. 440–454. Springer, Heidelberg (2008)
29. Patkos, T.: A formal theory for reasoning about action, knowledge and time. PhD thesis, Department of Computer Science, University of Crete, Greece (2010)
30. Patkos, T., Plexousakis, D.: Efficient epistemic reasoning in partially observable dynamic domains using hidden causal dependencies. In: Proc. 9th NRAC, pp. 55–62 (2011), `http://ijcai-11.iiia.csic.es/files/proceedings/W4-NRAC11-Proceedings.pdf#page=59`
31. Singh, M.P.: An ontology for commitments in multiagent systems: Toward a unification of normative concepts. Artificial Intelligence and Law 7, 97–113 (1999)
32. Son, T., Pontelli, E., Sakama, C.: Formalizing Commitments Using Action Languages. In: Sakama, C., et al. (eds.) DALT 2011. LNCS (LNAI), vol. 7169, pp. 67–83. Springer, Heidelberg (2012)
33. Son, T., Pontelli, E., Sakama, C.: Formalizing commitments using action languages. In: Proc. 10th Symposium on Logical Formalizations of Commonsense Reasoning. AAAI Spring Symposium Series. Stanford University (2011)
34. Torroni, P., Chesani, F., Mello, P., Montali, M.: Social Commitments in Time: Satisfied or Compensated. In: Baldoni, M., Bentahar, J., van Riemsdijk, M.B., Lloyd, J. (eds.) DALT 2009. LNCS, vol. 5948, pp. 228–243. Springer, Heidelberg (2010)
35. Torroni, P., Yolum, P., Singh, M.P., Alberti, M., Chesani, F., Gavanelli, M., Lamma, E., Mello, P.: Modelling interactions via commitments and expectations. In: Handbook of Research on Multi-Agent Systems: Semantics and Dynamics of Organizational Models, pp. 263–284. IGI Global, Hershey (2009)
36. Urovi, V., Bromuri, S., Stathis, K., Artikis, A.: Run-time support for norm-governed systems. Technical Report CSD-TR-10-01, Royal Holloway, University of London, UK (2010), `http://golem.cs.rhul.ac.uk/TR/CSD-TR-10-01.pdf`
37. Yolum, P., Singh, M.: Flexible protocol specification and execution: applying event calculus planning using commitments. In: Proc. 1st AAMAS, pp. 527–534. ACM Press (2002)

Web Service Composition via Organisation-Based (Re)Planning

David Corsar, Alison Chorley, and Wamberto W. Vasconcelos

Department of Computing Science, University of Aberdeen, Aberdeen, UK
{dcorsar,a.h.chorley,w.w.vasconcelos}@abdn.ac.uk

Abstract. The benefits of Service Oriented Architectures (SOA) for business, such as reduced costs and development time, are well recognised, however one of the most challenging steps in using SOA is defining the correct composition of services for a particular business process. Quickly recognised as a task where computer automation could help, various approaches have been proposed, including the use of AI techniques for planning service compositions. However, these techniques can perform poorly due to the search space explosion caused by dealing with the vast number of available services that must be composed. In this paper we present an approach to composing Web services, using software agents to enact plans of actions which achieve organisational goals, where each action specifies what should be achieved as opposed to which service to use. When enacting an action, agents use a matchmaking process to determine services that can be used to achieve the desired effects, intelligently handling any errors that may occur. The action plans are based on an organisation model in which organisational goals are refined into scenes, landmarks, and objectives, allowing the set of actions available to the plan synthesis mechanism to be tailored to the goal being targeted at that specific time, further reducing the planning search space.

1 Introduction

The Service Oriented Architectures (SOA) paradigm, in which services are composed to form systems which implement business processes, has various technological and business benefits. Given the (constantly increasing) vast number of services available on the web, and bearing in mind the dynamic nature of services (disappearing and re-appearing in different versions), manually building and managing such compositions (and keeping them up-to-date) has become very difficult [18,19], and (semi-)automated computer support is necessary.

With the creation of languages such as BPEL4WS [2] and OWL-S [11] for describing services, and defining the flow of a process with bindings between services, several researchers have proposed methods for computer support [7], including the use of AI planning techniques to automatically determine service compositions (surveyed in [19]). However, as [4] discusses, this task is hard as these approaches focus on composing stateless atomic services, failing to take into account the complex business protocols involved. Further, [9] argue that the

C. Sakama et al. (Eds.): DALT 2011, LNAI 7169, pp. 128–148, 2012.

high number of available services and service compositions create large planning search spaces making classical AI approaches to planning unfeasible for this task.

Once the difficult task of defining a composition has been achieved, either manually or automatically, it is natural to then want to execute and monitor the composition. While various platforms exist for enacting service compositions expressed in BPEL4WS (such as Eclipse BPEL[1], BPWS4J[2]), and OWL-S (OWL-S API[3]), few projects, such as CASCOM[4] and Astro[5], incorporate automated composition, execution, and monitoring. The handling of errors during the execution is also important for large scale, intelligent software, however there appears to be very little work on this (the Astro project and [20] are two exceptions).

The ALIVE project[6] [1,14,24] aims to address these issues, by providing a framework in which plans of abstract actions to achieve organisational goals are used by agents to dynamically produce a service composition. ALIVE plans do not refer to actual services; rather each action in a plan defines the preconditions that must be satisfied before the action is performed and the effects of performing the action. Agents within a multiagent system (MAS) coordinate the enactment of the plan, performing each step by selecting an appropriate service to achieve the action by using a semantic matchmaking process over a repository of service descriptions. A planning process is used to determine the action plan; however, as actions are more abstract than services, there should be far fewer actions than services, with multiple services matching any one action (for example, an action to purchase a book could be achieved through use of any one of a variety of services), which helps to reduce the planner's search space. Further, we make use of organisation concepts that describe, at an abstract level, how processes are performed in a given organisation. These descriptions consist of a set of scenes, each consisting of a set of landmarks which are in turn decomposed into objectives, to further reduce the planning search space.

ALIVE agents have the ability to manage the service invocation, monitor the plan enactment, and handle any errors that occur. Error handling is performed at several levels: errors with service invocation are handled autonomously, with alternative services being used if possible; if an action cannot be performed, the agents attempt to produce an alternative plan to achieve the goal; if this is not possible, organisational changes can be suggested to resolve the problem.

This paper is an extended version of the work reported in [5], and contains material used in the tutorial "Organisation, Coordination and Norms for Multi-Agent Systems", given at the First International Spring School on Declarative Agent Languages and Technologies (DALT School 2011, Bertinoro, Italy, 10-15 April 2011)[7]. The paper is structured as follows. In section 2 we discuss related

[1] http://www.eclipse.org/bpel/

[2] http://www.alphaworks.ibm.com/tech/bpws4j

[3] http://www.mindswap.org/2004/owl-s/api/

[4] http://www.ist-cascom.org/

[5] http://www.astroproject.org/

[6] The ALIVE project has been co-funded by the European Commission under the 7th Framework Programme for RTD (FP7 215890).

[7] http://lia.deis.unibo.it/confs/dalt_school/

service composition approaches. In section 3 we provide an illustrative use case. In section 4 we introduce the ALIVE architecture. In section 5 we discuss how model-driven development is used in ALIVE for the purposes of planning. In section 6 we discuss how organisation-based plans for service composition are generated and enacted. In section 7 we evaluate our approach, and in section 8 we provide concluding remarks.

2 Related Work

Various approaches to automated service composition have been proposed in the literature, in this section we briefly present approaches based on two different planning frameworks, namely centralised and decentralised [9].

Centralised approaches are characterised by the synthesis of plans composed of basic actions, defined in terms of preconditions and effects, that move from an initial world state to some goal state. To achieve this, centralised approaches make use of AI planning techniques combined with service descriptions defined in terms of preconditions and effects. Roa et al [19] survey a variety of such approaches for web service composition, which make use of mechanisms such as HTN planing [22], planning rules [13], or logic programming [12].

Decentralised approaches attempt to develop plans through the use of agents, each of which has access to a set of Web services and the agents work together to develop a plan (service composition) that will take them from an initial state to a goal state. A key step in the decentralised approach is that, before agents can work together to build a plan, a filtering process is performed to restrict the services available to each agent, in order to make the problem tractable.

The CASCOM project is one of only two approaches we have found using this approach. In the CASCOM approach [10], organisation information is used to filter the services available to each agent, and for selecting services to be considered for inclusion in a composition. An ontology of roles and interactions is used to define the roles each agent plays and to extend service descriptions to specify the roles that provide the service and who the service depends on. These are then used in service matchmaking and service filtering for composition. In service matchmaking, agents requesting a service pass a query which includes the desired provider roles and the roles the requestor can play; this is used by the matchmaker along with the role ontology's taxonomy to select and rank services based on which roles provide the service and which roles the service is dependent on. In service filtering for composition, when no single suitable service can be found, all the plans (composite services) that were created in the past are examined, and ranked according to their relevance based on the class of the roles in the request and those roles used by the services within the plan.

Falou et al. [9], assume that filtering has been performed, and describe a subsequent graph theory-based approach to plan building. Briefly, each agent has a graph of how services available to them can be composed (which are considered to be partial plans), with a planning agent responsible for receiving an initial and goal state and determining a combination of partial plans that will achieve the goal state.

The ALIVE approach to service composition sits between these two approaches: a centralised style planning process is used to determine a plan of actions, with the actual composition evolving as the decentralised agents enact the plan. As we discuss in section 6, the ALIVE approach also makes more extensive use of organisation information than [10], and does not require additional service markup.

3 Example Scenario

We explore a scenario to highlight the challenges involved in providing portability of communication services to which a customer has subscribed; in such scenarios, customers, depending on their context, dynamically request new communication services, as well as change and cancel some of their currently contracted services. More specifically, let us assume that a large cell phone operator would like to extend their communication services to on-line social networks and virtual communities such as SecondLife[8] (SL) or Bebo[9].

These services should support communication through a number of distinct types of media channels such as mobile telephony, plain old telephony services (POTS), video, SMS, e-mail, and instant messaging[10] (IM). We notice that when connecting such disparate channels, our aim is to bring them together to offer users the experience of a seamless cross-channel communication service. Crucially though, it is not realistic to pursue naïve unifications of the underlying technologies: our aim is to produce a virtual communication device – not an IM client glued on to a mobile phone glued on to an e-mail client. The goal should be to allow *the dynamic reconfiguration of communication pathways* based, on the one hand, *on the availability of services* (Does the user have a phone? Is the user currently registered to receive voice-mail messages in Bebo? Is the user currently signed up for a VoIP provider?) and on the other hand, *on the availability of the user.*

Social context, once formally captured, provides knowledge that can be exploited in routing and configuring calls. Players of SL have a social context represented within SL, such as groups, tribes, friends, and so on, but those players also have identities on Facebook[11], Bebo, Orkut[12] and so on. By connecting these identities (through mechanisms such as OpenID[13]) social context can be used to

[8] `http://secondlife.com/`

[9] `http://www.bebo.com/`

[10] Instant messaging puts together various technologies to allow real-time text-based communication between two or more participants over the Internet or some form of internal network/intranet.

[11] `http://www.facebook.com/`

[12] `http://www.orkut.com`

[13] OpenID (`http://openid.net/`) is an open standard for authenticating users which can be used for access control, allowing users to log on to different services with the same digital identity where these services trust the authentication body. OpenID replaces the common login process that uses a login-name and a password, by allowing a user to log in once and gain access to the resources of multiple software systems.The term OpenID can also refer to an ID used in the standard.

reconfigure the services required to effect communication on-the-fly. These social structures involve normative relationships: if A and B are friends on Facebook, they can write on each others' "walls", but that does not mean that, say, they have rights to view each other's data on LinkedIn[14]. However, it might mean that if A wants to communicate with B, A has permission to use a Facebook wall as a medium.

In addition to the technological and social constraints above, software solutions to such scenarios must factor in any regulations governing communication over electronic media. An example of a regulation is the ban the French government imposed in 2005 on research institutes and universities, preventing them from using Skype[15], a popular voice-over the Internet protocol (VoIP) that allows users on its peer-to-peer network to speak to each other over the Internet for free. This ban was due to concerns over the proprietary encryption mechanisms in Skype, and fears that eavesdropping and unauthorised decryption was technically possible. We thus consider in our scenario explicit regulations from the real-world which must be factored into the software solution; we observe that ultimately such regulations should change the behaviour of the software, but encoding regulations in some source programming language is very labour-intensive. We argue that regulations are more naturally captured via an explicit specification of norms (namely, permissions, prohibitions and obligations on components of the solution) that, together with the social context, should define the design space of software solutions.

We call the system under study a "Service Communication Router" (SCR). The main business goals the SCR has to achieve are:

- To satisfy national and European regulations;
- To make portability and customisation of services as transparent as possible to the customer; and
- To provide new added-value services.

Within the broad class of scenarios sketched above, we want to make the discussion more concrete and detail a more concrete example. Let us suppose that Bob is in a band, the AliveA5Os. They have decided to preview their new track in SL. Bob uses his SL communicator to send a message to all of his friends. He types in: "Hi all! Come hear AliveA5Os' new song, Hawaiian Mussels, at 1900CET at Alive Island". The following sequence of events unfolds:

1. Alice is in Bob's tribe on SL. She's tinkering in SL and receives a message through her SL IM client.
2. Henry is a friend of Bob on facebook, and also in Bob's IM friends list. He's working at home and receives the message through his MSN client.
3. Hirta and Max are on holiday. They're friends of Bob on Bebo: when they next check in to an internet cafe, they notice the message waiting for them on Bebo.

---

[14] `http://www.linkedin.com/`

[15] `http://www.skype.com`

4. Verig is the A&R man at Irish Beach records, and is in Bob's LinkedIn network. He's on the move, and receives a call to his mobile; an automated voice reads out the message.
5. Estragon is a close friend of Henry; they're friends on Facebook and in SL. Estragon is in a meeting at work. When he gets out, he has an email in his inbox containing the message.
6. Pandora is using Facebook. Her wall is updated with the message from Bob, and she's impressed and forwards it to her network of friends. They each receive the message in the channel, and on the device most appropriate to them, including Vladimir, who's playing SL and receives a voice call on his SL communicator reading him the message forwarded via Pandora.

3.1 Components of the Scenario

In this section we outline the various components of our scenario. Initially, we list its various stakeholders: we refer to these in a generic fashion, using the *roles* they play. The roles we have chosen to represent in our scenario are:

- *customers* – initiate and receive messages/calls.
- *managers* – represent interfaces to static or dynamic information repositories
- *subscription managers* – responsible for subscription look-up
- *context managers* – responsible for interfacing with the emergent presence determination service
- *profile managers* – responsible for handling user preferences.

The following data are available from customers:

- a set of *subscribed communication services*, each element of which is a tag corresponding to a particular application (*e.g.*, Facebook, SL, etc.)
- a set of *preferences*, comprising a specification of mappings from contexts to channels
- a *context* that can be determined by accessing the emergent presence engine; a context is resolved as a set of tags corresponding to contextual states (*e.g.*, "*in a meeting*", "*at work*", etc.).

The channels are the following communication media:

- *IM* is text-based instant messaging communicated (typically) over XMPP
- *SL-Text* is text-based communications coming from bespoke subsystems in SecondLife
- *POTS* is traditional voice telephony
- *VoIP* is packet-switched voice over IP infrastructure
- *SMS* is standard mobile text messaging.

To deal with messages coming into and going out of the SCR we have various handlers. For the incoming material we have *handle_im* for IM, *handle_pots* for voice calls over POTS, *handle_sms* for text messages and *handle_SL_text* for chat from SecondLife. For outgoing material we provide delivery components, namely, *deliver_sms* to deliver text messages, *deliver_pots* to deliver voice calls and *deliver_email* to deliver email. We also consider transformations that are responsible for performing transcoding tasks. We have *perform_asr* for automated speech recognition and *perform_tts* for text to speech transformation.

When selecting which channel to use, the SCR makes use of functionality *determine_possible* that identifies possible communication channels for a participant and *determine_appropriate*, that identifies appropriate communication channels for a participant (based on the participant's profile and preferences). The SCR accesses a reasoning service *calculate_possible* that supports *determine_possible* and *calculate_appropriate* that supports *determine_appropriate.* The SCR uses functionalities to access other sources of information, namely, *get_preferences*, that accesses the customers' profile data, *get_context*, that accesses emergent presence data, and *get_subscription*, that accesses subscription data.

4 ALIVE Architecture

Figure 1 outlines the key components of the ALIVE architecture related to planning and service composition. Each layer models different aspects of the system, with links between the layers defining correspondences between them. The *Organisation Layer* (OL) provides an abstract model of an agent organisation, including concepts such as roles and their high level objectives (which are shared with the organisation). Combined with landmarks and scenes (discussed in section 5.1) the OL provides an abstract specification of tasks performed in an

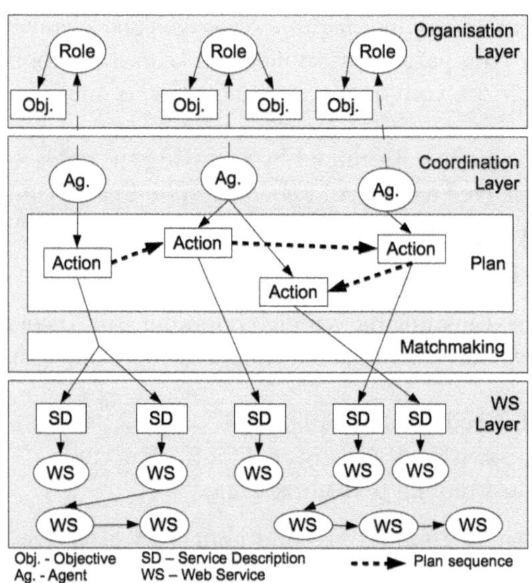

Fig. 1. ALIVE 3-layered architecture

organisation and how they are achieved. The *Coordination Layer* (CL) contains components that are used to synthesise a MAS for the organisation model (OM). Agents in the MAS play organisational roles, and actions define how organisational objectives can actually be achieved. This enables the agents to produce a plan of actions that will achieve those objectives. Agents then coordinate the plan enactment, enacting actions relevant to their role through use of a matchmaking process with the service layer. The matchmaking process analyses service descriptions to determine a set of service(s) that achieve the desired effects of a given action. The agent then selects the "best" service and uses it to enact the action. The *Service Layer* (SL) uses the OWL-S model to provide semantic service descriptions (SDs), in terms of a signature and capabilities. The SD can describe a single service, or act as a façade for describing a composition of services. A framework for invoking services is also provided.

5 ALIVE Models

The ALIVE approach is based on the Eclipse Modeling Framework (EMF)[16] implementation of the Model-Driven Development (MDD) [3] approach to software engineering. In this approach, models are systematically used to represent the important artifacts of a system, with model transformations used to convert instances of one model to instances of another. The ALIVE architecture uses three meta-models (top level models), one for each layer, which developers instantiate using graphical editors we have developed, to create models of the different layers of their system. In this section we provide a summary of the organisation model (OM) (section 5.1) and coordination model (CM) (section 5.2); the service model, which provides the service descriptions, is an EMF representation of the OWL-S ontologies, and so not discussed here (for a description of the OWL-S ontologies, see [11]).

5.1 The Organisation Model

The Organisation Model (OM) describes an agent organisation, defining the structure of the society, roles and interactions as intended by the organisation's stakeholders. The OM is strongly based on the OperettA approach to organisation modeling; for more details on OperettA see [15].

Briefly, an organisation model is composed of two structures relevant here. We have a social structure (SS), which describes the society's objectives (which can be recursively decomposed in terms of their sub-objectives), roles (in terms of their name and objectives shared with the organisation), and coordination mechanisms (dependencies) between roles. We also have an Interaction Structure (IS), which describes, at an abstract level, patterns of interaction within the organisation.

An IS consists of (multiple) scene(s), each describing a scenario of activity within the organisation, and the acceptable scene transitions (the order in which

[16] `http://www.eclipse.org/emf`

scenes can be enacted). Each scene is described by its players (roles involved in the scene), results (achieved landmarks), and landmark patterns. Each landmark pattern defines a series of landmarks (important states in the scene's execution, defined by objectives achieved when that landmark is reached) which along with partial orderings between the landmarks (specifying that one landmark must be achieved before another), specify one way to complete the scene.

The use case OM is as outlined in Figure 2, which decomposes (top-down) the various OM concepts, and shows ordering (left-to-right) between scenes and landmarks. Briefly, our SCR's IS contains three scenes, one of which,

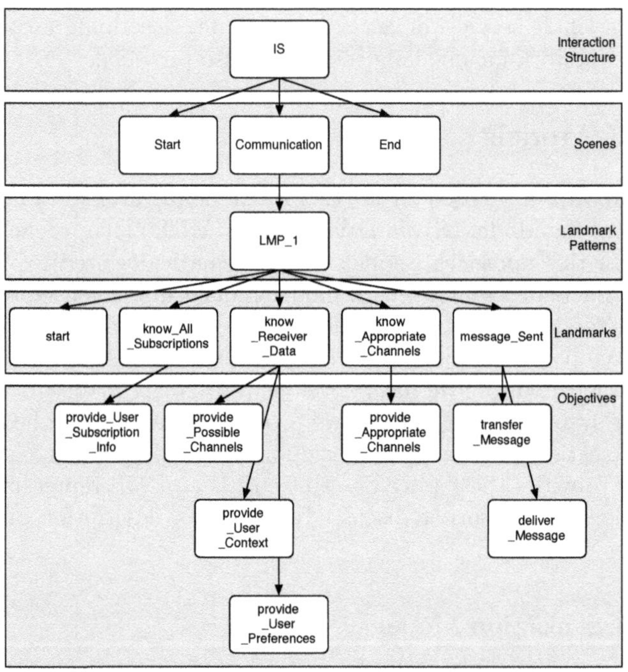

Fig. 2. Organisation Model for the Service Communication Router (SCR)

Communication is expanded further. The *Communication* scene has one landmark pattern, which has five landmarks, ordered via partial orderings into the sequence: *start*, *know_ All_Subscriptions*, *know_Receiver_data*, *know_Appropriate_ Channels*, and *message_Sent*. The last four landmarks entail the objectives that must be achieved for the landmark to be reached (for example, the objective *provide_User_Subscript-ion_Info* must be achieved to reach the *know_All_Subscriptions* landmark). Table 1 specifies the role associated with each objective (the table also presents actions – these will be introduced and discussed below).

Table 1. Correspondences between the OL and CL for the SCR Models

Objective	Role	Action
provide_User_Subscription_Info	*Subscription_Manager*	*provide_User_Subscription_Info*
provide_Possible_Channels	*Channel_Manager*	*provide_Possible_Channels*
provide_User_Context	*Context_Manager*	*provide_User_Context*
provide_User_Preferences	*Profile_Manager*	*provide_User_Preferences*
provide_Appropriate_Channels	*Channel_Manager*	*provide_Appropriate_Channels*
transform_Message	*Transformation_Manager*	*transform_message*
deliver_Message	*Delivery_Manager*	*deliver_message*

5.2 The Coordination Model

The Coordination Model (CM) is composed of three sub-models, each of which describes a different aspect of the CL. The three sub-models are: the action model, which describes activities that can be carried out at the CL; the agent model, which describes the agents that will enact the actions, and the plan/task model which describes plans of actions and the tasks (planning problems) the plans are designed to achieve. All these are presented in Section 5.2.

Describing Actions. The action model describes the CL behaviours that achieve aspects of the OM, such as the objectives, landmarks, and scenes. The action model is based on the OWL-S process model [11], and describes an action in terms of its name, inputs, outputs, preconditions, and effect. There are two types of actions: atomic actions, which are standalone actions that have a direct effect on the world when performed; and composite actions, which are composed of other actions and have an indirect effect on the world (the actual effect is defined by the atomic actions selected to perform the composite action).

There are seven different constructs available for describing how the referenced actions of a composite action are composed, most of which recursively refer to other constructs:

1. *any-order*: a set of constructs to be performed in any order.
2. *choice*: a set of constructs, one of which should be performed.
3. *if-then-else*: under a certain condition, perform one construct, else perform another.
4. *perform*: refers to an action to be performed.
5. *repeat-until*: repeat a construct until a condition is true.
6. *repeat-while*: repeat a construct while a condition is true.
7. *sequence*: a list of constructs to be performed in order.
8. *split*: a set of constructs to be performed in parallel.
9. *split-join*: like split, but control flow should wait for all constructs to be completed before continuing.

Describing an Agent System. The agent model describes the different agents that constitute a MAS representing the organisation. Each agent in the MAS is described in terms of its name, the role(s) from the organisation that it is playing, and the (CL) action(s) it is capable of performing.

Describing Plans and Tasks. The plan/task model describes the action plans that the agents attempt to enact. The plan model is similar to a grounding of OWL-S services [11], consisting of a sequence of action groundings. Each action grounding references the action that should be performed at that point in the plan and bindings between inputs of that action and actual values. Tasks, which are used as planning problems for a planner (currently JSHOP2), describe the initial world state and the action(s) that the planner should attempt to generate a plan to perform, along with any input values for those action(s).

5.3 Deriving Models

One of the strengths of the Model-Driven Development (MDD) approach is that it provides strong support for model transformations. Model transformations are essentially a script consisting of rules specifying how to generate new artifacts from elements of existing models. There are two types of transformation: model-to-model (M2M), which generate a new model (instances of a meta-model) from an existing model (instances of another meta-model); and model-to-text, which populates templates with values from a model, for example, generating text specifying a planning domain and problem for a planner. In this section we describe two M2M transformations used by ALIVE for deriving action (section 5.3) and agent (section 5.4) models.

Deriving Organisational Actions. The OM provides abstract descriptions of the processes undertaken by an organisation, while the CL actions describe how OM processes can be achieved by agents. To ensure the agents can determine how to achieve each OM process, we have defined an M2M transformation script which generates a set of CL actions from relevant OM concepts. Briefly, the rules of this M2M transformation are:

1. A composite action with the name "IS" is created based on the Interaction Structure (IS) in the organisation model. This action is composed of the following scene actions.
2. For each scene in the IS, a composite action with name "scene_<scene-name>" is created. These actions are composed of the following landmark pattern actions.
3. For each landmark pattern in a scene, a composite action with name "LMP_X" is created. This action is composed of the following landmark actions.
4. For each landmark in a landmark pattern, a composite action with name "LM_<landmark-name>" is created. This action is composed of the following objective actions for every objective entailed by the landmark.
5. For objectives with sub-objectives, a composite action with name "<objective-name>" is created, composed of objective actions for each sub-objective of the objective.
6. For objectives with no sub-objectives, an atomic action with name "<objective-name>" is created.

The rules also attempt to add as much detail as possible from the OM, such as using the scene transitions and landmark patterns to infer an ordering for the corresponding actions through the use of appropriate control constructs. Further, every action generated from an objective is assigned as being performed by the role(s) that include that objective as part of their objectives. However, the actions produced by these rules are still incomplete: they do not include details such as inputs, outputs, preconditions, or effects, and it is up to the developer to use the provided editors to add these details. We explain below how these rules operate in our example.

5.4 The Derived SCR Action Model

Figure 3 outlines the action model generated by applying the above transformations to the OM outlined in Figure 2. Briefly, going top-down, a composite action is generated for the IS, composed of a sequence of composite actions for each scene. As the *start* and *end* scenes have no landmark patterns, the corresponding actions are not composed of any actions. The *scene_Communication* action is composed of the landmark pattern composite action *LMP_1*, which in turn

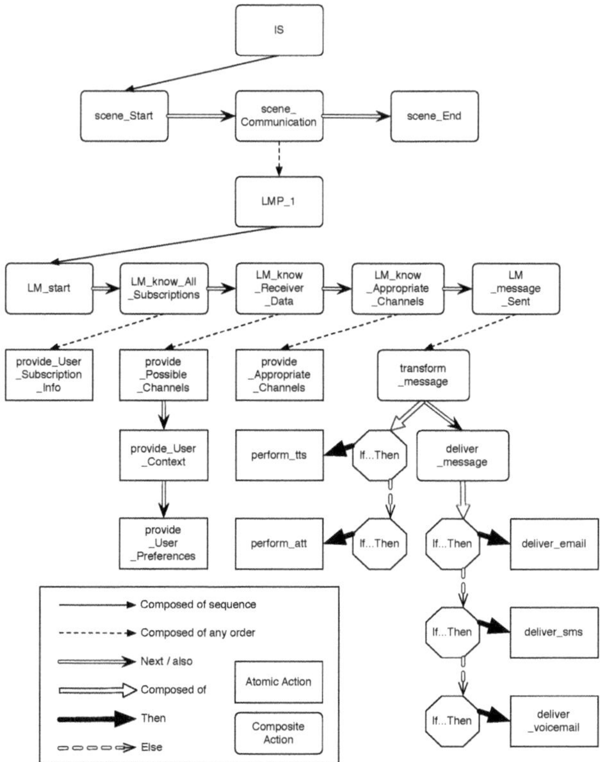

Fig. 3. SCR actions derived from the OM in Figure 2

is composed of a sequence of landmark composite actions. Each landmark action is composed of an any-order set of actions (so the *LM_know_Receiver_Data* action is composed of the atomic actions *provide_Possible_Channels*, *provide_User_Context*, and *provide_User_Preferences* which can be performed in any order). All objectives are initially transformed to atomic actions, however, the actions for the objectives *transform_message* and *deliver_message* have been manually changed to composite actions, which further break down how to achieve the objective (for example, the *transform_message* action selects the appropriate transformation action based on the channel type of the message and the selected appropriate channel[17]). The "If... Then" octagon stands for the "if-then-else" construct to combine actions (with outgoing arrows specifying the "if" and "else" parts).

Along with generating actions, the transformation script also generates a mapping file, which specifies mappings between OM concepts and the corresponding action. Table 1 lists the objective-action correspondences/mappings for the SCR example.

Deriving an Agent Model. Once an OM and corresponding set of actions have been defined, it is possible to derive an agent model for the organisation. We have defined a M2M transformation script which achieves this using the following rules:

1. One agent is generated for each role in the organisation. The agent's name is generated automatically, and the agent is assigned as playing that role.
2. For every action in the action model, if the action is set as being performed by the same role that the agent is playing, then that action is added to the agent's set of actions.

5.5 Code Generation

In addition to the above M2M transformations, the ALIVE architecture also uses M2T transformations to generate program code used for plan synthesis and executable agents. This transformation uses an agent model to generate the code for a MAS for the AgentScape environment[18]. The executable MAS consists of generic agents for planning, event reporting, and service matchmaking, along with a customised agent for each agent defined in the agent model. The functionalities of the agents are discussed in section 6.

6 Organisation-Based Service Compositions

After the generation of the MAS code, the agents can be injected into AgentScape from where they plan for and produce Web service compositions to achieve

[17] The action *perform_tts* performs a text-to-speech transformation, the action *perform_att* performs an audio-to-text transformation.

[18] `http://www.agentscape.org/`

organisational objectives, landmarks, scenes, and ultimately the entire interaction structure. In this section we discuss how plans are generated and enacted to produce Web service compositions dynamically generated at runtime.

6.1 Organisation-Based Planning for Web Service Composition

The planning agent is responsible for generating the necessary plan(s) to achieve the goals of the organisation. To generate plans, the planning agent makes use of the plan synthesis component, which in turn makes use of the JSHOP2 planner. We believe however, that the process is general enough to substitute JSHOP2 for another planner:

Step 1 - Action model instance(s) and a task model instance are passed to the planning component.
Step 2 - The action instance(s) are converted into a planning domain specification, expressed in the chosen planner's syntax through a M2T transformation; the task model is transformed into the planning problem specification for the planner.
Step 3 - The (underlying) planner is then invoked, using the generated planning domain and problem.
Step 4 - Plans generated by the planner are then converted to instances of the plan model, and returned.

One of the key responsibilities of the planning agent is to decide which action(s) the task should refer to. At this point, the planning agent makes use of the OM to reduce the search space for the planner: for example, if the MAS is attempting to achieve the entire IS, the planning agent can set the task action to be the action corresponding to the IS; however, the planning agent may decide (depending on the size of the IS) to split the process down, and produce plans for each scene, landmark pattern, or landmark by using the corresponding action for the task. Due to dependencies between the landmarks that often cannot be handled by the planner (for example, the planner cannot produce a plan for the *LM_message_sent* landmark action until the appropriate channel is known), the planning agent will typically break down the IS to the low-level landmarks and use the corresponding actions to create tasks to perform each landmark in turn.

Having selected the level that planning will be performed for (landmark, landmark pattern, scene, or IS) the planning agent builds the first task (in our example, this would refer to the *LM_know_All_Subscriptions* action), and requests plans from the plan synthesis component to perform that task. The returned plans are checked for norm compliance[19] and the "best" plan (the one(s) that satisfies the most norms and violated the least) is then distributed to the other agents to perform. Once execution of that plan is complete, the planning agent will use the agent's world state (a record of the post-conditions of all actions performed so far) at that point as the precondition of a task to achieve the

[19] Although not discussed in this paper, the OM also defines norms that the agents must comply with when enacting plans.

next landmark (the *LM_know_Receiver_Data* action) and repeat the plan synthesis/selection/distribution steps. This process is repeated until all landmarks (and so the scene) are achieved, at which point the planning agent moves on to the next scene, repeating the process until all the scenes are complete. The post-conditions of actions are recorded with actual values, and these represent the state of the world; having the agents probing and sensing the world is not an option here: for instance, an agent cannot find out whether it sent a message, or that it received a message by sensing the world, unless we made provisions for recording, in a persistent fashion, all messages (and these should be differentiated, when sent twice or more).

6.2 Dynamic Web Service Compositions

Each of the agents interacts with the others to decide on the scheduling of the plan. Once the plan has been scheduled, the agents dynamically build a composition of Web services to perform the plan. For each action in the scheduled plan the agent performing the action follows a set sequence:

1. The precondition of the action is checked against the state of the world to ensure the action can be performed at this time.
2. The agent asks the matchmaking agent for services that will perform the action.
3. The agent chooses a service and invokes it.
4. The agent updates the state of the world and informs the next agent that it has finished successfully.

The agents enact all the actions in the plan until the plan is completed, whereby they inform the planning agent of success. The planning agent will then create a task for the next landmark and the cycle starts again. It is only at this point that it is possible to determine the composition of Web services that were used to perform the plan.

This sequence may fail at several places and is handled in different ways by the agents:

- The plan synthesis component may return zero plans indicating that there is no sequence of actions that can perform the task. If this happens, feedback is provided to the OL suggesting changes to the OM which should help avoid this problem in the future.
- The scheduling of the plan may fail with the agents unable to decide who will do which action and when. If this happens, the agents will inform the planning agent that they need an alternative plan from the set returned by the plan synthesis component.
- The precondition checking may fail, which means that the action cannot be performed in the current state of the world. This may be because the action cannot be performed until another action is performed first, or a preceding

action has caused unexpected side effects when it was performed. If this happens, the agent will call for the other agents to stop enacting the plan and inform the planning agent of the need to replan from the current state of the world.
- The matchmaker agent may return zero services, indicating that there are no services currently available that can perform the action. If this happens, the agent will call for the other agents to stop enacting the plan and inform the planning agent that it is necessary to replan from the current world state avoiding the use of this particular action.
- The invocation of a particular service may fail. If this happens, the agent will try alternative services, possibly asking the matchmaker agent for additional services, until one succeeds or it runs out of services. If there are no services that can perform the action then the agent will call for the other agents to stop enacting the plan and inform the planning agent that it is necessary to replan from the current world state avoiding the use of this particular action.

When it is necessary to replan due to failure, the planning agent has two strategies for replanning: first it will attempt to replan from the current world state but removing the problematic action from the actions passed to the plan synthesis component. If this fails then the planning agent will attempt to find an alternative way to complete the scene, for example by using an alternative landmark pattern.

7 Evaluation

We evaluate our approach in two ways. Initially, we address the adequacy of our approach with respect to desirable features which approaches for engineering the new generation of open software should possess. Then we contrast the planning aspects of ALIVE against exhaustive planning approaches.

7.1 Adequacy of Architecture

Approaches (and associated methodologies and tools) for designing and engineering the new generation of open software should possess the following key features (with their motivation):

1. They should scale up to tackle large-scale applications consisting of hundreds or thousands of components.
2. Due to the sheer size of the applications being built, they should support self-governing software, that is, the engineered applications should "look after themselves". Approaches should thus explicitly factor in feedback loops that enable the connection of runtime phenomena with design-time models and artifacts.
3. To increase application transparency, approaches should accommodate humans in the feedback and governance loops, allowing for potential human intervention in the software management processes.

4. Approaches should allow alternative points of entry in the design process, both to accommodate existing systems (and let developers add further missing parts gradually), as well as different development styles and needs.
5. They should provide a methodology to support and guide the use of (semi-)automatic tools.
6. They should factor in and incorporate existing open standards, allowing for extensions to be easily integrated.

We do not claim that this list is exhaustive, nor that it is novel. It overlaps with challenges and "wish-lists" compiled by the Web services [8], distributed systems [6] and autonomic computing [17,21] communities; we have, however, provided a simple rationale for the inclusion of each item in the list, and we picked those which we can relate with our proposal.

Our approach scales up naturally, addressing item 1 above, as we can accommodate arbitrarily large and complex organisations which, on their turn, will give rise to a high number of software agents; each agent is a self-contained relatively small program, and agents could run in different computers, with more computers being added when needed (and this without changing our architecture). Similarly, the matchmaking mechanism could be replicated in many different computers, avoiding any bottleneck and single-point of failure.

Although not detailed in this paper, an important novelty of the ALIVE architecture is the explicit modelling of feedback loops. The execution of a system engineered with the suite of ALIVE tools causes events to happen; these events concern invocations of Web services (and their responses), the messages the agents exchange among themselves and with the matchmaker, and so on. We have defined an event meta-model, which we use to transform raw events onto alternative formats for different feedback mechanisms. A first feedback loop connects the events stemming from the service layer onto the coordination layer, possibly leading to re-planning. For instance, if attempts to perform an action (possibly using various different service descriptions and Web services) all failed, then the agents should re-plan, avoiding that action. A second feedback loop connects the coordination layer with the organisation layer: if the agents run out of planning options (that is, all plans they attempted failed), then the designers of the organisation should reassess their specification, paying attention to particular points highlighted by the feedback mechanism. For instance, an objective may be unachievable with the current scenes and description of actions and thus an alternative organisation should be designed. These feedback loops address points 2 and 3 of the list above.

The ALIVE approach does not advocate a specific entry point in the three-layered architecture. Indeed, we accommodate three possible development paths, namely, top-down, bottom-up and middle-out, detailed as follows. The top-down path starts from the OL, then moves on to the CL and finally the SL. The bottom-up path addresses legacy systems (making use of Web services): such systems will generate raw events which are mapped onto our event meta-model, thus allowing the feedback mechanisms to process them. The feedback mechanism to the CL is also able to suggest a skeleton for a workflow, based on the partial order among the events, and this workflow is then used to provide a design pattern to the OL. The middle-out path explores the CL-OL bottom-up connection and the CL-SL top-down connection. The different development paths address desirable feature 4 of the list above.

We developed a methodology to support the design, execution and monitoring of systems produced via the suite of ALIVE tools. We detail the model-driven methodology in [23], addressing point 5 of the list of desirable features above. Finally, we adopted open standards throughout the suite of tools, allowing us to incorporate (as well as extend) technologies such as Protégé[20] to edit parts of the models, JSHOP2 for planning, and so on. The adoption of standards was largely facilitated by the meta-modelling development of the ALIVE framework.

7.2 Organisation-Based Planning vs. Exhaustive Planning

We now contrast the organisation-based planning with exhaustive planning. The organisation model can be seen as a template for partial plans, and these could be as fine-grained and detailed as the designers wish to (or as the application requires it to be). The more finely detailed the organisation is, the more restricted the search space for plans becomes. For instance, a scene with many intermediate landmarks will give rise to fewer plans than a scene with only a few landmarks – planning aims at finding a sequence of actions connecting landmarks, and the more landmarks, the fewer options of actions to connect them.

Another source of simplification in the ALIVE planning activity relates to the level of abstraction of actions. In our approach actions are not necessarily equated with individual Web services. Instead, an action is mapped, via the matchmaking, to a semantic description of a Web service or, potentially, a Web service composition. The matchmaker thus provides, upon request, different alternative Web services (and/or their compositions) which fulfil the action. Web service compositions performed by the matchmaker are attempts to fulfil an action, and this is a simpler problem than assembling a composition for a full-fledged business workflow. Moreover, the mapping of an action to a Web service composition could be cached and re-used without the need to assemble the composition afresh next time an agent contacts the matchmaker to find means to execute the same action.

The organisation-based planning thus provides two layers of abstractions which help reduce the search space of the planning efforts. The first abstraction layer concerns organisational features such as landmarks and objectives, which narrow down the planning with abstract actions. The second abstraction layer stems from the coarse-grained actions, and to which the matchmaker provides candidate Web services and their compositions. If, however, we have an organisation model that is underspecified and the actions are defined to reflect too closely individual Web services, then the benefits stemming from the abstraction layers disappear and the ALIVE approach will have a similar performance as ordinary planning for Web service composition.

[20] `http://protege.stanford.edu`

Although the performance improvement of ALIVE is a function of the quality of the design (which is difficult, if not impossible to objectively measure and provide feedback about), there is an important benefit of our approach when re-planning is needed. The levels of abstraction mentioned above allows re-planning in two stages, namely, when choosing actions to connect landmarks (and fulfil organisational objectives), and when choosing how individual actions are matched by which Web services. The action-level planning is more stable: when an ALIVE plan fails, our agents first try to achieve their actions using different Web services, but still sticking to their original actions. Only when the agents attempt all possible means to achieve an action (using the matchmaker to find out about them), is that an action-level re-planning is performed.

8 Conclusions, Discussion and Future Work

We have presented an organisation-based approach to Web service composition, using off-the-shelf planning techniques. This approach was investigated within the EU-funded project ALIVE (FP7 215890), which used knowledge-rich means to support the engineering of open systems. The approach split the design process into three concerns, namely, those relating with organisation (the context), coordination (how stakeholders acted together) and services (how it was done). These concerns shaped the layered architecture and model-driven development allowed these layers/concerns to be formally related.

The task of building Web service compositions was quickly recognised as one in which automated computer support was not only necessary, but could potentially be provided through the use of techniques such as workflow composition and traditional AI planning. However, given the vast number of services available with which to plan, traditional approaches to planning can quickly suffer from search space explosion. Within the ALIVE project, we have addressed the task of building Web service compositions by using plans of actions, which specify preconditions and effects expected of services, but not the actual services themselves. This allows for runtime selection of services by agents, capable of not only consuming the services, but also handling any errors in a variety of ways, including planning for alternative compositions. By incorporating organisational knowledge into the process, we further reduce the planner's workload.

We plan to extend the work in various directions. We have been looking into ways to formally connect normative aspects and planning, both during the planning activity (centralised and distributed) as well as its distributed enactment [16]. This would allow norms to influence planning, but to be kept separate from plan representation and mechanisms, and achieving a separation of concerns which encourages re-use of norms, and interchangeability of planning representations and mechanisms. We are also looking into how normative and organisational aspects can be formally related, with a view to defining mechanisms to check for properties such as "potential for normative compliance/violation", whereby roles, their goals and roles' relationships may jeopardise compliance with particular norms (or encourage norm compliance). The ALIVE framework and methodology have been used to model two other scenarios, namely, service/information provision via a portal, and simulation of emergency relief efforts [1,14]. The use cases have provided useful feedback on the various ALIVE tools and models and how these can be made more useful; this feedback will help us improving the next versions. The complete ALIVE suite of tools is available at `http://ict-alive.sourceforge.net/`.

References

1. Aldewereld, H., Padget, J., Vasconcelos, W., Vázquez-Salceda, J., Sergeant, P., Staikopoulos, A.: Adaptable, organization-aware, service-oriented computing. IEEE Intelligent Systems 25(4), 26–35 (2010)
2. Andrews, T., Curbera, F., Dholakia, H., Goland, Y., Klein, J., Leymann, F., Liu, K., Roller, D., Smith, D., Thatte, S., Trickovic, I., Weerawarana, S.: Business process execution language for web services version 1.1 (May 2003), `http://www.oasis-open.org/committees/download.php/2046/BPELV1-1May52003Final.pdf` (last accessed June 22, 2010)
3. Atkinson, C., Kuhne, T.: Model-driven development: a metamodeling foundation. IEEE Software 20(5), 36–41 (2003)
4. Bertoli, P., Kazhamiakin, R., Paolucci, M., Pistore, M., Raik, H., Wagner, M.: Continuous orchestration of web services via planning. In: Procs. 19th Int'l Conf. on Automated Planning and Scheduling (ICAPS 2009). AAAI (2009)
5. Corsar, D., Chorley, A., Vasconcelos, W.: Organisation-based (re-)planning for web service composition. In: Procs. 12th Int'l Conf. on Information Integration, Web-based Applications & Services (iiWAS 2010), pp. 649–652. ACM, New York (2010)
6. Coulouris, G.F., Dollimore, J., Kindberg, T.: Distributed Systems: Concepts and Design (International Computer Science), 4th edn. Addison-Wesley Longman Publishing Co., Inc., Boston (2005)
7. Dustdar, S., Schreiner, W.: A survey on web services composition. Int. J. Web and Grid Services 1(1), 1–30 (2005)
8. Ermolayev, V., Keberle, N., Plaksin, S., Kononenko, R., Terziyan, V.: Towards a framework for agent-enabled semantic web service composition. Int. J. of Web Services Research 1, 63–87 (2004)
9. Falou, M.E., Bouzid, M., Mouaddib, A.-I., Vidal, T.: Automated web service composition: A decentralised multi-agent approach. In: Procs. IEEE/WIC/ACM Int'l Conf. on Web Intelligence and Intelligent Agent Technology, vol. 1, pp. 387–394. IEEE Computer Society, Los Alamitos (2009)
10. Fernández, A., Ossowski, S.: Exploiting organisational information for service coordination in multiagent systems. In: AAMAS 2008: Proceedings of the 7th International Joint Conference on Autonomous Agents and Multiagent Systems, pp. 257–264. IFAAMAS (2008)
11. Martin, D., Burstein, M., Hobbs, J., Lassila, O., McDermott, D., McIlraith, S., Narayanan, S., Paolucci, M., Parsia, B., Payne, T., Sirin, E., Scinivasan, N., Sycara, K.: Owl-s: Semantic markup for web services. W3C Member Submission (November 2004), `http://www.w3.org/Submission/OWL-S/`
12. McIlraith, S., Son, T.: Adapting Golog for composition of semantic web services. In: Procs. 8th Int'l Conf. on Knowledge Representation and Reasoning (KR 2002), pp. 482–496. Morgan Kaufmann (2002)

13. Medjahed, B., Bouguettaya, A., Elmagarmid, A.K.: Composing web services on the semantic web. The VLDB Journal 12(4) (November 2003)
14. Nieves, J.C., Padget, J., Vasconcelos, W.W., Staikopoulos, A., Cliffe, O., Dignum, F., Vázquez-Salceda, J., Clarke, S., Reed, C.: Coordination, Organisation and Model-Driven Approaches for Dynamic, Flexible, Robust Software and Services Engineering. In: Dustdar, S., Li, F. (eds.) Service Engineering, pp. 85–115. Springer, Heidelberg (2011)
15. Okouya, D., Dignum, V.: Operetta: a prototype tool for the design, analysis and development of multi-agent organizations. In: Proceedings of the 7th International Joint Conference on Autonomous Agents and Multiagent Systems, AAMAS 2008, pp. 1677–1678. IFAAMAS, Richland (2008)
16. Oren, N., Vasconcelos, W., Meneguzzi, F., Luck, M.: Acting on Norm Constrained Plans. In: Leite, J., Torroni, P., Ågotnes, T., Boella, G., van der Torre, L. (eds.) CLIMA XII 2011. LNCS, vol. 6814, pp. 347–363. Springer, Heidelberg (2011)
17. Parashar, M., Hariri, S.: Autonomic Computing: An Overview. In: Banâtre, J.-P., Fradet, P., Giavitto, J.-L., Michel, O. (eds.) UPP 2004. LNCS, vol. 3566, pp. 257–269. Springer, Heidelberg (2005)
18. Pistore, M., Barbon, F., Bertoli, P.G., Shaparau, D., Traverso, P.: Planning and Monitoring Web Service Composition. In: Bussler, C.J., Fensel, D. (eds.) AIMSA 2004. LNCS (LNAI), vol. 3192, pp. 106–115. Springer, Heidelberg (2004)
19. Rao, J., Su, X.: A Survey of Automated Web Service Composition Methods. In: Cardoso, J., Sheth, A.P. (eds.) SWSWPC 2004. LNCS, vol. 3387, pp. 43–54. Springer, Heidelberg (2005)
20. Saboohi, H., Amini, A., Abolhassani, H.: Failure recovery of composite semantic web services using subgraph replacement. In: Procs. Int'l Conf. on Computer and Communication Engineering (ICCCE 2008), pp. 489–493 (2008)
21. Salehie, M., Tahvildari, L.: Autonomic computing: emerging trends and open problems. SIGSOFT Softw. Eng. Notes 30, 1–7 (2005)
22. Sirin, E., Parsia, B., Wu, D., Hendler, J., Nau, D.: HTN Planning for Web Service Composition Using SHOP2. Journal of Web Semantics 1(4), 296–377 (2004)
23. Staikopoulos, A., Saudrais, S., Clarke, S., Riveret, R., Dignum, V.: The ALIVE methodology. Deliverable 6.1b, version 2.0 (October 2009), http://www.ist-alive.eu/index.php?option=com_docman&task=doc_download&gid=31&Itemid=49 (last accessed June 22, 2010)
24. Vázquez-Salceda, J., Vasconcelos, W.W., Padget, J., Dignum, F., Clarke, S., Roig, M.P.: ALIVE: an agent-based framework for dynamic and robust service-oriented applications. In: Procs. 9th Int'l Conf. on Autonomous Agents and Multiagent Systems(AAMAS 2010), pp. 1637–1638. IFAAMAS, Richland (2010)

Agent and Multi-Agent Software Engineering: Modelling, Programming, and Verification

Extended Abstract for a Course at DALT Spring School 2011

Rafael H. Bordini

Institute of Informatics
Federal University of Rio Grande do Sul
CP 15064, CEP 91501-970, Porto Alegre – RS, Brazil
R.Bordini@inf.ufrgs.br

In this extended abstract, I shall briefly describe the course I gave at the DALT International Spring School that took place at the University Residential Centre in Bertinoro, Italy, in April 2011. Before I do so, I feel compelled to say, although this was supposed to be a technical paper, that participating in that School was the most fabulous experience of my academic career. I attended many conferences and summer schools over the last decade, and in particular all the summer schools were incredible experiences, but none matched that of the DALT School in Bertinoro. The University Centre is located in an astounding medieval castle, where even Dante stayed for some time. The castle is at the top of a hill and the views from the castle where we were also accommodated are just breathtaking. The food was excellent and the people involved at all levels incredibly friendly; the organisation was impeccable. Of course just atmosphere does not make an academic event that memorable. Perhaps because this was the most specific summer school I ever attend in regards to the topics covered, which allowed the courses to go into much more depth than usual, but certainly not only because of that but also other factors such as the particular combination of people in that School, that was definitely the most technically productive school I ever attended. All the attendants cannot possibly thank enough the organisers for the amazing experience they created for us. Unfortunately, nothing is perfect. As memorable as the school was, I will never be able to forget the suffering it was to walk up those extremely steep hills either.

The course was commissioned by the School organisers with the specific title "Agent and Multi-Agent Software Engineering: Modelling, Programming, and Verification". I liked the title for various reasons. First because it makes explicit the move from single to multi agent that is an important development in agent programming languages. Second because it covers two areas that have been at the centre of my research over many years: programming and verification of multi-agent systems. Modelling is not an area I have contributed to significantly, so I used less time of the course for this part. It consisted simply of mentioning a selection of the best-known methodologies for agent-oriented software engineering as well as an overview of key concepts in modelling multi-agent systems. That

C. Sakama et al. (Eds.): DALT 2011, LNAI 7169, pp. 149–151, 2012.

was after a brief motivation to the development of *autonomous* software, showing the growing number of commercial application of autonomous software as well as pointing out that all current trends in computer science point to directions that are only possible if autonomy in software becomes commonplace. References to some of the main researchers and academic events in the area were made in the modelling as well as later in the agent programming and verification parts of the course. All the material used in the course, including the slides are available online at `http://www.inf.ufrgs.br/~bordini/DALT-SpringSchool-2011`.

The part of the course about programming referred to the variety of agent languages in the literature but focused on the AgentSpeak variant used in the *Jason* platform [5] available at `http://jason.sourceforge.net`. AgentSpeak is a BDI-based agent-oriented programming language, influenced also by logic programming. It has been much referred to in the AAMAS literature and is widely known, perhaps for being both simple and elegant, yet faithful to the BDI architecture and reactive planning systems. *Jason* is a platform that has become rather popular, with some 500 downloads a month on average. While *Jason* includes many extensions of the original AgentSpeak(L) language, and allow multiple agents and also has some support for simulating shared environments, its main strength in the language for programming autonomous (communicating) agents rather than agent organisations or agent environments. Yet both sophisticated social structures and shared environments are equally important to agent programming in complex multi-agent systems.

A platform called JaCaMo was created very recently which addresses that problem. The platform is based on *Jason* for programming agents, $\mathcal{M}$OISE [8,7] (`http://moise.sourceforge.net`) for programming organisations, and CArtAgO [10,9] (`http://cartago.sourceforge.net`) for programming environments. This course briefly presented $\mathcal{M}$OISE and CArtAgO so that JaCaMo could then be presented; JaCaMo is available at `http://jacamo.sourceforge.net`. A didactic example was presented that allowed the demonstrations of the use of first-class programming abstractions at the three levels of a multi-agent systems: social, individual, and environment; the example is available with the course material and also in the JaCaMo releases on Source Forge. For those used to traditional agent-oriented programming, it is quite revealing to see how full multi-agent oriented programming as embodied in JaCaMo can lead to much more powerful programming.

The last part of the course was about verification. As with the other parts, references to other researchers who contributed to agent verification and relevant survey papers were given and then the course centred on the work I have done with various colleagues. Our early work [3] aimed at allowing the use of model checking techniques on systems programmed in AgentSpeak particularly. Later, in a joint project with Michael Fisher and Louise Dennis [6,2], we developed an approach to model check systems programmed in various BDI-based agent languages, including systems where different agents were programmed in different agent programming languages, and focusing on the use of Java Pathfinder [12] (`http://javapathfinder.sourceforge.net/`) as the underlying model checker. In program model checking [11], the well-known state-space explosion problem is particularly difficult, so it is even more important to use abstraction techniques. The course also mentioned briefly work we have done on property-based slicing for AgentSpeak [4]; property-based slicing is interesting because it is a *precise* form of under-approximation. It was also pointed out that model checking can be useful in practical software development even when full verification is not possible, for example model checking can be used for test case generation [1].

References

1. Artho, C., Barringer, H., Goldberg, A., Havelund, K., Khurshid, S., Lowry, M.R., Pasareanu, C.S., Rosu, G., Sen, K., Visser, W., Washington, R.: Combining test case generation and runtime verification. Theor. Comput. Sci. 336(2-3), 209–234 (2005)
2. Bordini, R.H., Dennis, L.A., Farwer, B., Fisher, M.: Automated verification of multi-agent programs. In: ASE, pp. 69–78. IEEE (2008)
3. Bordini, R.H., Fisher, M., Visser, W., Wooldridge, M.: Verifying multi-agent programs by model checking. Autonomous Agents and Multi-Agent Systems 12(2), 239–256 (2006)
4. Bordini, R.H., Fisher, M., Wooldridge, M., Visser, W.: Property-based slicing for agent verification. J. Log. Comput. 19(6), 1385–1425 (2009)
5. Bordini, R.H., Hübner, J.F., Wooldridge, M.: Programming Multi-Agent Systems in AgentSpeak Using *Jason*. Wiley Series in Agent Technology. John Wiley & Sons (2007)
6. Dennis, L., Fisher, M., Webster, M., Bordini, R.: Model checking agent programming languages. Automated Software Engineering, 1–59 (2011), `http://dx.doi.org/10.1007/s10515-011-0088-x`
7. Hübner, J.F., Boissier, O., Kitio, R., Ricci, A.: Instrumenting multi-agent organisations with organisational artifacts and agents. Autonomous Agents and Multi-Agent Systems 20, 369–400 (2010)
8. Hübner, J.F., Sichman, J.S., Boissier, O.: Developing Organised Multi-Agent Systems Using the MOISE+ Model: Programming Issues at the System and Agent Levels. Agent-Oriented Software Engineering 1(3/4), 370–395 (2007)
9. Omicini, A., Ricci, A., Viroli, M.: Artifacts in the AandA meta-model for multi-agent systems. Autonomous Agents and Multi-Agent Systems 17(3), 432–456 (2008)
10. Ricci, A., Piunti, M., Viroli, M.: Environment programming in multi-agent systems: an artifact-based perspective. Autonomous Agents and Multi-Agent Systems 23(2), 158–192 (2011)
11. Visser, W., Havelund, K., Brat, G.P., Park, S., Lerda, F.: Model checking programs. Autom. Softw. Eng. 10(2), 203–232 (2003)
12. Visser, W., Mehlitz, P.C.: Model Checking Programs with Java PathFinder. In: Godefroid, P. (ed.) SPIN 2005. LNCS, vol. 3639, pp. 27–27. Springer, Heidelberg (2005)

Author Index

GPSR Compliance

The European Union's (EU) General Product Safety Regulation (GPSR) is a set of rules that requires consumer products to be safe and our obligations to ensure this.

If you have any concerns about our products, you can contact us on ProductSafety@springernature.com

In case Publisher is established outside the EU, the EU authorized representative is:

Springer Nature Customer Service Center GmbH
Europaplatz 3
69115 Heidelberg, Germany

Batch number: 09474016

Printed by Printforce, the Netherlands